C0-DKM-268

An Alternative History of Bicycles and Motorcycles

An Alternative History of Bicycles and Motorcycles

Two-Wheeled Transportation and Material Culture

Steven E. Alford and
Suzanne Ferriss

LEXINGTON BOOKS
Lanham • Boulder • New York • London

Quotes from *Motorcycle* by Steven E. Alford and Suzanne Ferriss reprinted by permission of the authors, Steven E. Alford and Suzanne Ferriss, 2007.

Published by Rowman & Littlefield
A wholly owned subsidiary of The Rowman & Littlefield Publishing Group, Inc.
4501 Forbes Boulevard, Suite 200, Lanham, Maryland 20706
www.rowman.com

Unit A, Whitacre Mews, 26-34 Stannary Street, London SE11 4AB

Copyright © 2016 by Lexington Books

All rights reserved. No part of this book may be reproduced in any form or by any electronic or mechanical means, including information storage and retrieval systems, without written permission from the publisher, except by a reviewer who may quote passages in a review.

British Library Cataloguing in Publication Information Available

Library of Congress Cataloging-in-Publication Data Is Available

ISBN 978-1-4985-2879-5 (cloth : alk. paper) — ISBN 978-1-4985-2880-1 (electronic)

∞™ The paper used in this publication meets the minimum requirements of American National Standard for Information Sciences—Permanence of Paper for Printed Library Materials, ANSI/NISO Z39.48-1992.

Printed in the United States of America

For our friends and supporters of *IJMS*

Contents

Acknowledgments

This book would not have been possible without the generous support of Nova Southeastern University, including our chair Marlisa Santos and Don Rosenblum, who, as dean of the Farquhar College of Arts and Sciences, granted us the course releases, sabbatical leaves, and travel funding that enabled us to complete it.

In 2009, the American Studies Department at the University of Trier, Germany, hosted a motorcycle-themed conference organized around our previous book, *Motorcycle*. The lectures and conversations at that conference, *Motorrad: Beschleunigung und Rebellion?* (Motorcycle: Acceleration and Rebellion?), sparked the ideas that began our lengthy trek resulting in the completion of this book. Our thanks go especially to Professor Gerd Hurm and his lovely wife Petra Adam, whose support and friendship for more than thirty years has been invaluable to our professional development, as well as the genial and welcoming Klaus and Maria Steinmann, whose inventive motorcycle-themed artwork, housing, and free drinks made our participation in the conference far better than we could have imagined.

Our friends Steve Gardner, Susie Higgins, and Lee Perez extended us serene spaces in their mountain homes where we conducted research and wrote substantial portions of this book. Andres Ocampo and Melissa Hartmann de Barros encouraged our personal and intellectual interest in bicycling. Tennille Shuster created our cover image and Jon Shuster advised us with web design. Our thanks go to them and to the anonymous reviewer of this manuscript who offered insightful observations and suggestions for its improvement. Our editor Lindsey Porambo extended genial, professional, and efficient support throughout the publication process.

We gratefully acknowledge the support of our friends and colleagues at the *International Journal of Motorcycle Studies*, who have sustained our work on this project for more than five years, patiently listening to presentations of our ideas at conferences in Colorado Springs and London, and inspired us with their own cutting-edge research and passionate attachment to cycling including Ted Bishop, Michael Chappell, Marina Cianferoni, Geoff and Cynthia Crowther, Tim Fransen, Lisa Garber, Leland Giovanelli and Jim Everett, Tom Goodmann, Miguel Grunstein, Alex Ilyasova, Gary Kieffner, Steve Koerner, Melissa Lambert, Michael Lichter, Sheila Malone, Randy McBee, Christian Pierce and Jessica Keesee, Caryn Simonson and Kadett Hulsman, Kris Slawinski and Dick Watts, John Sumser, Katherine Sutherland, David Walton, and Jim Ward. This book is dedicated to them—and to the many others who have attended the *IJMS* conferences and read the journal.

Introduction

> How we desire, produce, and discard the durables of existence helps form who we are, how we connect to one another, and what we do to the earth. In addition to ordering intimacies, these urges and actions influence the way peoples across large stretches of time, cultures, and geographies align, exchange, and conflict.
>
> —Harvey Molotch, *Where Stuff Comes From*

Of the many gifts of the Italian Renaissance to the West is the concept of the genius. Exemplified in Vasari's *Lives of the Most Eminent Painters, Sculptors, and Architects*, the creation of the artist came to be seen as a product not of the guild members' studio—a shop filled with individuals working together to collectively produce "masterworks"—but as the result of the "genius" of the creator, a da Vinci (Vasari's example) or a Michelangelo or a Donatello.[1] The mental processes of the genius were conceptualized as beyond the understanding of the ordinary individual, and the process itself was not the result of the ordinary prerequisites of education or skill, but a special, inner way of seeing the world and creating concrete products based on that mysterious interior vision. The later manifestation of the artistic genius was one of the cornerstones of European Romanticism, with Byron's Manfred standing for many others, and well into the nineteenth century critic John Ruskin crowned J. M. W. Turner the greatest genius of English painting, while Gustave Courbet crafted his image as a celebrity artist.[2]

Despite Edison's contention that 99 percent of genius is perspiration, the idea of the genius persists. We have read that the recently departed Steven Jobs was a "genius," and to many it was not clear at the time of his death whether Apple, an enormous international corporation with thousands of talented employees, could survive economically without his guidance. (Jony

Ive, Apple's principal designer, was also the subject of a 2013 biography proclaiming him the company's resident genius: *Jony Ive: The Genius Behind Apple's Greatest Products*).[3] The history of significant technological milestones of Western culture is characterized as the innovations of the geniuses—from military leaders to industrial designers—who advanced them.

In the mechanical arts, we have another historical figure who pops up periodically, the tinkerer. Perhaps lacking the cerebral gifts of the genius, the tinkerer substitutes physical gifts: the tinkerer's knowledge rests in his or her hands and the willingness to pursue in solitude an idea that others have either discarded or ignored.[4] Legendary Kiwi motorcyclist Burt Munro was a tinkerer, and lived up to the image of a solitary crank who nonetheless was capable of extraordinary mechanical innovations.[5]

Hence, in the mechanical arts, the progress of technological innovation is frequently personalized: without the contribution of Morse we would never have had the telegraph, or without Bell we would never have had the telephone. While it's instructive to look to the tinkerer-geniuses in transportation, we would like to suggest that understanding technological innovation is a bit more complex than it first appears. Karl von Drais, Kirkpatrick MacMillan, Pierre Lallement, Pierre Michaux, John Kemp Starley: without them, the bicycle wouldn't exist. Perhaps. Perhaps not. Innovation results not from an individual, but from the *convergence* of a number of forces, not all of which can be understood as emanating from a single individual.

It is a commonplace to note that technology produces social and cultural changes. For example, it is often observed how the bicycle transformed the social and romantic opportunities of women, both in Britain and America. However, for socially transforming technology to exist, a series of seemingly unrelated events—both in technological development and social condition—has to occur for said technology to be possible. Hence, our focus would be improved by looking not so much at the geniuses and how their inventions led to social change, but rather by asking, *how did individuals find themselves in a position to invent the technology responsible for social change*?[6] The conditions involve a complex interaction of politics, economics, religion, and available environmental materials, among others, and, in the intellectual realm, a peculiar set of assumptions about cultural legitimacy or superiority based on levels of technological progress.[7] While this list of influences is by no means exhaustive, it does illuminate just how difficult the search for historical causes for technological innovation can be.

MATERIALS AND MATERIAL CULTURE

Just as we cannot privilege the mental or mechanical work of a singular individual as the source of innovation, nor can we assume that objects themselves propel technological progress. This deterministic view holds that a device, such as the bicycle, has a social impact but ignores its own social origins. Devices have "developmental trajectories that are either entirely obscured or seen as governed by a sort of natural law which makes their forms (and presence) seem inevitable."[8] In this unilineal model of development, the horse, which carried one, perhaps two, riders, led inevitably to the creation of the *cheval de bois* (1791), a "wooden horse," on which a rider sat and propelled himself into motion using his feet. Inevitably, others improved on this design, adding steering to create the draisine or velocipede (1817). That led to more complex forms of propulsion: like the *cheval de bois*, the velocipede was simply an aid to walking or a "running machine," in that it relied on the rider to use his feet to push it forward—and to stop it, since it also lacked brakes. Inevitably, then, the developing bicycle gained pedals and brakes (1861), and later a chain (1879), becoming self-propelled, though still reliant on human energy for movement.[9] Affixing a motor was the next logical step, so the determinist argument goes, freeing the device from its dependence on human power alone, enabling it to go faster. And then motorcycle gave way to the automobile. In this narrative, the device rides a steady road of progressive development.[10]

But it could have been otherwise. This is the guiding principle of a countermodel—the social constructionist model—that considers "technological forms and histories of innovation are far more contingent on social factors than the technological determinist position indicates."[11] As Harvey Molotch argues in *Where Stuff Comes From*, "nothing stands alone—to understand any one thing you have to learn how it fits into larger arrays of physical objects, social sentiments, and ways of being. In the world of goods, as in

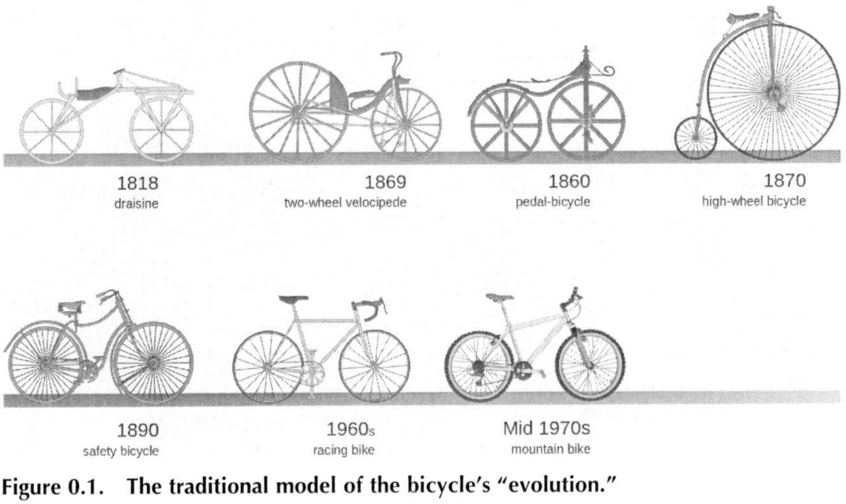

Figure 0.1. The traditional model of the bicycle's "evolution."

worlds of any other sort, each element is just one interdependent fragment of a larger whole."[12] The determinist narrative of the bicycle's development, for example, isolates certain *parts* of the device—steering, pedals, brakes, chain—while neglecting the *materials* that shape them—wood, metal, rubber—each with its own complex development, each a product, as it were, of an equally complex social dynamic.

Materials are obviously fundamental to creating any object of use, such that we can trace eras of human history on the basis of the available materials: Bronze Age, Iron Age, and others. The existence of raw materials is a precondition of their being fashioned into objects of use, but first these materials have to be recognized as *materials*. Asphalt, rubber, and petroleum literally form part of the earth, and always have, yet using asphalt for road surfaces, rubber for insulation and shock absorption, or petroleum to power vehicles are practices that developed only yesterday in the span of human history. Even when discovered, they are often not deployed in any socially useful way, and are frequently regarded as physical nuisances, such as gooey tar pits or crude petroleum that bubbles to the surface and creates dangerous oil slicks. Until the nineteenth century, rubber was never processed to improve it (eliminating, for example, its tendency to solidify in cold weather), and its only use, other than as a child's toy, was as a projectile in Amerindian games. The fact that it existed and was recognized as a material meant nothing as to whether it was employed as part of an object of use, such as a bicycle or motorcycle tire.[13]

The roads that tires now cross offer another compelling example. Following the great era of Roman road building (and their use by the Romans to dominate, through swift transportation and communication, those around them), road maintenance fell by the wayside, as it were, creating serious challenges not only for warfare, but also for the simple circulation of trade goods. In America in the mid-nineteenth century, road conditions were scandalous and, in general, worse than those in Italy 1,500 years before. Not until a hundred years ago was there a general understanding as to whose responsibility the planning for, establishment of, and maintenance of roads was. At the dawn of the twentieth century the American federal government did begin to systematically take the responsibility for roads that connected towns. Before that road crews attended to their small geographical areas either to work off local taxes or on the theory that an improved road in front of one's property increased its value. British road builder John Louden McAdam developed new techniques of road building, using crushed rock and rock dust in a novel technique described in his 1816 book, *Remarks on the Present System of Road Making*, but asphalt, found in surface tar pits, was considered a nuisance to agriculture and, owing to its smell, to local inhabitants until the twentieth century (today, known as Alberta's tar sands, it has returned to the public eye to create a new set of controversies). Note again that the presence of the raw material for technological advance was there all along; but a confluence of events (social acceptance of taxation, cultural understanding of the need for maintained roads to improve prosperity, political agreement on whose shoulders responsibility for road building fell, adaptation of vehicles for novel kinds of roads, warfare's need for swift movement, etc.) were required for the "genius" of a McAdam and others to originate one of America's grandest (and most maligned) contemporary contributions: the Interstate Highway System. And, as we shall see, this movement originated with an unlikely group of good-roads proselytizers: bicyclists.

Although the frames of bicycles (and early motorcycles) were made from a number of different materials, from wood to bamboo, for modern bicycles and motorcycles to exist, the technology for forming strong, reliable tubular steel had to be perfected. The motive force behind this development was not the need for two-wheeled transportation, but the need for breech-loading rifles. Rifles were needed as a force superior to the muskets (originally used by imperialist invaders, but later sold to non-Western people), used by the colonized to fight against the exploitation by their occupiers. The British and other imperial nations needed to maintain superiority to continue the flow of agricultural goods and raw materials from the colonies to Europe and America.

As the history of rubber production and use demonstrates, the demands of empire stimulated the need for newer and more sophisticated weapons to physically control markets of desired overseas goods, which in turn stimulated the development of ever more sophisticated armaments once older ones had fallen, inevitably, into the hands of the colonized, which then stimulated developments in metallurgy, and a transition from iron to steel, particularly strong tubular steel to fashion rifle barrels. These steel tubes became, along with rubber, the "raw" materials of the bicycle, a device universally acknowledged to be instrumental in the social, economic, and political progress of European men and women, as the history of road construction reveals.

These various strands combine to form a complex web, fusing materials with culture. One thread linking the two is actual thread: an essential component of early tires was cotton. Cords of cotton, coated in rubber, formed the layers (called "plies") of bicycle (and later motorcycle and automobile) tires, to offer much needed cushioning against the uneven surfaces of early roads. But the same fibers were woven into the fabrics protecting riders from the dust and mud the vehicles produced. As in the case of rubber, however, cotton was not cultivated directly for such purposes (although Dunlop and Goodyear later established farms and textile factories in Arizona in the

1920s to meet demand). Instead, global processes of trade and conquest were responsible. An ancient material, cotton's precise origins are murky, with evidence of ancient cultivation and use in India, Pakistan, and Egypt, as well as in Mesoamerica and Peru. Arab traders brought cotton cloth to Europe around AD 800 and, during the Medieval era, manufacture arose after Muslim conquest of the Iberian Peninsula and Sicily. Subsequent conquest of Sicily by the Normans in the twelfth century was responsible for the spread of manufacturing throughout Europe. But its development as the "fabric of our lives" rested on a foundation of colonial invasion, when Britain's East India Company began importing calico—cheap, colorful cotton—and then slavery as European nations devised their own alternative processes of manufacture, spurring demand for cheap raw materials.

Simultaneously, textile manufacture was central to the Industrial Revolution responsible for the engine that transformed the bicycle into the motorcycle, and the sewing machine provided early bicycle manufacturers with inspirations for propulsion and pedal design. Unsurprisingly, many early bicycles were produced by sewing machine manufacturers such as Singer, Coventry, and Weed. Yet, the sewing machine also transferred stigmas to early female riders of the bicycle, who faced the same charge plaguing seamstresses: use of the machine led to nymphomania. Paradoxically, the bicycle energized dress reform, an essential component of early feminism, as well as trends in sporting dress for both sexes that propelled not simply fashion but the fashion for bicycling. The fashioning of the rider remains central to the image, if not the identity, of the motorcyclist. Complicated to an extraordinary degree are the threads linking human and machine.

MACHINES AND THEIR RIDERS

Both the bicycle and the motorcycle are understood popularly as transportation devices, the latter resulting from strapping a motor onto a bicycle. The bicycle (whose design has not changed appreciably since 1885), after an initial rocky integration into daily life (it scares the horses, it subjects its rider to physical danger, it moves so quickly pedestrians are subject to risk, etc.), has become a ubiquitous part of public life. For many, it's the perfect vehicle for human self-propulsion, a testament to the perfection of its design. For the economically minded, it provides transportation for the poor. For the ecologically minded, it provides reliable conveyance absent of the evils of burning fossil fuels. For the health-minded, it gets you where you want to go, and you arrive in better shape than when you started.

The first motorcycle, Daimler's Einspur, showcased in 1885, the same year as the introduction of the Safety bicycle, has had a more checkered history than the bicycle, particularly in America.[14] Suffering the usual criticisms, fist-fights, arrests, and other indignities suffered by the bicyclist, the motorcyclist was dependent not only on the mechanical reliability of the engine, but also on the lack of infrastructure, given the early absence of gasoline stations (an analogous problem for today's drivers of electric automobiles). Despite the stir early female riders caused in the 1890s, the bicyclist has never experienced the radical transformation in his/her image as the motorcyclist did in the late 1940s and early 1950s with the emergence of the "outlaw" motorcyclist and the subsequent dominance of this imagined creature in the popular media. One of the lessons of the early young "scorchers" flying about on their Ordinaries and the "outlaws" lumbering loudly down quiet suburban streets is that both devices aren't simple transportation machines. Like the telephone, originally understood as a business device (and initially barred from use by women, who, men feared, would fritter their days away on it with idle gossip), the bicycle and the motorcycle find themselves always already *within* a culture, with its consequent arrangements of class, economics, politics, aesthetics, and gender. Analogous to Marshall McLuhan's notion that information itself changes owing to the medium in which it appears, it would be reductive to, for example, suggest that the motorcycle purchased in Lhasa by a Tibetan herder is the same device ridden by a fifteen-year-old dirt biker in California. (The infamous Coke bottle in the film *The Gods Must Be Crazy* is another humorous illustration of how a "technological" device can only be understood for what it is when we see it in the context of the culture in which it appears.) Studying technologies entails attending to their "'context of use'—the society and the web of other artifacts within which technologies are always embedded."[15] For, as Wiebe Bijker reminds us, "technology and society are both human constructs."[16]

THE SPOKES OF THE WHEEL

The common evolutionary model of development from the bicycle to the motorcycle oversimplifies both the technology and its origins. Stripping the vehicles of all their material and cultural associations, such a model fails to advance our understanding of the devices, their creators, and their riders. The "invention" of the bicycle, much less the motorcycle, simply cannot be understood in the context of the model of a series of British and French tinkerers, whose persistence and imagination led to this remarkable device. Instead, we need to understand the role of these men as midwives of a machine with many mothers and fathers, Asian, African, and South American, and whose countries' resources, unknown to the British before the imperial period, were not only instrumental, but necessary to the idea of the bicycle and its serial developments. In addition, as an operating principle for any technology, but particularly for the two under review, we need to recognize that how we understand what a technological device is—and what it is for—is dependent on a host of social, cultural, economic, and political assumptions that go largely unrecognized in the history of a developing technology. As Molotch has argued, "Somehow, everything must—and this is the crucial idea—'lash up' such that the otherwise loose elements adhere; only then can there be a new thing in the world. Like a plant variety in the forest or a microbe among the animal species, a product comes about and stays around—sometimes for a relatively short time and sometimes for epochs—to the degree that the diverse elements that make it up continue to be."[17]

This complex "lashing up"—or synergy—defies a straightforward unilinear or teleological explanation. Each piece of the bicycle and motorcycle's physical components—rubber, metals, fabrics—contributed simultaneously to their development. As we will argue, the vehicle's development was not linear, nor was it the product of an individual inventor or invention.[18] Instead, it was the product of a synergistic set of developments in material culture, understood not simply as physical products but as the social, intellectual, and political processes that undergird them. For this reason, we have adopted the metaphor of the wheel for our book's title and organization. The wheel, naturally, is foundational to the construction of the bicycle and motorcycle. It also connects the devices to the road, enabling mobility, and to the rider who guides their movement (and propels it, in the case of the bicycle). Yet the wheel itself is a complex creation, composed of a variety of materials—from wood and textiles to rubber and metal—enmeshed in a history of social production and consumption as ancient as human civilization. It thus both grounds and embodies the dynamic system at the core of our investigation of the bicycle and motorcycle. These two-wheeled vehicles are the hub, as it were, of our inquiry, with various spokes radiating outward, each representing pieces of the interlocking elements of material culture (see graphic below).

Part 1 considers the development of two-wheeled vehicles, noting the simultaneous appearance of the Safety bicycle (the Rover) and motorcycle (the Einspur) in 1885, and outlines how the two devices' development matched one another and how they differed. While we invoke the key individuals and milestones common to the traditional narrative of progressive development, we emphasize that it could have been otherwise. We highlight the often ingenious alternative designs that fell by the wayside and discuss how larger cul-

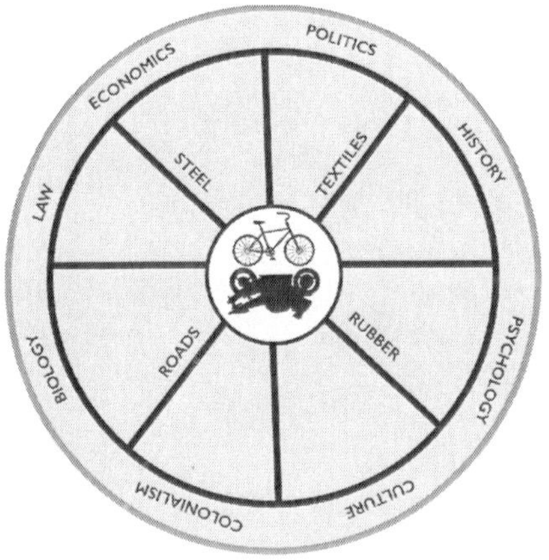

Figure 0.2. Spokes of the Wheel.

tural forces were responsible for what mistakenly appears to be the inevitable triumph of one design over another.

In part 2, we turn our attention to the material components—roads, rubber, steel, textiles—central to the vehicles' construction and use by riders. As we have already suggested, humans—creators and users, producers and consumers—shaped the transformation of these materials into the devices, as well as the devices themselves. Each part or "spoke" can be taken up independently, in any order, but each connects or overlaps with the other.

The rider, who has been described as the upper-half of the vehicle,[19] is the focus of part 3, which considers social relations that conditioned the meaning of these devices, including those of class and gender, and the ideas shaping their cultural value, from the physiological and psychological lure of speed to philosophical and political notions of "freedom." Women writers encouraged bicycling as a means toward greater female health, and one area of "scholarly" conflict concerned bicycling's effect on women's reproductive health and viability. Part 3 brings the argument full circle: culture affected materials, which produced the bicycle and motorcycle, which affected culture.

We have tried to construct the text to offer a model of dynamic convergence, while necessarily extracting individual elements—material and cultural—as temporary points of focus. Imagine, if you will, riding a two-wheeled vehicle along a road, first focusing your attention on the place (literally) where the rubber meets the road, the metals that support its movement, and the fabrics that unite the rider and machine. Then, as any rider might, consider why you are riding. What motivates you (and others)? What enhances or restricts your mobility? What arouses pleasure? Or fear?

We invite you to start from the beginning and join us for the entire ride—or dip in for brief spin.

IMAGES

In addition to the thirty images in the present volume, additional illustrations and resources keyed to each chapter can be found at http://www.themotorcyclebook.com.

A NOTE ABOUT TERMINOLOGY

In what follows we will be making observations about bicycles and motorcycles, which logic suggests could take three forms: observations about bicycles (in contrast to motorcycles), observations about motorcycles (in contrast to bicycles), and observations about both (that is, ways in which they share properties or qualities). Since the populations of bicycle riders and motorcycle riders are generally, but not always distinct, within the two communities various shorthand terms have been adopted that, if we followed them, could lead to confusion. For example, both groups commonly refer to "my bike," and "bike" doesn't clearly delineate whether one is referring to a bicycle or a motorcycle. Designating someone a "biker" generally, but not necessarily, refers to a motorcyclist, but within the motorcycle community this term can also refer to a segment of the motorcycling community often referred to as "outlaws."

To forestall confusion, we will adopt the following conventions, even if they don't necessarily reflect usage in the two communities.

We will try to avoid using "bike" altogether, instead using "bicycle" and "motorcycle" to refer to the two devices (keeping in mind that there is some difference of opinion as to the difference between a "motorized bicycle" and a "motorcycle," that is, what constitutes a "real" motorcycle). In some instances this sounds silly, so we will endeavor, against our instincts, to avoid silliness in referring, for example, to a "dirt motorcycle," instead using the common "dirt bike" to refer to an off-road vehicle that could be considered the motorcycle equivalent of a mountain bicycle.

When referring to riders, we will use "bicyclist" and "motorcyclist." We will avoid, unless referring specifically to popular culture references, calling someone who rides a motorcycle a "weekend warrior," a "biker," a "squid," or other terms that seek to distinguish motorcyclists into categories, usually for the purpose of valorizing one group of riders at the expense of another.

In instances in which we are discussing issues that pertain equally to bicycles and motorcycles, we will use the term "cyclist," that, to repeat, could refer to a bicyclist or a motorcyclist. In this case, the topic under discussion is assumed to apply to two-wheeled vehicles, regardless of their source of propulsion.

NOTES

1. Giorgio Vasari, *Lives of the Most Eminent Painters, Sculptors, and Architects*, trans. Gaston du C. de Vere (London: Macmillan and Co. & The Medici Society, 1912–1914).

2. For Ruskin's defense of Turner as greater than the "Old Masters," see *The Works of John Ruskin: Modern Painters, Vols. 1–5* (New York: J. Wiley, 1890). Courbet's *The Painter's Studio: A Real Allegory Summing Up a Seven-Year Phase of My Artistic Life* (1855) is representative of this impulse toward self-promotion. See Mary Morton, "To Create a Living Art: Rethinking Courbet's Landscape Painting," in *Courbet and the Modern Landscape* (Los Angeles: Getty Publications, 2006), 1–20.

3. Leander Kahney, *Jony Ive: The Genius Behind Apple's Greatest Products* (New York: Portfolio, 2013).

4. The tinkerer was a critical figure in the Industrial Revolution. As Joel Mokyr notes, "During the Industrial Revolution, technological progress was usually the result of the joint and cumulative efforts of many individuals. A typical innovator in those years was a dexterous and mechanically inclined person who became aware of a technical problem to be solved and guessed approximately how to go about solving it. The successful inventors were those who put the pieces together better than their colleagues, or those who managed to resolve one final stubborn difficulty blocking the realization of a new technique" (*The Lever of Riches: Technological Creativity and Economic Progress* [New York: Oxford University Press, 1992], Kindle loc. 946–49).

5. Munro's achievements were fictionalized in the film *The World's Fastest Indian* (2005), based on a previous television documentary by Roger Donaldson, *Offerings to the God of Speed* (1973). Donaldson later produced a book, *The World's Fastest Indian: Burt Munro—A Scrapbook of his Life* (Auckland, New Zealand: Random House, 2010). For his biography, see Tim Hanna, *One Good Run: The Legend of Burt Munro* (London: Penguin Global, 2006).

6. Mokyr suggests a balance between external forces and individual inventors. "The changes in the British economy during the Industrial Revolution were no doubt the result of profound economic, social, and demographic forces. But ingenious, practical, mechanically minded people came up with the ideas that changed the world. . . . The supply of talent is surely not completely exogenous; it responds to incentives and attitudes. The question that must be confronted is why in some societies talent is unleashed upon technical problems that eventually change the entire productive economy, whereas in others this kind of talent is either repressed or directed elsewhere" (*Lever of Riches*, Kindle loc. 1245–259).

7. This is the central concern of Michael Adas's fine book *Machines as the Measure of Men: Science, Technology, and Ideologies of Western Dominance* (Ithaca, NY: Cornell University Press, 1989).

8. Ron Eglash, "Technology as Material Culture," in *Handbook of Material Culture*, ed. Christopher Tilley, Webb Keane, Susanne Küchler, Michael Rowlands, and Patricia Spyer (London: Sage, 2006), 331.

9. Each of these steps forward is also commonly presented as the work of individuals: Comte Mede de Sivrac, in the case of the *cheval de bois*, Karl Friedrich von Drais, for the draisine, Pierre Lallement or Pierre Michaux for the pedals/brakes, and Harry Lawson for the chain.

10. Note that this interpretative pattern works backward as well as forward with, for example, the motorcycle, which is understood by its more nostalgic riders as an "iron steed" or "chrome horse." This view, in turn, leads to the individual's self-fashioning as a throwback to a simpler era where a person could light out for the interstate territories on his or her faithful motorcycle. See Steven E. Alford, "Riding Your Harley Back Into Nature: Hobbes, Rousseau, and the Paradox of Biker Identity," in *Harley-Davidson and Philosophy*, ed. Bernard E. Rollin, Cynthia Pineo, Kerri Mommer, and Carolyn M. Gray (Chicago: Open Court Press, 2006), 145–54.

11. Eglash, "Technology as Material Culture," 332. The social constructionist model of technology (or SCOT) emerged in the 1980s, with Wiebe E. Bijker, Thomas Parke Hughes, and Trevor J. Pinch, *The Social Construction of Technological Systems: New Directions in the Sociology and History of Technology* (Cambridge, MA: MIT Press, 1987) and Pierre Lemonnier, ed., *Technological Choices: Transformation in Materials since the Neolithic* (London: Routledge, 1993), now regarded as seminal texts.

12. Harvey Molotch, *Where Stuff Comes From: How Toasters, Toilets, Cars, Computers, and Many Other Things Come to Be as They Are* (New York: Routledge, 2003), 1.

13. Indeed, the same could be said not only of materials, but of what we might regard as inventions: "[Voltaire] noted that the Chinese were the originators of key inventions—printing, the compass, gunpowder—but that these devices had remained 'mere curiosities' until the Europeans obtained them and carry them to a 'high level of perfection'" (Adas, *Machines*, 88–89). Adas further indicates that, for Enlightenment thinkers, the source of this "backwardness" was political. "The backward state of scientific inquiry in China, for example, and the Chinese failure to develop the full potential of such key inventions as gunpowder and paper were linked to the despotic character of the Chinese government. In this view, corrupt and oppressive bureaucrats, acting on behalf of an aristocratic Emperor, stifled the free expression, experimentation, and the exchange of ideas or 'freedom of the pen' that most Enlightenment thinkers were convinced constituted the sine qua non of a healthy social order" (123).

14. As we shall see, there is no consensus as to the "first" motorcycle. The Einspur featured odd "training wheels," making it not technically a two-wheeler. Source of propulsion would be another consideration, whether steam or petrol. Strapping a motor onto a bicycle results not in a motorcycle, but a motorized bicycle, some would say. While early and late, the engine has migrated around the frame, as well as into

the wheels, an engine fitted into a loop frame or bolted fore and aft where a bicycle's pedals would be makes for a motorcycle. Given the many incommensurable arguments, the authors remain agnostic, given that this embodies the principle that "it could have been otherwise."

15. Nelly Oudshoorn and Trevor J. Pinch, "Introduction," in *How Users Matter: The Co-construction of Users and Technologies*, ed. Nelly Oudshoorn and Trevor J. Pinch (Cambridge, MA: MIT Press, 2003), 2.

16. Wiebe Bijker, *Of Bicycles, Bakelites, and Bulbs: Toward a Theory of Sociotechnical Change* (Cambridge, MA: MIT Press, 1997), 3.

17. Molotch, *Where Stuff Comes From*, 2.

18. We agree with Oudshoorn and Pinch that "the co-construction of users and technologies . . . go beyond technological determinist views of technology and essentialist views of users' identities" (*How Users Matter*, 3).

19. Bernt Spiegel, *The Upper Half of the Motorcycle: On the Unity of Rider and Machine* (North Conway, NH: Whitehorse Press, 2010).

Part I

MACHINES

Chapter One

"It Could Have Been Otherwise"

Bicycles and Motorcycles

> The inevitability of the present violates the contingency of the past, which involves alternative choices and outcomes that could have produced alternative presents. To deny the contingency of the past deprives us of alternative futures, for the present is the future's past. Contingency, in turn, demands hypotheticals about what might have happened. They are fictions, but necessary fictions. It is only by conceiving of alternative worlds that people in the past themselves imagined that we can begin to think historically, to escape the inevitability of the present, and get another perspective on issues that concern us still.
>
> —Richard White, *Railroaded*

As we argued in our introduction, technological and design histories offer an evolutionary model of the motorcycle's development from the bicycle. In this unilineal model, their forms appear to have resulted from an inevitable progression: the horse led its wooden equivalent, the *cheval de bois* (1791), the rider's feet substituting for the horse's hooves. The draisine or velocipede (1817) added steering and, through later improvements, gained pedals and brakes (1861), and later a chain (1879). While self-propelled, the device still depended on human energy for movement, until affixing a motor freed it from its dependence on human power alone, enabling it to go faster. And then the motorcycle gave way to the automobile. In this narrative, the device rides a steady road of progressive development, each step forward is commonly presented as the work of individuals: Comte Mede de Sivrac, in the case of the *cheval de bois*, Karl Friedrich von Drais, for the draisine, Pierre Lallement or Pierre Michaux for the pedals/brakes, Henry Lawson for the chain, German inventors Gottlieb Daimler and Wilhelm Maybach for the Einspur, and Karl Benz for the first internal combustion automobile.

But the development of two-wheeled vehicles could have been—and was—otherwise. Rather than one device antedating the other, for instance, note that the bicycle and motorcycle appeared simultaneously. What has become the universal bicycle design—two same-sized wheels and chain drive—originated with the introduction of the Rover Safety bicycle at the annual cycle industry exhibition, the Stanley Show, in London 1885.[1] In November of the same year, the Einspur—a two-wheeled device propelled by a single-cylinder, four-stroke, gasoline-powered engine generally credited as the first motorcycle—took its inaugural ride in Canstatt, Germany.[2] Nor was this motorcycle conceived to improve on the bicycle. Its creator Gottlieb Daimler saw it as simply a device for testing an engine to be used in four-wheeled vehicles, a feat he achieved later with Karl Benz.[3] These designs may now be recognized as the prevailing models of two-wheeled transport. But attention to the often ingenious, alternative designs surrounding their development reveals that larger cultural forces were responsible for what might appear to be the inevitable triumph of one design over another.

Our goal is not to quibble over dates, historical evidence, and individuals or to debate whether steam-powered devices count as motorcycles or automobiles. (If so, then François Isaac de Rivaz "invented" the car before Benz by using a steam engine on four wheels, Sylvester Howard Roper did the equivalent for the motorcycle in 1867, and Edward Butler's Petrol cycle beat Daimler's Einspur by a year.)[4] Nor is it to debate whether the *célérifères* (wooden horses) even existed (according to the author of *Legendary Bicycles* they did not)[5] or if draisines had brakes (evidence and patents suggest they did)[6] or if Pierre Lallement beat Pierre Michaux to the punch by adding pedals (the patent record is maddeningly inconclusive).[7] Such debates are largely futile for they ignore myriads of other possibilities, fixated as they are on sustaining an evolutionary model in which the device in question originated with a single inventor.

Peter Cox and Frederick Van De Walle have described this "evolinear" model:

> The history of the bicycle with which we are most familiar tends to present a story of a machine undergoing a series of logical changes over time, much as any other technology. This history takes us from the bicycle's primitive first beginnings, through succession of rational, progressive steps, to a final, mature form in the classic diamond-framed machine we recognise today. A few evolutionary side branches and dead ends are noted along the way, reflecting the oddities and novelties that occasionally curve but do not distract from the main narrative. It is a story that can be told in isolation from other forms of personal road transport, since the bicycle achieved its final form before the end of the nineteenth century. Indeed, when framed through this dominant historical narra-

> tive, it can be tempting to portray the bicycle as fundamentally anachronistic in today's society, as superseded or out-evolved by motorcycles and motor cars.[8]

Such accounts, they argue, ignore the sheer diversity of alternative designs. *Griffin's Bicycles and Tricycles of the Year 1886*, for instance, lists 89 bicycles and 106 tricycles.[9]

The evolinear models, applied retrospectively, assume a teleological endpoint—the eventual triumph, in the case of the bicycle and motorcycle, of two same-sized wheels arranged in a single line, propelled by an internal combustion engine fueled by petroleum—and select, out of a group of experimenters and innovators working simultaneously and often collectively, certain individuals as solely responsible for key moments of insight or entrepreneurship. Looking back from the contemporary moment, historians trace causal connections retrospectively, which reinforces the inevitability of the present device making it appear to be a "technologically predestined form," to borrow a phrase from Henry Petroski.[10] Understanding results in their then-contemporaneous complexity suggests a more accidental relation among forces than a causal one. If Molotch is right that "social sentiments and ways of being"[11] influence design, then human perception, guided by preexisting conceptions of individual mobility, configured the bicycle's and motorcycle's development.

THE HORSE

"Man is the animal which rides," pronounced Charles Pratt in the opening to *The American Bicycler*, which pictured the author next to his "steed," his high-wheeler.[12] If the model for individual, assisted transport in the late eighteenth century was the horse, then inevitably designs conforming most to this model would find social acceptance. The primacy of the equestrian model can easily be seen in designating the draisine as the first human-propelled two-wheeled vehicle.[13] The device's inventor, Karl von Drais dubbed it a *Laufmaschine*, or "running machine," conceiving it as augmenting human leg power. The term employed in the French patent filed on 19 January 1818 was *vélocipède* (from the Latin words meaning fast foot).[14] However, others—from Drais's contemporaries to modern historians—have tended to follow the British in conceiving it as a "hobby horse."

David Herlihy's influential *Bicycle: The History* presents the culmination of the seventeenth-century search for "the elusive mechanical horse," as the design solution to "the vexing problem of the horseless carriage."[15] Historical circumstances support this interpretation: Drais had earlier designed a four-wheeled carriage and his device employed elements of "the carriage technology of the time," as it was made of wood with "two miniature carriage wheels in a line."[16] Drais's invention appeared in a response to a severe horse shortage in Germany, following the 1815 eruption of the Tambora volcano in Indonesia. The ash spewed into the atmosphere traveled around the globe, blotting out the summer sun in Europe in 1816. Crop failures made oats scarce and expensive, leading to horse deaths.[17]

However, the designer's intent alone had little influence on how others perceived the device. As Thomas Cameron Burr has noted, a successful product hinges on its "cognitive legitimacy," that is, "the social *perception* of functionality. It is not about whether the product works; cognitive legitimacy is about whether many people perceive that it works, and tell each other that it does or does not. And 'works,' of course, depends on what the product is purported to do."[18] Thus, potential users situated the draisine by analogy to preexisting modes of transport that "worked." One dismissed draisine riding to "working a passage up a canal by towing a boat," referring to the practice of walking on shore, using ropes to pull floating cargo forward. Others derided the device as a "strange invention" that "turned a man into a horse and carriage."[19] The draisine was dehumanizing, turning its riders into animals. Critics such as these did not perceive the act of riding one as equivalent to traveling by horse, which freed the rider from labor, but as shifting the horse's labor to the rider, turning humans into beasts of burden. The analogy was not bicycle = horse, but rider = horse, transferring the work of four legs to two.

Note, as well, that criticisms such as these share the additional assumption that transport devices have a utilitarian purpose, that technology advances work. The English term "hobby horse" sustains the equestrian analogy but shifts the context to play: the draisine was touted as a recreational device for harmless, purposeless exercise. Caricatures in the popular press derided early riders as careless aristocrats, parading their devices and themselves. One 1819 drawing titled "Royal Hobby's" [sic] pictures a drunken prince regent mounting a maid in one frame, while sitting primly on a draisine with his paunch leaned against the push bar in another, doffing his hat to a disapproving onlooker as his wife perches in an undignified crouch behind him. Captions contrast his smug satisfaction at his "Windsor job" with the outraged disapproval of a working father with starving children.

The draisine represents aristocratic excess and frippery, an image repeated in caricatures and conveyed by the alternate term "dandy horse." The cartoonish images reflected the reality that, at least initially, draisines were affordable only to aristocrats.[20] The fictional worker's outrage in Cruickshank's cartoon had its basis in fact, as well, and not simply for capturing the generalized resistance to mechanization common in the era.[21] Those whose livelihoods

Figure 1.1. Thomas Cruickshank, "Royal Hobby's" (1819).

depended on horses perceived their wooden replacements as an economic threat: "Blacksmiths are reported to have smashed hobbyhorses that passed through their villages. This horse, they pointed out, required no shoeing."[22]

But the general public appears to have rejected the equestrian equation. Caricatures abound mocking the horse's extinction, such as "The Pedestrian Hobbies" (William Heath, 1819), which wittily points out a singular weakness of the draisine in its verse:

> You have heard of Pegasus flying no doubt
> But our Hobbies now beat him good back
> For when you are tired of riding about
> You may carry your horse on your back.

Again, the caricature captures the device's flaws while skewering recreation and the rich, and implicitly valuing work and utility. Top-hatted dandies are shown careening downhill astride the draisine, only to plunge out of control in the absence of brakes, and then lug it uphill, the device riding the human beast of burden. The central figure adopts the same posture and dress of the painting of Drais astride his machine, pointedly mocking its creator.[23]

The draisine's ultimate failure with the public stemmed less from the influence of popular images on the imagination of potential riders than on the biases at the root of their criticism. The device could not be fit neatly into the prevailing equestrian model of individual transport. Instead, it occupied an

Figure 1.2. William Heath, "The Pedestrian Hobbies" (1819).

Figure 1.3. Detail from "The Pedestrian Hobbies" compared to a portrait of Karl Von Drais (1817).

indeterminate status: it was neither truly a substitute horse nor an aid to walking. Drais's own patent points to the vehicle's ambivalent position between man and beast. He claims, on the one hand, that it can "travel uphill as fast as a man can walk" and on a plain is "swift as a courier." Thus, it resembles a human, but can only match its speed on hills or flat ground. However, Drais claims that on dry, fast roads it can attain speeds "equal to a horse's gallop" and on descent "equals a horse at full speed."[24] It can rival a horse, but only under perfect conditions. Its climbing abilities require "a well-maintained post road" and speeds only "when the roads are dry and firm."[25] While a horse could speed uphill or traverse uneven, muddy roads, the draisine was incapable of riding easily on poorly constructed or maintained roads, and excelled on descents but failed on ascents. (For more on roads, see part 2.)

Still, the device's two-wheeled structure endured. And while subsequent designs, such as the high-wheeler or Ordinary featured disparately sized wheels, its evenly sized wheels became the norm. Constrained by its failure to fit the equestrian model, the drasine ironically established the basic two-wheel structure or "type form" that we associate with the bicycle to this day. And, while failing to supplant the horse, the bicycle retains its early equestrian pretensions. We still refer to the "saddle" of a bicycle, and to the "rider" who perches upright on it, positioned midway between the front and rear. While pedals and/or an engine enabled self-propulsion, the rider still guides direction using his body, applying pressure through the arms and legs, as on a horse. Common, if nostalgic, references to motorcycles as "iron steeds" or "chrome horses" sustain these indelible associations, as do Italian references to racers as *centauri* (centaurs), mythical beasts that are half man, half horse. Even the anachronistic reference to horsepower as a measure of power sustains the analogy.[26] (Note that this is a recurring pattern of thought: we refer to digital messages as email, as though they are the equivalent of handwritten letters, and organize our digital materials in folders as though they are all pieces of paper in a file cabinet, blithely ignoring that such a definition glosses over whether we mean text, photos, or audiovisual recordings.) The stubborn persistence of this "type form" despite its engineering limitations reveals the influence of less rational—if not irrational—influences of rider perceptions and expectations.

SPEED AND ACCELERATION

Consider how competing models of early transport influenced alternative designs that proved less popular and enduring. Figure 1.4, an 1869 Currier & Ives painting, pictures the modern velocipede prevailing over the horse, but also points to an alternative source of early bicycle design innovation: the horse cart or carriage (and the chariot well before that). The "horseless carriage" model prevailed in automobile design, but failed to gain traction in cycle design. A wealth of competing designs featuring more than two wheels or alternative configurations of two wheels resolved many of the design limitations of both the draisine and its pedal-driven successor, the velocipede, but were not embraced by consumers.[27]

Tricycles, for instance, provided greater stability than two wheels, and historians note that in 1819, as draisine riders were being caricatured in the press, Italian, French, and Scottish engineers produced three-wheeled devices that presented a variety of solutions: they enhanced stability, elevated the rider's feet, and added mechanical propulsion, not by foot-driven pedals, but hand-driven levers or cranks.[28] It could be that, as Herlihy suggests, such devices had their own limitations, lacking the "simplicity, compactness, and convenience of a personal vehicle on the order of a draisine,"[29] but additional biases were surely at work. The carriage industry produced three-wheeled devices during the 1840s and 1850s as "wheelchairs for the disabled and lever-driven tricycles for children."[30] Augmenting the existing dismissal of human-propelled devices as merely toys was rejection of wheeled devices as facilitators, rather than accelerators, of movement. They were "*voitures de malades*" (carriages for the sick),[31] associated with the infirm and debilitated, with "elderly and middle-aged gentlemen whose weight or nerve renders

Figure 1.4. Currier & Ives, "The Velocipede" (1869).

them unsuited for bicycling."[32] One writer in 1869 lamented, "In these days of invention, improvement and locomotion, why cannot we poor pedestrians be helped forward by some new kind of velocipede or accelerator?"[33]

Drais's initial claims that his device would allow humans to equal a horse's speed suggest the traction of the equestrian model as well as his two-wheeled, inline design. For, as imperfect as it was, the draisine could augment walking and running speeds. The three-wheeled models, by contrast, stressed practicality and assistance over speed and independence. (We explore the confluence of acceleration and freedom in greater detail in part 3.) Heavier and more difficult to steer, they provided mobility and stability at the sacrifice of maneuverability and speed. Even as late as 1901 the device was still equated with "the elderly, nervous and less venturesome."[34]

What other than this irrational attachment to speed explains the phenomenon of the Ordinary? Privileging inline design led to obvious limitations and flaws. The Ordinary, with its oversized front wheel, provided challenges in mounting and balancing, and, with a displaced center of gravity, the rider was in constant danger of being pitched forward over the handlebars at high speeds (the origins of the phrase "taking a header"). And there was no way of braking. Still, the Ordinary was supposedly an "advance" from the earlier designs featuring wheels of similar size because, in the absence of gearing, speed could only be increased by enlarging the size of the wheel, so that each pedal drive applied to the front wheel produced greater distance. Speed and daring trumped practicality and safety.

Wiebe Bijker argues, simply, that from its inception the high-wheeled bicycle was presented as "a sports machine," recounting how James Starley and William Hillman introduced their Ariel to the market by racing each other from London to Coventry in one day in 1871.[35] Their promotional feat associated bicycling with speed, and not simply for the racers developing the sport. "Whereas skiing began as a means of getting about and evolved into a sport," Bijker notes, "bicycling began as a sport and evolved into a means of transport."[36] "Evolved" is not an accurate description, given that, at the time of Starley and Hillman's race, high wheelers were competing with monocycles, dicycles, and multi-wheel cycles. As Bijker himself notes, "the tricycle was a very viable alternative to the bicycle . . . and not 'some historical mistake,' as it may seem now."[37] Instead, the Ordinary's association with athleticism and daring granted it a romantic appeal to those capable of mounting—and purchasing—one.[38] As with the draisine, consumers were wealthy, young males.

In fact, "The Ordinary gave bicycling an aura of elite snobbery and dangerousness that many wanted and few could previously afford."[39] Aggressively marketing his version, the Columbia, to American consumers beginning in the 1870s, Alfred Pope featured well-dressed men displayed on the latest models. Employing a technique that would become predominant in advertising in the twentieth-century, Pope focused as much, if not more, on the consumer, than the product.[40] (For more on fashion and consumerism, see part 2.) Initially, his Ordinary featured a dashing and daring gentleman:

> When Albert Pope put his first Columbias on the road, most Americans would have found the very idea that a man could remain upright on a machine with two in-line wheels preposterous. Some very early cyclists reported that they were actually mistaken for demons gliding down the road a few feet off the ground. Less than a decade later, even a preschooler deep in the slums of the lower east side knew what a bicyclist was: a rich, imperious Wall Streeter with neither the time nor the inclination to leave way for a ghetto girl.[41]

Impervious to both danger and cost, the Ordinary owner embraced and embodied a divisive identity. The device defined its rider as upper class, athletic and masculine.

GENDER

Complex associations of speed with gender also configured early bicycle and motorcycle design. The athleticism required to mount and propel the Ordinary limited its appeal to men, and bicycle manufacturers capitalized on "the upsurge enthusiasm for outdoor recreation and physical culture" in the late nineteenth century, an essential component of what John Higham has described as a cult of masculinity.[42] Speed, combined with the leisure afforded to men of means, fused into a fashionable image of manliness. "Cycling as sport and leisure initially conformed to a limited, or exclusive, definition of manhood. Advocates from the middle and upper classes promoted it as a healthy and manly activity, but one that was refined and therefore more civilized than brute sports like football or pugilism."[43]

Manufacturers, as well as cycling advocates, touted the Ordinary as a tool of masculine self-definition. Pratt wrote that cycling was "manly, innocent, humane and rational," that it was a "gentlemanly recreation, a refined sport."[44] Riding clubs and organizations such as the League of American Wheelmen were the equivalent of gentlemen's clubs, equally exclusionary but promoting healthier modes of male bonding than drinking and smoking.

Alternatives to the Ordinary promised a safer, more stable ride attractive to a wider array of riders. A model designed by Edward C. F. Otto featuring two wheels arranged side-by-side was popular for a time in the 1870s for this very reason. The rider perched on a saddle centered between two evenly sized wheels, using his feet on the pedals to provide forward motion and using handles fixed to the axle to steer "indirectly" by slackening or tightening a band brake on one or the other wheel.

Offering even greater stability and ease of operation, the tricycle became particularly popular with women in the late 1880s and instituted a definitive gendering of wheeled transport, linking safe, stable devices with the feminine,

Figure 1.5. Advertisement for Columbia Bicycles and Tricycles (1885).

and the high wheeling Ordinary with the masculine. The ad for Columbia cycles (figure 1.5) is representative of the nascent division. Pratt extended damning praise when he noted tricycles were "much used by ladies and elderly gentlemen who desire a vehicle that keeps its equilibrium."[45] The device became a means of signaling gender distinction, as "the conspicuous use of the highwheel bicycle" could be seen as "an overt expression of 'cavalier masculinity' . . . and a resistance to bourgeois domestic propriety."[46] Other configurations of three or even four wheels enabled pointedly domestic arrangements. Photographs feature ingenious methods for pairing couples, including this image of a husband and wife atop matching Ordinaries, supported by a rear wheel doubling as a baby carriage.

Figure 1.6. A "domestic" arrangement.

When the Safety bicycle (see below) added gearing, a device with two equally sized wheels was able to match the speed of the Ordinary,[47] with the added benefit of stability. This made bicycling accessible to riders of all ages and abilities, especially women, undercutting the association of two-wheeling with daring, or cavalier, masculinity. (We consider women riders, as well as the intersection of class and gender, in greater detail in part 3.) The bicycle's early development demonstrates that speed alone was not—and is not—considered masculine. Instead, distinctions in degree and quality, defined along gendered lines, characterize speed, and the devices that provide it, as either masculine or feminine. Devices that propel riders beyond ordinary limits, enhancing danger, gain masculine association, while those keeping speed under control while offering stability, become feminized.

These associations endure whether the two-wheeled device is human-propelled or motorized. The scooter is to the motorcycle, what the Safety was to the Ordinary. In "Object as Image," Dick Hebdige uses the scooter as an example of "sexing the object." He notes that from their initial appearance in the 1920s, scooters were marketed to women and acquired feminine associations, such that "despite modifications in designs over the years, the overall conception and placement of the scooter—its projected market, its general shape, its public image—remained fixed in the formula—motorcycles:scooters as men:women and children. Scooters were permanently wedded to motorcycles in a relation of inferiority and dependence."[48] (Note this phenomenon underscores the culturally specific nature of such associations, which don't apply, for instance, in Italy or in other parts of the world where scooters are ubiquitous forms of practical transport.) But in North America and Britain at least, such biases mean that contemporary scooter manufacturers face a challenge in marketing models such as the Burgman, which Suzuki has addressed in part by deliberately styling the bike's fairing to resemble that of a sport bike and emphasizing its 650-cc engine. Still, reviewers for motorcycle magazines felt compelled to address the scooters' implied inferiority. An American magazine headline read, "Scooter on the Outside, Sportbike on the inside."[49] One UK writer opened his review by stating, "'Proper' bikers may turn up their noses at Suzuki's Burgman just because it's a scooter, but let's get this straight right from the off—I loved it."[50] Interestingly, Suzuki seeks to mute gender anxieties by describing the Burgman 650 as redefining the "two-wheeled luxury scooter experience." Like Lambretta in the 1960s, which advertised its scooters in the United Kingdom as "sports car[s] on two wheels,"[51] Suzuki is appealing to riders' desires for elegance and comfort, hoping that class trumps gender and performance outweighs stigmas based on aesthetics.[52]

TYPE FORM

The bicycle and motorcycle, human accelerators with two, inline wheels, occupy a narrow course between speed and safety, propelled less by engineering and design considerations than social expectations, not simply about gender but about function and aesthetics. Molotch argues that objects acquire a specific "type form" and "people resist variations that depart too strongly from what they think 'a thing like that' ought to be."[53]

When the Safety bicycle, with similar-sized wheels and a chain linked to the rear wheel, appeared in the mid-1880s, it not only eclipsed the Ordinary but alternative unicycle, dicycle and tricycle designs, reinforcing the "iron steed" model that propelled the bicycle boom in the 1890s and that endures to this day. The Ordinary, with its limited appeal and high price tag, was fashionable for a time among a limited market of wealthy young men. Once, however, its speed was combined with stability, the revised bicycle became accessible to the general populace and its ubiquity established its type form. As Bruce Epperson describes, "when the technological leap to the safety bicycle made cycling physically accessible to everybody but the very poor and the elderly, the nation fell over itself in its rush to grasp a piece of that allure, igniting cycling's great golden era of the 1890s."[54] So ubiquitous were bicycles and bicyclists by the turn of the century that they were indeed ordinary. "Cyclists, much more than their predecessors a decade earlier, could ride the urban scene unnoticed, on machines as anonymous as they were," according to Nicholas Oddy. "Never before in the history of cycling had it been possible to cycle with so little attention being paid to one, and furthermore, that this was true for both genders."[55]

The type form that emerged came from the tricycle design initially rejected in the rush for speed:

> In September 1885, the British firm of Starley and Sutton introduced its "Rover" safety bicycle, designed by John Kemp Starley, James Starley's nephew. The first Rover, using a 36-inch front wheel borrowed from the firm's tricycle and indirect steering through bridle rods, was not a technical or commercial success. A second version, introduced a month later, was vastly improved. It had almost equal-sized wheels and direct steering made possible by sloping the head tube back and sweeping the handlebars toward the rider. The following February, the definitive version was introduced with equal-sized wheels and an almost fully triangulated frame.[56]

The rider sat between the wheels, not above the front wheel as on the Ordinary, redistributing the center of balance for stability. With her feet in reach of the ground, the rider could stop the bicycle, even in the absence of brakes. Power came from the rear wheel, operated by treadles initially, and then pedals linked

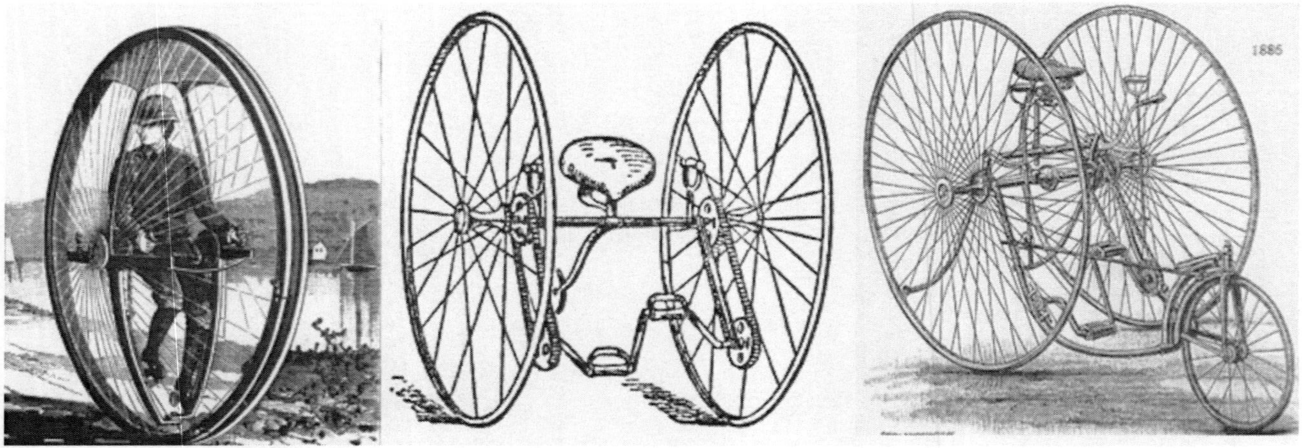

Figure 1.7. Monocycle, dicycle, and tricycle designs.

by a chain. Sprockets—a larger attached to the front wheel and a smaller to the back wheel—multiplied the revolution of the pedals, adding speed without increasing wheel size. The addition of pneumatic tires greatly enhanced ride comfort. (For more on rubber, see part 2.) In their advertisements, Starley and Sutton boasted that it was both "safer than any Tricycle" and "faster and easier than any Bicycle ever made."[57]

By 1900 or so, both the technology and aesthetics of the device had achieved "closure," acquiring a specific "type form."[58] As Oddy notes, "at even fairly close inspection it is difficult to tell the difference between standard road machines built in 1905 and 1925 by the vast bulk of manufacturers, not only in layout and structure, but also in finish, even down to graphic details such as transfers and lining."[59] But such details only distract from the basic and enduring architecture of the diamond-frame and two wheels of identical (or nearly identical) size, readily visible and identifiable in contemporary road signs. As in Pratt's 1879 definition, it is "a skeleton vehicle, consisting primarily of two wheels and a perch."[60]

As a transportation device developing simultaneously with the bicycle, the motorcycle was, then, equally constrained by social adherence to the "type form" expected of two-wheeled transportation. It is worth repeating that the motorcycle developed alongside the bicycle, rather than evolving from it, as a transitional device culminating in the triumph of the automobile.[61] Affixing a steam engine, the power fueling the Industrial age, was an aspiration from the time of the draisine—at least on paper. A caricaturist "whimsically depicted a draisine with a steam engine" in 1818.[62] His vision was realized in the 1860s. Coincident with the rush of experimentation on the velocipede were initial designs for motorized versions. Louis Perreaux created a metal velocipede in 1871 with an alcohol-powered steam engine tucked under the seat and over the rear wheel, attached to the motor by a belt drive. At about the same time, Sylvester H. Roper constructed one with a coal-powered steam engine. In the late 1880s, Marquis Albert de Dion and his mechanics Georges Bouton and Charles Trépardoux created steam-powered tricycles and quadricycles.[63] Steam engines, which were bulky, required frequent refilling and "half roasted"[64] the rider, proved impractical. As a result, Daimler is generally credited with "inventing" the first motorcycle, the Einspur, in 1885, but only because the engine he perfected—the internal combustion engine—came to prevail in motorcycle and automotive design. His intent was not to motorize a cycle: he initially placed his engine on a boat and then a carriage before building a crude wooden frame that necessitated adding two small wheels for stability.[65] The device was derisively nicknamed the "Bonecrusher," because it was "more like an old 'boneshaker' than the new Safety bicycles with tubular frames and wire wheels which were just coming into use in England."[66] It was not recognized as a motorized bicycle but an oddity harkening back to the velocipede era.

Once the Safety established bicycle type form in the 1890s, continued experiments in affixing a motor to a cycle were constrained both pragmatically and aesthetically by its design. In *The Evolution of Useful Things*, Petroski analyzes this 1977 cover of *Science* magazine illustrating eight possible turn-of-the-century solutions.

He argues that the components—the motor, plus a fuel tank and battery—and how they fit together on the existing bicycle frame, determined the design (rather than individual inventiveness). While, as we've seen, bicycle design was constrained by equestrian precedents, motorcycle design was constrained by two-wheeled precedents, as though guided by the imperative of "fitting a motor to a bicycle."[67] And the emerging form, like that of the bicycle before it, acquired a specific "type form" or "motorcycleness" divorced from questions of use and shaped by social expectations. Petroski's example is the "vestigial" tank first noted by John Heskett. Bikes that store fuel in the rear or even in

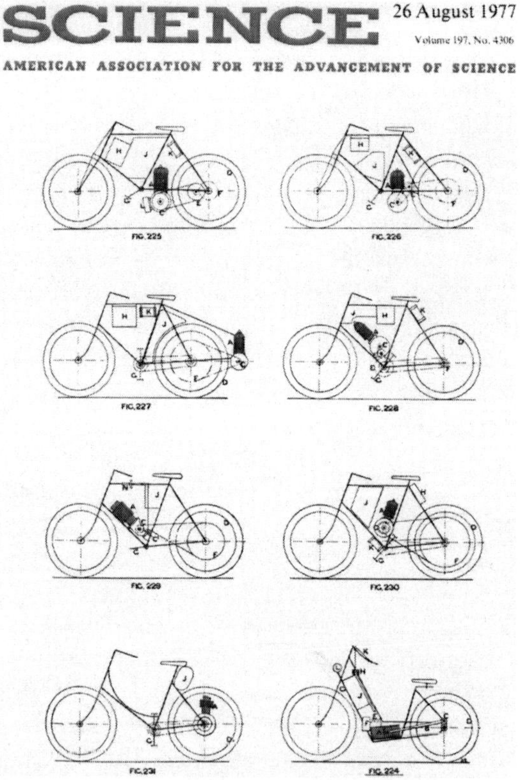

Figure 1.8. The cover of *Science* magazine, 26 August 1977.

the frame, such as the 1958 Ariel Leader, or under the seat, such as the 2001 BMW F650 CS, still feature a dummy tank (repurposed for storing tools, gear, or makeup) attesting to the power of the conventional visual image.

The type form of the bicycle constrained motorcycle design, but the reverse has also been true. Pryor Dodge describes a "motorbike"—a bicycle designed to look like a motorcycle—that appeared in the United States following World War I:

> The deluxe models had "tanks" (built-in or bolted-on tool boxes imitating early motorcycle gas tanks), headlights, full mudguards, and occasionally front fork spring suspension. With the addition of balloon tires, adapted to bicycles by Goodyear, the motorized look was complete; all that separated the "motorbike" from the motorcycle was the engine.[68]

The circle is completed here: the motorcycle, modeled on the bicycle, creates a bicycle modeled on the motorcycle, a phenomenon seen again and again as one device gains favor over the other. During the 1960s and 1970s, for example, popular culture granted motorcyclists and their machines greater visibility. In their hit song "Leader of the Pack" (1964) the Shangri-Las romanticized the rebel biker and the sound of his engine,[69] while the film *Easy Rider* (1969) glamorized customized bikes. In response, manufacturers such as Schwinn and Raleigh produced bicycles styled like choppers, with banana seats, elongated backrests, and high-rise handlebars.

The endurance of both bicycle- and motorcycle-type forms has nothing to do with design or performance advantages and everything to do with human perception, shaped by cultural conventions that are remarkably persistent. These tend, however, to stress the visual.[70] So long as devices sustain an exterior appearance of "cycleness," designers are free to tinker with internal components. This is best exemplified in recent advances in electric vehicles. Note that the Zero, for instance, is indistinguishable from gasoline-powered sport bikes. The same applies to motorized bicycles, which artfully incorporate battery power under the seat or in the frame and secrete the motor in the wheel hub (recalling Megola's 1920 design for a motorcycle with a rotary engine in its front wheel)—or, in the case of the Copenhagen Wheel developed at MIT, place all the components in the wheel itself, which can be mounted on any bicycle.[71] If the fuel source—be it electricity or gasoline or steam—is hidden from view, then engineers are freed to experiment and innovate.

But are motorized bicycles motorcycles? Cox and Van De Walle question the distinction between the two:

> But where, empirically, does the boundary between cycle and motorcycle lie? The EU regulates categorical distinctions on the basis of the wattage available

> (250 W) and maximum speed for the assist engine (25 km/h), below which thresholds the vehicle is defined not as a motorcycle but as an 'assisted cycle'. According to individual national laws, however, only certain forms of power are deemed viable to be used as 'assist'. A sub-250 W petrol assist, whilst practical, remains illegal in the UK. To note these confusions is not to argue that cycles and motorcycles are conceptually indistinguishable, but to suggest that their distinctions may best be conceived as an axis along which there are many possible stopping points. Between the fully motorised and the entirely pedal powered lies a range of limited power output vehicles, not just mopeds. Today, a range of "e-bikes" (electrically assisted or powered cycles) fills the market niche once filled by petrol-driven motor-assisted pedal cycles (Méneret and Méneret, 2004). Assuming we can set aside discussions over the relevant number of wheels, the continuum of cycle to motorcycle is a question of the variability of power and its source, from the smallest power assist, incapable of movement without pedal input, through mopeds to various categories of motorcycle.[72]

Focusing on the motor alone, however, is unlikely to erase the distinction between the two cycle type forms.

Contemporary suspicions of electric bicycles, for instance, as inauthentic for providing motorized assistance in place of leg power alone echo arguments from 1896 rejecting the marketability of a "power bicycle." Pope proclaimed, "I do not believe that the great army of bicycle riders throughout the country will take kindly to the idea of sitting idly in the saddle, and merely balancing the machine while the motor does the work." Such machines would appeal only to those "too indolent or feeble" to pedal.[73] (Unsurprisingly, Pope also envisioned that such motorized devices would have three or four wheels, sustaining the equation of cycling on two wheels with manly, physical exertion.)

The motorcycle type form is equally persistent—and resistant to visual alteration of rider position and wheel alignment, images fixed by the bicycle type form on which it is derived. Cycles with fewer or more than two wheels, with upright or recumbent riding positions, with inadequate or oversize wheels violate the type forms of "bicycleness" and "motorcycleness." Most individuals, for instance, are unwilling to accept that trikes or their inverse, Can-Ams, count as motorcycles, for their added wheel violates the culturally constructed concept of motorcycleness. For this reason, it is also unlikely that recumbent or "feet-first" motorcycle designs are going to ever find more than a small group of passionate adherents, even if, as Paul Blezard has contended, they have performance advantages.[74]

Instead, contemporary and innovative motorcycle designs are more likely to succeed if they retain traditional emblems of motorcycleness while pushing boundaries. J. T. Nesbitt's Bienville Legacy, a part of the American Design and Master Craft Initiative, is a case in point. Intended to be, in Nesbitt's words, "a true American four-cylinder superbike,"[75] it employs innovative strategies for suspension, for instance, using a single, centrally located composite leaf spring for both the front and rear suspension to eliminate steel coils further away from the mass center of the motorcycle, and is crafted from contemporary materials, including titanium, aluminum, and carbon composites. And yet Nesbitt took his inspiration from the 1923 Ace XP4 and deliberately invokes the equestrian model in the bike's ergonomic saddle, attesting simultaneously to the influence of motorcycle type form and the persistence of the horse as the original model for individual transport on two wheels.

As we have seen, most accounts of the development of two-wheeled transport rely on a developmental model, in which the "end product," whether it is a Rover bicycle or a motorcycle, results from what we might call technical reason applied to problem solving in device design. In an historical narrative, this analysis results in the "evolutionary" model of product development, in lieu of a more comprehensive understanding of the contingencies—social, economic, political, etc.—that impinge on product creation. We have suggested instead that what we now call end-user perceptions and cultural biases have as much to do with design as the technical solution approach. As such, the evolutionary model, while useful, should be understood contextually, alongside approaches that stress the device's social positioning.

What accounts for the popularity of evolutionary explanations of the history of a product's development, whether in two-wheeled transport or other technical innovations? We argue that it originates in assigning an end point in the development of a device, suggesting a point of "perfection," or at least a moment of culmination of a series of competing design requirements, from which one solution is determined the best by those involved in its execution. (Our example here could be, for example, the remarkable consistency of the diamond-frame, two-wheeled design, following its introduction with the Rover.) Once the design historian fixes on this moment in the design process, previous designs that "led to" this design are highlighted, with the other, "failed" designs noted, but no longer attended to. We then move from point A to B to C, demonstrating how the culminating design "solved" the various competing issues in the design process. This historical sampling process—discovering prior designs that can compare in some way to the culminating design, while casting aside those that fail to match the sought-after elements—results in a conception of the historical inevitability of a particular design. Think, for example, of the "inevitability" of cars powered by internal combustion engines over their "cast aside" competitors, such as electric vehicles. We suggest it could have been otherwise.

Had we not, for example, been constrained by the equestrian model, would the dramatically elegant Jackson's Monocycle (1870) have been considered an ideal solution to individual wheeled transport: one individual, one wheel?

Figure 1.9. **The Wheelsurf (2015), *right*, compared to Jackson's Monocycle (1870). Monocycle photo by Damien Merle, courtesy of Claude Reynaud, *Legendary Bicycles* (Georges Naef, 2013)**

Equally precarious as the Ordinary, it might have captured the male consumer's predilection for danger. Given that it won a gold medal at a race in Vésinet, it would have satisfied the need for speed.[76] Historian Charles Meinert listed the monocycle's design merits: "less friction with a single axle, lighter machines because of a single wheel, greater speed with a large wheel, less arm exertion in steering, and the ability of women to ride side-saddle on some machines."[77] Still, like Lawson's derided "Bicyclette," its seat placed the rider too close to the ground, within the wheel rather than on top of it, the so-called proper "mount" for the rider who was expected, in the words of one contemporary commentator, to "get up and over his work."[78] Associations of unicycle designs with witch's brooms fused gender bias with irrational superstition.[79] In the absence of such culturally derived preconceptions and prejudices, leading to the monocycle's dismissal as a "curiosité acrobatique" fit only for clowns and acrobats,[80] the model for individual wheeled transport might have been the futuristic design of the Wheelsurf.[81]

It could have been otherwise—and for additional reasons than the "social sentiments and ways of being" we have discussed in this chapter. As part 2 will explore, not simply the devices' designs but the materials employed in their construction are themselves cultural products. The preconditions for the creation of bicycles and motorcycles involved roads, rubber, steel, and textiles, each with its own multifaceted developmental history involving equally complex social dynamics.

NOTES

1. See, for instance, David Herlihy's account in *Bicycle: The History* (New Haven, CT: Yale University Press, 2004), 225–50.

2. Mortiz Holfelder, *Das Buch vom Motorrad: Eine Kulturgeschichte auf zwei Rädern* (Husum: Husum, 1998), 10–16.

3. Holfelder, *Motorrad*, 14.

4. Erik Eckermann, *World History of the Automobile* (Warrendale, PA: Society of Automotive Engineers, 2001). Butler's device has also been credited as a precursor to Benz's automobile. See G. N. Georgano, *Cars: Early and Vintage 1886–1930* (New York: Crescent Books, 1990).

5. Claude Reynaud calls this "the great deception" of bicycle history, pointing to *Le Vélocipède Illustré* as originating the myth in 1870. See *Vélos de legend* [Bicycles of Legend] (Geneva: Georges Naef, 2013), 16, 47. For a brief overview of other mythical origins, see David B. Perry, *Bike Cult: The Ultimate Guide to Human Powered Vehicles* (New York: Four Walls Eight Windows, 1995), 4–5.

6. Reynaud includes an image of a French "horse" drasienne with a brake block and notes that Drais equipped his draisine with a brake called a "checker" in his patent of 1818. See *Vélos de legend* [Bicycles of Legend], 32. Also see Tony Hadland and

Hans-Erhard Lessing, *Bicycle Design: An Illustrated History* (Cambridge, MA: MIT Press, 2014), 258–59.

7. For an exhaustive comparison of the existing records, see Hadland and Lessing, *Bicycle Design*, 38–53.

8. Peter Cox with Frederick Van De Walle, "Bicycles Don't Evolve: Velomobiles and the Modelling of Transport Technologies," in *Cycling and Society*, ed. Dave Horton, Paul Rosen, and Peter Cox (Aldershot, UK: Ashgate, 2007): 120, 113. Writing about bicycles alone, Wiebe E. Bijker employs the term "false linearity" (*Of Bicycles, Bakelites, and Bulbs: Toward a Theory of Sociotechnical Change* [Cambridge, MA: MIT Press, 1997], 7).

9. Cox with Van de Walle, "Bicycles Don't Evolve," 123.

10. Henry Petroski, *The Evolution of Useful Things* (New York: Alfred A. Knopf, 1993), 174.

11. Harvey Molotch, *Where Stuff Comes From: How Toasters, Toilets, Cars, Computers, and Many Other Things Come to Be as They Are* (New York: Routledge, 2003), 1. Cox and Van de Walle similarly claim that the "persistence of particular technologies results from political, economic and social decisions. Transport technologies arise within complex cultural matrices and their form, use and practice are shaped by context. Values of technologies are also contextual: the technologies may become obdurate, their meanings are neither inherent nor static" ("Bicycles Don't Evolve," 119).

12. Charles E. Pratt, *The American Bicycler: A Manual for the Observer, the Learner, and the Expert* (Boston: Osgood and Company, 1879), 3. As a caption to the image, he included a line credited to Shakespeare: "Here is the steed, we the comparison."

13. On the distinction between the terms "draisine" and "bicycle," see Herlihy, *Bicycle*, 23.

14. Reynaud argues that then draisines are really "velocipedes" and what we call velocipedes (two-wheeled devices with pedals produced between 1865 and 1870) should really be called "velocipedes with pedals" (*Legendary Bicycles*, 47). To avoid confusion, we retain the common, if incorrect, distinction, using the term *draisine* to refer to devices without pedals and *velocipedes* for devices with pedals. Hadland and Lessing provide a useful chart delineating the names and spellings for various two-wheeled devices in German, French, and English (British and American). See *Bicycle Design*, xvii.

15. See Herlihy, *Bicycle*, chapter 1: "The Elusive Mechanical Horse," 15–30.

16. Herlihy, *Bicycle*, 21.

17. Hadland and Lessing, *Bicycle Design*, 8–10; Carlton Reid, *Roads Were Not Built for Cars: How Cyclists Were the First to Push for Good Roads & Became the Pioneers of Motoring* (Washington, DC: Island Press, 2015), Kindle loc. 2514. The 1816 European "year without summer" has also been credited with influencing the Romantic poets vacationing on the shores of Lake Geneva, inspiring Byron's poem "Darkness" and Mary Shelley's novel *Frankenstein*.

18. Thomas Cameron Burr, "Markets As Producers and Consumers: The French and U.S. National Bicycle Markets, 1875–1910" (PhD diss., University of California,

Davis, 2005), 59. He notes that the design concept itself borrowed so obviously from a previously existing cultural tradition—horse-riding—that both producers and consumers adapted some practices and some vocabulary of this old tradition to the new machines" (62).

19. Qtd. in Herlihy, *Bicycle*, 24.

20. Hadland and Lessing suggest that Cruikshank's animosity to the device might have originated in an accident he experienced while riding with his printer James Sidebethem. The two collided while riding down Highgate Hill and Sidebethem later died (*Bicycle Design*, 25).

21. The most famous, of course, were the machine-breaking protests of the textile workers and self-employed weavers (the Luddites) in the British countryside, 1811–1816.

22. Bijker, *Of Bicycles, Bakelites, and Bulbs*, 24. Pryor Dodge argues that the creation of riding academies in France and England followed the equestrian model as well (*The Bicycle* [Paris: Flammarion, 1996], 18–20).

23. Bijker notes that the colored lithograph of Drais was published in the *Weimarian Journal for Literature, Art and Fashion* in 1820 (*Of Bicycles, Bakelites, and Bulbs*, 23), underscoring the device's association with dandyism.

24. Qtd. in Perry, *Bike Cult*, 14.

25. Qtd. in Perry, *Bike Cult*, 14.

26. Geraldine Elizabeth Biddle-Perry argues the same equestrian analogies operated in France and England: "In France the bourgeois cyclist was called *le cavalier cycliste* (rather than *le cavalier equestrien*), his upright riding position was seen as akin to that of an equestrian rider, with pedals being rhetorically substituted for stirrups, the handlebars for reins and the machine itself often referred to in terms of a bestial analogy as a 'horse of steel' with a 'skin of nickel and enamel' or 'whinnying' when overworked. Equestrian terminology was also frequently used in the fashionable discourse of English specialist journals and fashion magazines where the bicycle was referred to as a 'steed' and discussions of aristocratic female participation and their clothing linked with the codes and conventions of English equestrianism" ("Fashioning Social Aspiration: Lower-middle-class rational recreational leisure participation and the evolution of popular recreational leisure clothing, c. 1880–1950" [PhD diss., University of the Arts London, September 2010], 113).

27. For an overview of the differing fates of the velocipede in France, America, and England from 1867 to 1869, see Burr, "Markets As Producers and Consumers," 67–72.

28. See Herlihy, *Bicycle*, 53–55.

29. Herlihy, *Bicycle*, 55.

30. Herlihy, *Bicycle*, 56.

31. Pratt, *The American Bicycler*, 11.

32. Qtd. in Dodge, *The Bicycle*, 72.

33. Qtd. in Herlihy, *Bicycle*, 64. One scientific study has confirmed that "the early part of cycling evolution (1820–1890) allowed individuals to increase their personal mobility at a remarkably fast pace" (Alberto E. Minetti, John Pinkerton, Paola Zamparo, "From Bipedalism to Bicyclism: Evolution in Energetics and Biomechanics of

Historic Bicycles," *Proceedings: Biological Sciences* 268 [July 7, 2001], 1358), but note that it does so by focusing solely on two-wheeled devices, embracing the determinist model while ignoring competing wheeled devices.

34. "Too Old for Cycling?" Ad for Tinkham Tricycles published in the April 25, 1901 issue of *The Youth's Companion*, http://www.magazineart.org/main.php/v/ads/bicyclesandmotorcycles/bicycles/Tinkham+Tricycles+-1901A.jpg.html.

35. Bijker, *Of Bicycles, Bakelites, and Bulbs*, 36–37.

36. Bijker, *Of Bicycles, Bakelites, and Bulbs*, 37.

37. Bijker, *Of Bicycles, Bakelites, and Bulbs*, 57.

38. Paul d'Orléans has argued that speed equally configured motorcycle advertising. See "Selling Speed," *The Vintagent*, January 30, 2012, http://thevintagent.blogspot.com/2012/01/selling-speed.html?m=1.

39. Bruce D. Epperson, *Peddling Bicycles to America: The Rise of an Industry* (Jefferson, NC: McFarland & Company, Inc., 2010), Kindle loc. 2499.

40. See Robert J. Turpin, "'Our Best Bet Is The Boy': A Cultural History of Bicycle Marketing and Consumption in The United States, 1880–1960" (PhD diss., University of Kentucky, 2013), 39, 43. Also see Burr, "Markets As Producers and Consumers," 84–89, who notes that Pope's methods were "unusually aggressive for the time" (87).

41. Epperson, *Peddling Bicycles to America*, Kindle loc. 1713.

42. John Higham, "The Reorientation of America in the 1890s," in *Writing American History*, ed. John Higham (Bloomington: Indiana University Press, 1970), 79. Higham may have been the first to identify the cult of masculinity, but his thesis has been echoed and expanded by a chorus of voices, including Clifford Putney. See *Muscular Christianity: Manhood and Sports in Protestant America, 1880–1920* (Cambridge, MA: Harvard, 2001). Gail Bederman points out that the adjective "masculine" did not come into widespread usage until the 1890s (*Manliness and Civilization: A Cultural History of Gender and Race in the United States, 1880–1917* [Chicago: University of Chicago Press, 1995], 6, 18–19), and Ann Douglas notes that the cultivation of manly men during the period emerged in reaction to the perceived "feminization of American culture" (*The Feminization of American Culture* [New York: Doubleday, 1988]). As Highman notes, virility was opposed to the "effeteness" of late-nineteenth-century culture.

43. Turpin, "'Our Best Bet Is The Boy,'" 43. He notes that the definition of American masculinity at the time was not fixed, but changing and refines the concept of masculinity to note its racial definition: "White men who participated in cycling used the bicycle not only as a means of reaffirming their strength, perseverance, independence, courage, adventurism, temperance, and virility, but also as a means of exercising authority through the manner in which they attempted to control access to cycling. In essence, white, middle-class men demonstrated their manliness through their participation in cycling and their attempts to exclude others" (25).

44. Pratt, *The American Bicycler*, 30. Burr sees such insistence on gentlemanliness as defensive, suggesting "an underlying lack of social legitimacy" behind the device ("Markets As Producers and Consumers," 91). Pratt, hired as Pope's in-house patent attorney in 1881, was clearly engaged in marketing his employer's devices (Burr,

"Markets As Producers and Consumers," 105). For more on Pope's involvement with the League of American Wheelmen and the Good Roads movement as part of his promotional efforts, see part 2.

45. Pratt, *The American Bicycler*, 6. Note that the tricycle was not, in fact, safer. Bijker points out that tricycles, which were heavier and more difficult to steer, outnumbered accidents on bicycles (*Of Bicycles, Bakelites, and Bulbs*, 60). However, we cannot agree that the device's failure to solve the safety issue explains its eventual eclipse in popularity.

46. Phillip Gordon Mackintosh and Glen Norcliffe, "Men, Women and the Bicycle: Gender and Social Geography of Cycling in the Late Nineteenth-Century," in *Cycling and Society*, ed. Dave Horton, Paul Rosen and Peter Cox (Aldershot: Ashgate, 2007), 153–54. Ellen Gruber Garvey notes that popular fiction supported this separation of spheres. She cites a 1888 *Godey's Lady's Book* story, Max Vander Weyde's "A Turn of the Wheel," arguing that "the man must be knocked off of his high wheeler to bring him within women's sphere and make him marriageable: he would go by too fast otherwise. As long as such a man was on a high wheeler, he was definitively outside women's sphere" ("Reframing the Bicycle: Advertising-Supported Magazines and Scorching Women," *American Quarterly* 47 [March 1995], 68). She notes, by contrast, that later stories featuring the bicycle emphasized marriage: "Stories that incorporated bicycles within a courtship plot (and courtship stories were themselves ubiquitous in middle-class magazines) use formulas that defuse the threat of women's bicycling" (85) and "the bicycle is simply an aid to making an improved version of heterosexual marriage" (95).

47. Herlihy, *Bicycle*, 169.

48. Dick Hebdige, *Hiding in the Light: On Images and Things* (London: Routledge, 1988), 84. One Internet meme puts the distinction more crudely, "Scooters are for men who want to ride motorcycles, but prefer to feel the wind in their vaginas." See, for instance, http://www.funnyquotesimg.com/874171/scooters-are-for-men-who-want-to-ride-motorcycles-but-prefer-to-feel-the-wind-on-their-vagina. One ecard features the quote with an image of a child on a trike.

49. Mike Hanlon, "Scooter on the Outside, Sportbike on the Inside," *Gizmag*, June 4, 2004: http://www.gizmag.com/futuristic-650-scooter/1909/.

50. Fraser Addecott, "Suzuki Burgman 650 Executive review: Real sharp scooter," *Mirror*, November 7, 2013, http://www.mirror.co.uk/lifestyle/motoring/suzuki-burgman-650-executive-review-2688112.

51. Hebdige, *Hiding in the Light*, 96.

52. Interestingly, this campaign runs counter to the scooter revival in urban centers in the United States and Europe, which has based itself on economic practicality, rather than luxury, and, in some cases, deliberately defied conventional aesthetics through an embrace of recycling and do-it-yourself styling. See Klaus Neumann-Braun, "Retro Meets Rat, or the Vespa Legacy in the Hands of Young People," *International Journal of Motorcycle Studies* 6 (Spring 2010), http://ijms.nova.edu/Spring2010/IJMS_Artcl.NeumannBraun.html.

53. Molotch, *Where Stuff Comes From*, 97.

54. Epperson, *Peddling Bicycles to America*, Kindle loc. 1713.

55. Nicholas Oddy. "The Flaneur on Wheels?" in *Cycling and Society*, ed. Dave Horton, Paul Rosen, and Peter Cox (Aldershot, UK: Ashgate, 2007), 102.

56. Epperson, *Peddling Bicycles to America*, Kindle loc. 1959.

57. See http://www.roadswerenotbuiltforcars.com/wp-content/uploads/2012/12/starley-rover-safety-bicycle1884.jpg.

58. In the SCOT model outlined by Bijker, "closure leads to a decrease of interpretative flexibility—to one artifact becoming dominant and others ceasing to exist" (*Of Bicycles, Bakelites, and Bulbs*, 87).

59. Oddy, "The Flaneur on Wheels?" 103. He notes that bicycle aesthetics were so fixed that an English murder trial hinged on the color of the criminal's bike: green, rather than the ubiquitous black (107–8). Epperson quotes Frank Schwinn as recalling that the period between 1903 and 1925 was defined by "the almost complete standardization of all bicycle parts," bemoaning that fact that "the bicycle was so completely standardized that one bicycle looked, and was, almost exactly like another" (*Peddling Bicycles to America*, Kindle loc. 5148).

60. Pratt, *The American Bicycler*, 26.

61. In fact, most bicycle historians, including Dodge and Herlihy, either ignore the motorcycle entirely or treat its development superficially, focusing instead on how the bicycle paved the way for the automobile and airplane.

62. Herlihy, *Bicycle*, 301.

63. Dodge, *The Bicycle*, 146.

64. Qtd. in Herlihy, *Bicycle*, 303.

65. Dodge, *The Bicycle*, 150.

66. G. N. Georgano, *Cars: Early and Vintage 1886–1930* (New York: Crescent Books, 1990), 13.

67. Petroski, *Evolution of Useful Things*, 174.

68. Dodge, *The Bicycle*, 175.

69. Lisa MacKinney, "'Mmmm, he's good-bad, but he's not evil': The Shangri-Las, "Leader of the Pack," and the Cultural Context of the Motorcycle Rider," *International Journal of Motorcycle Studies* 4 (Spring 2008), http://ijms.nova.edu/March2008/IJMS_Artcl.MacKinney.html.

70. Consider that both devices were created at the same time as photography and film were invented. Bicycle advertising has also been credited with developing an emerging art form: the poster (see Ross D. Petty, "Peddling the Bicycle in the 1890s: Mass Marketing Shifts into High Gear," *Journal of Macromarketing* 15 [Spring 1995], 32–46).

71. On the Copenhagen wheel, see http://senseable.mit.edu/copenhagenwheel/. The motor is produced by Ducati Energia, which was formed after the Ducati brothers split their company into two in 1948: DUCATI Elettrotecnica and DUCATI Meccanica. The innovative product was featured in the Showtime series *Weeds* (Season 7, June 11, 2011–September 26, 2011). See Alissa Walker, "How 'Weeds' Became a Marketing High For MIT's Hybrid Bike Wheel," September 15, 2011, http://www.fastcodesign.com/1665013/how-weeds-became-a-marketing-high-for-mits-hybrid-bike-wheel.

72. Peter Cox with Frederick Van De Walle, "Bicycles Don't Evolve," 124. Applying a SCOT analysis to the development of motorcycles in New Zealand

1895–1915, Reg Eyre agrees that the distinction between motorized bicycle and motorcycle is moot. He notes that "even the most modern machines still have the engine placed centrally between the wheels and the steering column in the same position as the first 'modern' Werner motorised bicycle of 1902" ("Understanding the History of the Motor Cycle from a Sociotechnological Perspective with Examples from New Zealand, 1895–1915" [paper presented at the *International Journal of Motorcycle Studies* Conference + Exhibition, Chelsea College of Art and Design, University of the Arts London, July 5, 2013]).

73. Qtd. in Herlihy, *Bicycle*, 411.

74. Paul Blezard, "Feet First into the Future (if only we had the sense)" (paper presented at the *International Journal of Motorcycle Studies* Conference + Exhibition, Chelsea College of Art and Design, University of the Arts London, July 5, 2013).

75. Quoted in Alan Cathcart, "Bienville Legacy Motus V-4 Project," *Motorcyclist*, March 31, 2014, http://www.motorcyclistonline.com/news/bienville-legacy-motus-v-4-project-wild-file. Also see J. T. Nesbitt, "Legacy Motorcycle Commission Design Brief," http://commission.admci.org/design-brief.

76. Louis Baudry de Saunier, *Le Cyclisme: Théorique et Pratique* (Paris: La Librairie Illustrée, 1893), 97.

77. Qtd. in Pryor, *The Bicycle*, 55.

78. Robert P. Scott, *Cycling Art, Energy and Locomotion: A Series of Remarks on the Development of Bicycles, Tricycles and Man-Motor Carriages* (Philadelphia: J. B. Lippincott Company, 1889), 32.

79. Famously, the association with witches and cycling was exploited in *The Wizard of Oz* (1939), as Miss Gulch riding her bicycle is transformed during Dorothy's vision of the tornado into the Wicked Witch on her broom. For a clip, see https://www.youtube.com/watch?v=NA42WWfh1xQ.

80. De Saunier, *Le Cyclisme*, 97, 99.

81. Others include the various monocycle versions created by Kerry McLean: http://www.mcleanmonocycle.com/mclean-monocycle/. A motorized concept vehicle based on the unicycle, the Bombardier Embrio, won a gold Annual Design Award in 2003 from the Industrial Design Society of America & *Business Week* Magazine: http://www.brp.com/en-us/company/news/bombardierr-embrio-concept. Despite its name (and image in profile), the Uno, designed by Benjamin Gulak, is actually a dicycle, with two wheels arranged tight together to give the appearance of one: http://bengulak.com/innovation_UNO.html.

Part II

MATERIALS

Chapter Two

Roads

Mobility, Bicycles, Motorcycles

One of our central goals is to understand technological devices in context: seeking to comprehend a device on the basis of what it's *for* is reductive and fails to consider that while utility is obviously behind the invention of a device (i.e., we seek new devices to extend human capabilities), devices always already appear, inseparably, in a socio-cultural and economic context. In this chapter we'll consider another facet of this embeddedness: the connection of the device to its physical environment.

The title of Bernt Spiegel's book on motorcycling, *The Upper Half of the Motorcycle*, proclaims that in the act of riding a type of unity occurs between the rider and the machine, a claim that could be understood neurologically, psychologically, and even metaphysically (as we will discuss in part 3).[1] In the case of two-wheeled vehicles, we must consider another connection as well: not only from a design standpoint, but as a precondition to their existence, we must have roads. These "roads" may be a simple dirt pathway (engendering the existence of mountain bikes and dirt motorbikes). The road could be an interstate highway, allowing for rapid transit of a motorcycle, but denying entry to any bicycle. In between these two extremes we have varying types of passageways for two-wheeled vehicles. However, except in certain exceptional cases (elevated bikeways erected at the end of the nineteenth century, bikeways in places such as Amsterdam, Asian cities where the sheer number of bicycles dominate the roadways), bicycles and motorcycles have been a secondary presence on roads, and a secondary consideration in roads' construction. Yet, the contact between a two-wheeled vehicle and a road is critical. Whether it be from the standpoint of a pneumatic tire or the type of road (wooden, gravel, asphalt, concrete), this paired relationship is reciprocally determinative, both of the machine and of the road. Hence, in understanding roads we are simultaneously broadening our understanding of two-wheeled vehicles and, in understanding bicycles and motorcycles, we gain insight into roads.

While engineered roads are not indispensable to the existence of two-wheeled vehicles, the presence of roads allowed the bicycle and motorcycle to develop into essential means of personal transportation. But the devices alone did not influence road development. Equally significant were human imperatives for and understandings of movement or mobility.

The relationship between a two-wheeled vehicle and the road that bears it can be unpacked as a greater complex of values within which riding occurs. While we unreflectively assume that roads are there for our commuting purpose or traveling pleasure, the sheer presence of a road is a consequence of a series of decisions: Where? Why? For whom? How long? Of what substance? Who pays for it? More generally, a road's existence results from the realization of a set of social and economic values. In America, we have grown to expect safe, straight, huge Interstates and quiet suburban streets. We expect quiet on rural pathways and tolerate street noise in a big city, yet the experiences we have on all these roads reflect the culture in which they arise. Roads may serve cultural imperatives when they quickly move the weapons of war, or when they bypass communities without political clout, or ignore such obligations when, for example, their known danger to two-wheeled vehicles is ignored. Roads don't simply allow for human movement; they are part of the system we call mobility.

MOBILITY

Following Tim Creswell, we can distinguish between movement and mobility. As he notes, movement is a kind of abstraction from mobility, shorn of all its cultural and ideological content. Pure movement from one place to the next occurs. However, while such movement can be understood in, for example, the equations of physics, such an understanding is an abstraction from our experience of movement, which always occurs within a human context—that is, movement is always embedded in a complex nexus of cultural and/or ideological elements. When we understand that any kind of movement always already finds itself embedded in culture, we may call that mobility.[2] As such, any discussion of roads and their function can understand them in the context we first encounter them—that is, as aids to *mobility*—or, reductively, as a solution to a technological problem—the human need for *movement*. For example, in demonstrating how concrete has a superior wear resistance relative to asphalt, we would be discussing how concrete is a better material to facilitate human *movement*. Analyzing the torturous process that led to the creation of the (concrete-based) American interstate highway system—from securing legal and political access to the economics of material production—we would be examining how Americans achieved their contemporary *mobility*. Thus, we should understand that any encounter with transport of any kind is always already grounded in mobility, and that any discussion of movement is an abstraction from issues of mobility.

Of course, humans physically moving their bodies through space aren't engaged in the only kind of mobility. As Jonas Larsen, John Urry, and Kay Axhausen note, physical travel—the kind we do on two-wheeled vehicles—is only one way to understand mobility. In addition, we can consider the movement of objects (as occurs in trade), imaginative movement (such as we experience in film, television, texts, and on our computer screens), communicative travel (via telephones, letters, Skyping, etc.), and virtual travel, as we find on the Internet.[3] Indeed, when we consider two-wheeled vehicles in the context of cultural studies, we are actually exploring the reciprocal relations between physical mobility—actually riding a two-wheeled vehicle—and imaginative and virtual mobility—how, for example, films parasitically appropriate the physical act of riding for narrative purposes, and in turn, how narratives influence our understanding of what we're doing when we are riding.[4] Like movement itself, the two-wheeled vehicle, understood as a pure technological solution to the problem of personal transportation, is an abstraction.

The two-wheeled vehicle as a technological object is embedded in the same cultural and ideological complex as is a road. For example, we might argue whether the Suzuki GSXR 1000 or the Yamaha R1 is faster, but sport bikes are encountered *as* sport bikes, that is, as "crotch rockets" ridden by "squids" who would reject any connection to a "cruiser." We might suggest that a fixie is a better solution to urban transportation than a mountain bike, but both types of bikes have embedded cultural associations that might cause a person to reject/accept one on the basis of those associations rather than the practical question of which would function better as transportation, given the environment.

Consider as well the step-through bicycle frame, originally designed to accommodate women's skirts. While a step-through frame might today be functionally more convenient, one can imagine men not allowing themselves to be seen on a "girl's bike." According to Harvey Molotch:

> Women's bicycles, with the dropped frames originally designed to handle large skirts, are more easily mounted by anybody—and also offer more comfortable rides. But now, even with heavy skirts gone, men do not go near the dropped frame. Females often use the male diamond form frame, as for competitive racing, but the "girl's bike"—like girls' names—stigmatize those of the opposite

> sex. They thus remain gendered, and hence when bikes are done up in pastels and with feminine baskets, they are of the dropped-frame variety.[5]

One could consider as well the inheritor of the step-through frame, the scooter, and its cultural associations, most notably for Italians with the priesthood, and for Americans, with Audrey Hepburn's ride through the city in *Roman Holiday* (1953).[6]

While a Japanese high performance motorcycle may have different cultural or ideological markers, depending on where in the world it is encountered and discussed, it will always find itself deployed in a relationship to other elements of culture: for instance, young versus old, "Jap bikes" or "rice rockets" versus the made-in-America cruiser, etc. Given the current state of bicycle production, where huge Chinese factories produce frames for a multitude of marques, the question of the cultural association of a specific brand becomes problematic (and something to highlight in marketing, for instance, Harley-Davidson as an "American" bike; BMW as a "German-engineered" bike; high-end Trek bikes as "made in Wisconsin," despite these brands employing vehicle parts that come from all over the world). In any discussion of other kinds of mobility—movement of objects, imaginative movement, communicative travel, virtual travel—we experience this same kind of cultural and ideological embeddedness.

FUNCTIONS OF ROADS

The concept of mobility implies a context for movement. Roads themselves occur in various environments, as the example of Rome suggests. For the Roman leadership, roads were one of the key instruments of empire, and, there, as in other dominant political orders, a precondition to a sense of nationhood.[7] In America, we can see roads manifesting themselves in differing cultural contexts.

> Roads served four different but interrelated components of American life, each of which contributed to the economic welfare of the nation: *agriculture*, farm-to-town or farm-to-city traffic—as well as "social, educational, and religious activities which produce traffic from farms to the schools, to the churches, and to the community centers"; *recreation*, the practice of combining business with pleasure travel, as well as the increasingly popular motor tour; *commerce*, the transport of goods between towns and cities about 100 miles apart; and *defense*, the use of road for military vehicles.[8]

Having long ago moved from an agricultural nation to a postindustrial one, we still employ the roads for moving goods in the commercial sense—today courtesy of UPS rather than a farmer's cart. Given the status of contemporary air travel, roads are becoming more important for recreational travel than ever. Of course, two-wheeled vehicle travel, when not made necessary by business, is a built-in form of recreation. Looking at two-wheeled vehicle use worldwide, however, we recognize that its contemporary American use—mainly as recreational vehicles, except in dense urban environments where bicycles may well trump other forms of transport—represents a tiny percentage of its functions in other cultures. Citizens of other countries use bicycles, scooters, and motorcycles much more often for moving agricultural goods (bringing, for example, fish to market), commerce (moving nonperishable goods), and work-related travel. The romantic, self-referential aspects of two-wheeled vehicles—relaxation, getting "in touch" with oneself, going on a "spiritual journey," constructing one's identity by identifying with a group ("outlaws," "fixie riders," etc.), or engaging in a long-distance test of one's endurance popularized in Western cycle literature—would be lost on the majority of the world's two-wheeled vehicle riders.[9]

MOVING PEOPLE, MOVING GOODS

As facilitators of movement, roads are the obvious focus, suggesting an inevitable development as animal and human paths became formalized as efficient means of travel from one point to the next. And indeed, histories of roads and road-making technology usually emphasize roads as sites of *movement*, ignoring issues of mobility. Yet, one should consider roads alongside other possible means of movement, such as waterways (in particular, canals), and, with the rise of the Industrial Revolution, rails (including both railroads and streetcars), which dominated, while not replacing, other forms of travel, such as horseback, cart, and coach travel. (The aqueous version of the railroad, the steamboat, is another significant alternative to road travel.)

To briefly rehearse the status of roads in the latter half of the nineteenth century, we can begin with the domestication of large animals around 7000 BCE, following which would naturally assume riding on animals would replace walking as a means of efficient transportation. However, until the development of the stirrup in India around 200 BCE, and its transmission to Europe around 700 CE, the original two-wheeled vehicle, the chariot—not the saddled horse—was the principal form of rapid transportation used by the military.[10] The development of metals for horseshoes and horse bits (700–900 CE) were another precondition to using horses for human transport.[11] Even then pedestrian movement continued alongside horse traffic for two thousand years: North and South American Indians (particularly the Iroquois and the

Inca) used human runners to transmit information, and "footmen" were a popular means of communication in Europe as well. The seventeenth century saw the development of "footposts" for these runners, which evolved into posthouses for horses, where horses could be rested or exchanged. Still, it was argued that a good footman could outdistance a horse over a period of seven or eight days.[12]

With respect to the movement of goods, following the development of the wheel in Mesopotamia in around 5000 BCE, carts were developed that greatly increased the load-bearing limits of the horse, since a cart could carry the equivalent of a horse pack train. But, the development of the chariot around 1700 BCE greatly increased the speed of individual travel. "The jump from 4 km/h in an ox cart and six km per hour on foot to 30 km/h in a chariot was not to be bettered until the coming of the steam engines 3 ½ millennia later."[13]

Canals, and then railroads, were other kinds of "roads" that, in their capacity to move both goods and groups of people, delayed demand for a reliable and efficient road system. Before railways superseded horse-drawn coaches, canals functioned as an important—and cost effective—link in the movement of people and goods. According to Winfried Wolf, "On land a horse could transport between 600 and 700 kg, but a single canal horse could move loads of up to 50 tons. Transport costs sank to a third of their previous level."[14] Indeed, "it was not until a full century after the beginning of the Industrial Revolution that the railways began to replace the canals and inland waterways, the arteries of the Industrial Revolution in England and Wales."[15] In America, canals functioned to improve commercial traffic until, of course, they found themselves in conflict with the new rail system, the latter supported by an aggressive cadre of rich investors and the politicians on their payrolls.[16]

While tracing the developing technologies of assisting human movement, from roads to the animals and machines that traversed them, understanding these developments in the context of mobility yields some intriguing insights. For example, the new railroad technology, like that of other transportation devices, was itself always already embedded in ideology. As Wolf argues, "In the 19th century the train was identified with egalitarian tendencies, the freedom from classes and the freedom of the collective."[17] Two-wheeled vehicles and the automobile, on the other hand, have been linked with personal freedoms, not collective egalitarianism. Note that the inherent contradiction between these two terms—freedom and equality—was precisely the incongruity de Tocqueville found at the heart of democracy as it was theorized by America's founders. Those who embrace individual "freedom" as the principal American political value are, consciously or not, favoring a value that is bound to increase social and/or economic inequality, given the natural difference in human intelligence, strength, and social skills, differences that tend to engender self-aggrandizement in various forms and, indirectly, inequality. Those who favor democratic "equality" implicitly support the notion of the limitation of certain citizens' endowments in favor of greater egalitarianism (for example, a progressive income tax, with at least a portion of the proceeds distributed to the less fortunate). As a group, riders of two-wheeled vehicles fall solidly on the side of "freedom," although the generally murky meaning of this term for them is open to debate.[18] What is clear is that, although transportation devices fall fairly squarely on one side or the other of this dichotomy—railroads enhance equality, while two-wheeled vehicles exemplify freedom—the roadways themselves seem to serve both constituencies. The wealthy get richer from road-building contracts, the award of which almost always relies on political influence (following the example of American railroad development), while the beneficiaries of its use are often the citizens of the country.

From bicycles to electric cars to motorcycles, we will find throughout the history of personal transport one or another form of conveyance publically demonized, not because it is antithetical to democratic freedom or equality, but because powerful financial interests see the mode of transport as an economic threat. Hence, when we speak of mobility as inherently ideological, we need to consider both political ideas (such as those of freedom and equality) as well as economic forces (such as the profound dynamics of capitalism). While the motorcycle emerged in Germany in the 1880s, Europeans, particularly the English, had already adopted a new form of personal transport, the Safety bicycle, which was met by business interests in places like Germany with as much enthusiasm as for a contagious disease.[19] "On 15 April 1864, the Prussian Government restricted 'the riding of bicycles, which has become fashionable' on most Berlin streets. The private owners of the urban transport systems pressured the government into banning the bike."[20] Given the rapid urbanization of Western nations and the growing size of their urban areas, bicycles and motorcycles were attractive alternatives to public transportation, particularly given the need for the emerging proletariat to commute between their dwellings and their bosses' factories.[21]

The geographical mapping of American cities, many of which were established on the basis of the needs of the railroad, did in part follow technological developments, such as the streetcar. As Earl Swift notes, "Streetcars, far faster than carriages, had lengthened the distance workers could cover on their morning and evening commutes; soon suburbs had sprung up within a short walk of the radiating streetcar lines, so that the settlement resembled the spokes of a wheel."[22] With the advent of the bicycle and the motorcycle, the rigid geometry of the rail lines could be replaced by roads more sensitive to the environment though which they passed, being traversed by the more maneuverable and flexible two-wheeled vehicles.

This developmental model would suggest that, as bicycles became more available to the working class, there was a "groundswell" of popular demand for housing that, while a sufficient distance from the noise and smell of the city, was close enough to make a bicycle a useful transportation device. Yet, the notion of consumers freely choosing transportation devices that suit their needs,[23] while simultaneously engendering changes in city and suburban geography, ignores the powerful determinative effects of transportation manufacturers, lobbyists, and others, on creating an arena of "free" choice for the consumer. Hence, the outline of the "development" of roads (like the brief excursus, above) fails to consider the context of roads and road building, a context we have, following Creswell, called mobility.

THE QUEST FOR BETTER ROADS

Until the development of personal transportation, there was no real impetus for improving the road system in either Europe or America. Given that, "until the 19th century, travel times, distances, cost, and capacities had altered little since the invention of the wheeled cart and the harnessing of the horse,"[24] there was no public demand that travel be made easier or faster. The main traffic on roads was agricultural. Until the relatively new concept of nationhood as coming into being as a result of a social contract—with reciprocal rights and responsibilities of both citizens and their representatives—there was no sense that the government had a public responsibility to citizens to maintain a network of roads linking cities and towns.

Despite the lack of public impetus for road improvement, moving faster was thought of as having a salutary effect on the individual, although it was an idea not universally shared. W. G. Lay notes that, "When in 1270 Bacon predicted, among other things, that 'one day we shall endow chariots with incredible speed without the aid of animals,' he was jailed for 14 years by his Franciscan order for being in league with devil."[25] In the eighteenth-century, Dr. Johnson famously asserted that his concept of the ideal life was to ride in a fast post-chaise with a pretty woman.[26] In the nineteenth century, we find the Duke of Wellington opposed railways as well as roads, because they would "only encourage the common people to move about needlessly."[27] The automobile fared no better in, for example, Tennessee, which had a "turn-of-the-century law that required a week's notice of any impending car trip."[28]

By the nineteenth century, what was historically acceptable as a pathway for horse and cart transport was found wanting in the age of self-propelled (either through muscle, steam, electricity, or gasoline power) vehicles. In both Europe and America, the physical threat to the development of personal transportation can be identified in a word: mud. Untended common pathways were at constant risk of being transformed into rivers of liquid, congealing, or frozen mud—difficult enough for a horse, but impossible for certain wheeled vehicles.

Exemplary of this experience is C. K. Shepherd's 4,500-mile "trot across America" in 1919, a trip made, like those of the young American motorcyclists after World War II, to forestall the seeming postwar necessity to settle down, find a wife, and get a job. Here he describes his experience of the state of America's roads:

> Ninety-five per cent or more, however, of America's highways are dirt roads, or what they are pleased to call "Natural Gravel." In many cases they comprise merely a much worn trail, and as often as not a pair of ruts worn in the prairie. Very often, instead of being a single pair of ruts, there are five or six or perhaps ten, where individual cars have manifested their own personality. When this multiplicity of ruts crosses and re-crosses in a desperate attempt to achieve the survival of the fittest, the resultant effect on the poor motor-cyclist is somewhat disconcerting.[29]

Here we find Shepherd outside of Philadelphia, on his way to San Francisco:

> At this juncture in my reveries the macadam road stopped and gave way to "natural gravel." That was quite sufficient to postpone any soliloquies I may have been indulging in until a later date. The entire sixty seconds in every minute were employed in keeping myself substantially upright. Small pot-holes gave place to larger ones, and they in turn to larger still. The loose sand, which was an inch or two deep at the start, soon assumed more considerable depths. As the detective books of our youth used to say, "the plot grew thicker and thicker." I was floundering about from right to left, prodding energetically on the ground each side with my feet to maintain some kind of balance. At times the back wheel turned up the sand aimlessly in an endeavor to get a grip on something solid. Here and there the sand and gravel were heaped in great ridges as if a mighty plough had been along that way. Getting through this stuff, thought I, was no joke. Furthermore, it was warm work; very warm work. Now and then I would find myself directed absolutely without control from one side of the road to the other, and only with the greatest strain could I keep the machine on its wheels. And with all of this the "highway" still maintained its regulation width of 90 feet! The casual observer from an aeroplane above would in all probability be attracted by its straightness, its whiteness, and its apparent uniformity. "What a splendid road!" he would think.[30]

While this may make for a fine adventure for an intrepid, ex-soldier, roads such as these could never support an emerging class of two-wheeled vehicle enthusiasts bent not only on getting to work, but exploring the country.

Although road building lacked a national mandate, there have been American roads since before its founding as a British colony. In *Ways of the World*, Lay argues, "The first manufactured road in the United States was probably a 70km length of road in Florida, running north from San Augustine to Fort Caroline. It was built by the Spanish in 1565, and the southern end is closely paralleled by Highway 1." However, hundreds of years were to pass before there existed a "national" road, one identified not as the province of local interests, but one for the citizens of a new America. "A formal road across the country was not available until the Lincoln Highway (or Route 30) was opened in 1923."[31]

In nineteenth- and early twentieth-century America, road tending was left to local groups organized for that purpose, with little training in road-making technology. Those employed on road crews sought the work as a means of paying off local taxes, or were charged for road surface work adjacent to their property on the theory that it increased the property's value. Indeed, it was not until 1916 that the U.S. government was persuaded to provide funds for roads that were increasingly not used for agriculture, nor fronting privately owned property, but instead connected cities and towns, snaking through long, uninhabited tracts of land, connections that yielded interurban traffic devoted to a diversity of purposes, only some of which were agricultural.[32] Various "solutions" to the ubiquitous mud—such as embedding wooden planks or half-logs into the dirt, or creating "corduroy" by placing logs side by side, perpendicular to the traffic—fared poorly. They were deadly slippery to a horse when covered in ice, required frequent maintenance by unspecified people, and, when in disrepair, were often worse than the road before its "improvement."

GOOD ROADS AND THE GOOD ROADS MOVEMENT

Ironically, the late-nineteenth-century push for improved roads came not from government but from organizations representing group of citizens who had no real economic interest in road improvement: bicyclists. Bicycle-related organizations and their members, "produced the first modern maps, were the first group tourists, were the founders of many of today's automobile clubs, and were the first organized protagonists for better roads through the Good Roads Association that arose in most developed countries."[33] Groups first developed a popular, dedicated cycle path in Brooklyn in 1895, and, as what was to become a "craze" in the late 1890s spread in the northeastern United States, greater demands were placed for road improvement.

> In Britain, the two national cycle clubs joined forces to create the Roads Improvement Association in 1886. . . . In the United States, the League of Ameri-

> can Wheelmen combined with the farmers group called National Grange of the Patrons of Husbandry (composed of state granges), to found the National League for Good Roads in 1892. . . . The league operated in 1905 at time when the cyclists' role began to decline relative to that of the motorist. . . . The League of American Wheelmen was also instrumental in 1902 in starting the American Road Makers, an organization that changed its name to the American Road Builders Association in 1910 and which has been active to the present day. The league itself became inactive in 1907.[34]

Thus, in America, the push for improved roadways did not result from an upsurge in pressure from individual citizens or, for that matter, from one concerned group of citizens: bicyclists.[35] Instead, one individual worked behind the scenes to organize popular advocacy, for less than altruistic purposes. Albert Pope made it his business to improve roads because it was good for his business—the manufacture and sale of bicycles. He organized, financed, and provided support for bicycling groups, principally the League of American Wheelmen.

Pope's story has been told often and well.[36] Born in 1843, Pope was a veteran of the Civil War. Attending Philadelphia's 1876 Centennial Exposition, he was fascinated by imported British bicycles on display, and the following year created the Pope Manufacturing Company. Through a partnership with the Weed Sewing Machine Company in Hartford, Connecticut (which, of interest to us, occupied the former factory of the Sharps Rifle Manufacturing Company), he began producing high-wheeler bicycles.[37] By 1886 he was producing the Safety, and by the 1890s his Columbia-branded bicycles were famous. The company was hugely successful, owing to the intersection of his business acumen and the growing demand for bicycles.[38]

As a businessman, Pope combined a sharp eye toward prices with a vision of the various promotional activities that would enhance his bottom line. These activities included political involvement, behind the scenes control of elements of the media, creating social clubs devoted to bicycles where there were none, and seeking out new markets—in this case, women—when spending on these enterprises increased the value of his own.

Perhaps Pope's most visible act of promotion was to found the League of American Wheelmen in 1880. Stephen Goddard notes that among the goals were to press state legislatures to improve roads, publish maps, endorse hotels and taverns along the road, shine a spotlight on road dangers that needed correcting, and fight tolls on bicycles. "In short, they would be the first to assert and defend the freedom of the American road, a mantra that would be echoed fervently by the automobile industry, not yet even in existence."[39] By 1887 Pope had successfully supported a New York effort to have bicycles accorded the same rights as carriages.[40] Starting in 1882, Pope sought to limit international competition through the erection of a tariff barrier (focused on

England), which, enacted as the McKinley Act in 1891, placed a 45-percent tariff on bicycles and bicycle parts.[41]

In addition to his political efforts, beginning 1892 the League of American Wheelmen began publishing *Good Roads*, a periodical listing the various challenges and accomplishments in improving roads. The magazine was originally edited by Sam McClure, who went on to found *McClure's* magazine. Pope maintained a relationship with McClure, resulting in a good deal of free and paid-for publicity for Pope's machines.[42] In the academic arena, Pope financed courses at Boston's Massachusetts Institute of Technology to develop road engineers, and he persuaded the Commonwealth of Massachusetts to set up a highway commission to improve the roads.[43]

Figure 2.1. The American Wheelman's *Bulletin and Good Roads*, Boston, May 27, 1898.

Pope also resorted to the usual promotional activities, sponsoring contests in which the prize was a new Columbia bicycle. In one instance, he offered a prize at a doll show for the doll best attired in a woman's cycling costume. One of the more notable contests was a nationwide poster contest, which, derided by art critics, was won by Maxfield Parrish.[44]

As the example of Pope suggests, the "demand" for improved roads did not result from some democratic uprising of citizens anxious for smooth, efficient transportation. Instead, better roads resulted from a number of external events and pressures. Tariffs promote domestic production and consumption, and thereby increase the need for road improvement, so the argument goes. Regardless of how fair or unfair they may be, the origins of Congressional support of the McKinley Act lie in the murky region of campaign contributions. What may seem to be popular culture reportage, in *Good Roads*, *McClure's* and elsewhere, may well have been financed by those whose business interests stood to benefit. Awards for doll costumes, a goofy but seemingly benign event, could well indirectly legitimize women's participation in bicycling. Pope's presence as the Man behind the Curtain in many of his promotional enterprises can represent how a set of economic forces, set in motion by self-interested parties, results in significant social and cultural changes.[45]

None of this is to suggest a conspiracy of capitalist fat cats controlling the economy, but rather to emphasize the importance of attending to the question of who gains economically from government-supported activities that benefit the citizenry generally, such as the enhanced quality of life that results from improved mobility. It is not a question of cynicism, but understanding the many forces that result in a singular phenomenon: good roads.

THE ROAD-MAKING DILEMMA

What constitutes a "good" road introduces further material complications. Building roads strong enough to bear wheeled vehicles involves a dilemma: "natural materials soft enough to be formed into a smooth, well-graded surface [are] rarely strong enough to bear the weight of a loaded wheeled vehicle, particularly when the material is wet. On the other hand, rock strong enough to carry wheel loads under all moisture conditions is rarely able to be easily formed into a suitable surface for traveling."[46]

While bitumen and asphalt were known to early civilizations, they were not used in road building.[47] The Romans' well-known development of roads, aiding military and administrative control as well as movement of goods, involved "good drainage, good material and good workmanship," alongside their invention of concrete, a development "which was lost for over 1000 years following their departure in AD 500."[48]

The greatest technological advance in road making, taking it beyond primitive mud-and-wood solutions, was made publically available a full one hundred years before active American government funding of road building, in British Road supervisor John Louden McAdam's 1816 work, *Remarks On The Present System Of Road Making*. His book described the technique for road building that bears his name, macadam (note the spelling variation).[49]

> The great secret of McAdam's method lay in the use of crushed stone in which the sharp fractured edges tended to lock together. When the voids between the pieces of crushed stone were filled with fine stone dust and repeatedly sprinkled and rolled to ensure adequate penetration, the result was a surface firm enough to shed water, but flexible enough to provide a suitable footing for horses.[50]

For the relatively vast distances required for American roads, even McAdam's technique faced two problems: the labor costs involved in producing the crushed stone, and the need to compact the mixture once it was laid down. Steam-based technology came to the rescue with "Eli Whitney Blake's 1852 invention of the steam-powered stone crusher, which drastically reduced the costs of broken stone," and the steam roller, which originated in France and Britain, with the design being copied by American manufacturers.[51] These two devices, along with the novel steam shovel, shifted the tremendous labor burden of road making from men and horses to steam-powered devices.[52]

It was not until the early twentieth century that asphalt (originally employed in Europe, but only on urban streets) and, later, concrete were used for road surfacing. In addition to various technical problems in the production of reliable asphalt and concrete, early asphalt was vulnerable to the weight of trucks concentrated on primitive tires, a problem that persisted until the development of pneumatic tires for vehicles.[53]

EARLY BICYCLE ROADWAYS

One of the assumptions of the narrative so far is that roadways were built for all vehicles to share—often at the expense of bicyclists, given their vehicle's size, openness, fragility, and general vulnerability to threats from other vehicles, pedestrians, animals, and weather. Our contemporary assumptions about road surfaces may block our imagination to just what there was to contend with on late-nineteenth-century urban roadways, namely horse manure. For example, as Swift notes, "In New York City, by one estimate, horses left behind 2.5 million pounds of manure and sixty thousand gallons of urine every day. That amounts to roughly four hundred thousand tons of manure a year—enough to float three Nimitz-class nuclear aircraft carriers and a half-dozen navy destroyers. Forget the smell and mess; imagine the flies."[54] Given animals' practice of relieving themselves at will, regardless of an urban locale's methods of dealing with this ongoing problem, one can only imagine piloting a bicycle down the street and the inevitable contact of the bicycle wheel with slick, smelly, slippery manure.

One solution to urban bicycle transport was the California Cycleway, connecting Los Angeles and Pasadena, a planned nine-mile-long elevated wooden "road" linking the two towns. This tollway (ten cents for a one-way ticket; fifteen for a round trip) originated with two wealthy residents, Horace Dobbins and ex-governor H. H. Markham. Four cyclists could ride abreast. As *Pearson's Magazine* notes, "The surface is perfectly free from all dust and mud, and nervous cyclists find the track safer than the widest roads, for there are no horses to avoid, no trains or trolley-cars, no stray dogs or wandering children."[55] A mile-and-a-quarter section opened in 1890 and, eventually, 1.25 million feet of Oregon timber were employed on the project, although the complete path was never finished. The *Pearson's* author rhapsodizes

> The cycle-track has pretty terminal stations and a Casino. The stations are little buildings of Moorish design, where cycles and motor cars may be hired and repaired and housed. The Casino sits on one of the loftiest hills in a beautiful tract of country that has been christened Merlemount Park, and which is now laid out as a peaceful retreat for the weary townsman.[56]

Unfortunately, the project failed for financial reasons, and was shut down by the turn of the century. The wood comprising the cycleway was sold, and the right of way was to become the Pasadena Freeway, signaling the victory of the automobile.

While the cycleway's history may support narratives of the inevitable progress of the automobile, as engines replace muscles in transport, consider Boston's contemporary Minuteman trail, a ten-mile (unelevated asphalt) bicycle route connecting Cambridge with Bedford (passing through Lexington and Arlington). Inaugurated in 1992, the trail follows (and supplants) a railroad line first built in 1846, thirty-nine years before the introduction of the Safety bicycle. Rail service was officially ended in 1981 and, by 1998, the path had been extended to Cambridge. (No motorcyclists are allowed, an interesting contrast with the Interstates.) In this case, motorized public transport was replaced by self-propelled individual transport suggesting, in the case of transportation developments, that not all "progress" moves in a unilateral direction.[57]

Figure 2.2. Cycleway looking from Hotel Green, circa 1901. Courtesy of the Archives, Pasadena Museum of History, Main Photo Collection, C16-12

THE GOLDEN ERA OF U.S. ROAD BUILDING

Despite the improvement of road-making technology, outside of concentrated urban areas, nineteenth-century American transportation economics were still largely focused on the railroads. Road improvements generally originated at the railway stop: given the railway's vast geographical reach, agricultural goods could find distant markets, but only if they could reach the railroad, so both railway companies and farmers found it in their mutual interest to improve the conduit from farm to railway station. Once at the station, both people and goods could find their way to other settled areas via the railroad. While this did improve the lot of farmers and increased the efficiency of agricultural transport, it did little to serve other American mobility needs.

The great American road-building era did not begin in earnest until the 1930s, but for most of us, the signal national road-building effort occurred in the 1950s with the construction of the Interstate Highway System. The political struggles and economic problems that energized the debate over its construction were eye-glazingly tedious, as a glance at Mark H. Rose's *Interstate: Express Highway Politics, 1939–1989*, will reveal.[58] But far from a gift to American drivers, "the interstate was initially justified to postwar American Congresses as a national defense system for the movement of military vehicles and the evacuation of civilians. . . . The formal name of the system was The National System of Interstate and Defense Highways."[59] President Eisenhower, as allied commander in Europe during World War II, was struck by the role the Autobahn played in Hitler's Blitzkrieg, and his support of the interstate system as part of war-preparedness—to have a land-based system of moving the instruments of war to wherever they were needed—resulted from his vision of the roadway as a component of our military defense strategy.

Both the bicycle and the motorcycle have been used in warfare, given their ability to cover uncertain terrain unsuitable for Jeeps, tanks, and other military vehicles. As Jim Fitzpatrick notes, bicyclist-warriors can be a flexible fighting force, first becoming wartime participants in 1901 in the Boer War, as members of the five-hundred-strong Cape Colony Cyclist Corps:

> While "riding a bicycle" is the usual image, bicycling is essentially a man-machine combination that allows mode to be matched to terrain, optimizing the use of wheel and foot. When sand, mud, obstacles, high winds, or a steep incline made pedaling difficult, the rider can get off and walk. The cycle can be pushed, carried, lifted over fences, and floated across rivers. Heavy weights and bulky loads can be transported on it. Moreover, man and machine can be readily carried on wagons, trucks, cars, boats, or trains. It was that combination that radically altered the human travel equation—for civilians and military alike.[60]

Motorcycles were employed in battle, from the dispatch riders of World War I, whose ranks included women, to the Nazis in World War II.[61] Steve McQueen's famous ride (and jump) in *The Great Escape* (1963) illustrated, for the popular imagination, the possibilities—and limits—of the motorcycle in wartime.[62]

Beyond military uses, however, the road system became an important component of the postwar recovery. The tremendous burst of economic activity and its concomitant prosperity following World War II was reflected in the increase in the number of vehicles on the roadway: the years of 1946 to 1950 saw a two-thirds increase in the number of motorized vehicles of all types on the road.[63]

As with all things American, the primary focus on, and justification for postwar road building was economic—with better roads, various elements of the economy could make more money. However, the transformative effects of roads don't simply involve dollars and cents. Consider, for example, the decisions made during the interstate era in linking city roads with the new interstate system, a process that often involved demolishing neighborhoods to provide access. As one might expect, older, poorer neighborhoods were chosen, and those neighborhoods often were populated by people of color. It could be argued then, that the racism that so permeated 1950s America manifested itself even in the building of a road. A road, in this respect, is a determinant of a nation's values, which in this case demonstrate that efficiency and commerce outweigh equal treatment of all citizens.

In addition to equal treatment of all citizens, one might add equal treatment of all modes of transportation. Ironically, while the bicyclists of the League of American Wheelmen and the Good Roads movement they inspired were responsible for influencing the growth of better roads, road design and proliferation summarily ignored the interests of bicyclists. Bike lanes, when they existed, were considered an addition to the leisure activities of a town's citizens, not an additional pathway for commuting, the transportation of goods, and travel to centers of consumption. While Albert Pope represented a powerful economic interest during his time, lending support to the growth of roads, subsequent support for road building came from those with an economic interest in either motorized transport or road construction.[64]

Consider as well the multiple-partner dance of road construction, the building of suburbs, the granting of the postwar G.I. Bill's mortgage benefits, and the ubiquitous spread of television, all of which not only served to promote the spread of suburbs and the consequent "mallification" of America (consider the huge automobile parking lots surrounding malls, relative to facilities for bicycle and motorcycle parking), but the correlative decline of some of our great cities, separating the rapidly increasing economic fortunes of the suburban gentry from those who once were their neighbors, the urban poor.[65] The growth of suburban single-family homes had justifiable benefits, such as (in tandem with the mortgage tax break) a powerful, positive jolt to many sections of the economy affiliated with construction, greater safety for growing (white) children, and personal financial security with the rapid growth of home values. But it also led to much greater use of private motorized transportation (with the needs of bicyclists and motorcyclists being ignored),[66] and the country has been dealing with the consequences of increased pollution—health and environmental concerns—ever since. While the era following that of great American road building seemed like an economic bonanza that would keep on giving, the current generation and its children will be dealing with the problems associated with this growth for some time. And, without good roads, none of the changes in our landscape, both physical and economic, would have been possible. Suffice to say that road building, while building a sense of nationhood, promoting economic prosperity, and providing for military readiness, is not an unalloyed good.

Two-wheeled vehicle riders, like other citizens, benefit from large, efficient means of travel, but, from their inception, bicycles and motorcycles were used for purposes other than travel: hill climbing, racing, off-road challenges, motocross, and the like. While citizens of the West have greatly benefited from advances in both road-building technology and the spread of roads, as riders we often seek to balance the value of accessibility with that of adventure. As such, while good roads are often our friends, we are reaching a point where some of the moral and spiritual opportunities inherent in two-wheeled vehicle travel are getting increasingly difficult to experience.

Political freedom was first understood as freedom to move, and twentieth-century governments' attempts at political repression can be understood as attempts to prevent movement, from the "homelands" of apartheid, to the camps of Siberia, to the house arrests of prominent opposition politicians worldwide. Roads exemplify, in a concrete (as it were) sense, freedom in modernity. Yet, this freedom needs to be understood in the context of other values—positive and negative—arising from the opportunity of mobility. Bicycles first allowed women to escape the patriarchal gaze of their family and community, a coincidence of movement and developing individual freedom we can understand as mobility. Correlatively, motorcycles allow us to light out for the territories, escaping, for however long, the confinements of jobs, relationships, and the oppressive quotidian. But part of our task of understanding what it means to be on the road—celebrated by figures from Mark Twain to Jack Kerouac to Willie Nelson—is that roads are not simple ribbons on which we travel, but social products entrenched in the values of our culture, for good or ill. Unraveling these value-riven strands of the roadways will make us more reflective riders and, one hopes, better citizens.

NOTES

1. Spiegel's book, originally published in German, is available in English: Bernt Spiegel, *The Upper Half of the Motorcycle: On the Unity of Rider and Machine* (North Conway, NH: Whitehorse Press, 2010).

2. Timothy Cresswell, *On the Move: Mobility in the Modern Western World* (New York: Routledge, 2006), 3.

3. Jonas Larsen, John Urry, and Kay Axhausen, *Mobilities, Networks, Geographies* (Aldershot, UK: Ashgate, 2006), 4.

4. While the road movie has many antecedents, from the Medieval processional, to the religious pilgrimage, to the quest narratives, it's an essentially American genre, rife with thematic significance (from Manifest Destiny to existential alienation). From covered wagons, as in *Meek's Cutoff* (2010) or cars, as in *Death Race 2000* (1975) and *Two Lane Blacktop* (1971), the roads have been populated by four- as well as two-wheeled vehicles. *Breaking Away* (1979) and *Easy Rider* (1969) exemplify how two wheels on the road can be fertile ground for an imaginative narrative.

5. Harvey Molotch, *Where Stuff Comes From: How Toasters, Toilets, Cars, Computers, and Many Other Things Come to Be as They Are* (New York: Routledge, 2003), 101.

6. Dick Hebdige discusses subsequent refashionings of the scooter's image during the conflict between the Mods and Rockers in England in the 1960s as pitting the feminized, Continental scooter favored by the style-conscious Mods against the motorbike, the preferred vehicle of the café-racing Rockers. See *Subculture: The Meaning of Style* (London: Methuen, 1979), as well as the section on gender in part 1.

7. At its founding, the Soviet Union was bereft of a road system linking its vast expanse. Leaders sought to employ film, distributed throughout the young nation, as a means of promoting national unity among diverse groups of people separated by language, religion, and culture. The contemporary emergence of the Internet, as a mode of virtual mobility, and one which also can supply a sense of unity (e.g., Facebook), may well augment the functions of roads in culture, just as film did for the Soviets.

8. Tom Lewis, *Divided Highways* (New York: Penguin, 1997), 12.

9. The list of two-wheeling memoirs is long and growing. Bicycling memoirs include Frances Willard's *A Wheel within a Wheel: How I Learned to Ride the Bicycle with Some Reflections by the Way* (Chicago: Woman's Temperance Publishing Association, 1895), Dervla Murphy's *Full Tilt* (New York: The Overlook Press, 1965, 1986), and Amy Snyder, *Hell on Two Wheels: An Astonishing Story of Suffering, Triumph, and the Most Extreme Endurance Race in the World* (Chicago: Triumph Books, 2011). Romantic celebrations of motorcycling include not only Robert Pirsig's *Zen and the Art of Motorcycle Maintenance: An Inquiry into Values* (New York: William Morrow, 1974, 1999) but Melissa Holbrook Pierson's *The Perfect Vehicle: What It Is about Motorcycles* (New York: W. W. Norton & Company, 1997). Travel and/or adventure memoirs predominate in motorcycle culture, from Theresa Wallach's account of her Africa crossing in 1936, *The Rugged Road* (London: Panther Publishing, 2001) to contemporary accounts, including Dave Barr, *Riding the Edge: An 83,000 Mile Motorcycle Adventure around the World!* (Bodfish, CA: Dave Barr Publishers, 1999), Jonny Bealby, *Running with the Moon* (London: Arrow Books, 1995). Andres Carlstein, *Odyssey to Ushuaia* (Chicago: Chicago Review Press, 2002), Robert Edison Fulton, Jr., *One Man Caravan* (North Conway, NH: Whitehorse Press, 1937, 1996), Glen Heggstad, *One More Day Everywhere: Crossing 50 Borders on the Road to Global Understanding* (Toronto: ECW Press, 2009), Karen Larsen, *Breaking the Limit: One Woman's Motorcycle Journey through*

America (New York: Hyperion, 2004), Gary Paulsen, *Pilgrimage on a Steel Ride* (New York: Harcourt Brace & Company, 1997), Allen Noren, *Storm: A Motorcycle Journey of Love, Endurance, and Transformation* (San Francisco: Travelers' Tales, 2000) and Ted Simon, *Jupiter's Travels* (Covelo, CA: Jupitalia, 1979, 1996). So numerous are the books, in fact, that one German collector boasts a collection of 800 and has catalogued more than 1,100: http://www.tukutuku.de/index.php. Tim Fransen has designed an interactive timeline as a virtual catalog: http://essex-dakar.org/motorcycle_travel_literature_timeline/.

10. Given the popularity and widespread dissemination of two versions of nineteenth-century bicycles, the Ordinary (aka, the High Wheeler, the Penny Farthing) and the Safety bicycle, it is assumed that to be a bicycle is to have two wheels in line with one another, thus distinguishing the bicycle from the chariot (and, of course, the chariot was pulled by animals, while the bicycle is self-propelled). However, many versions of two-wheeled vehicles existed in the nineteenth century that featured side-by-side wheels, rather than in-line wheels, including the Otto dicycle. See part 1.

11. M. G. Lay, *Ways of the World: A History of the World's Roads and of the Vehicles that Used Them* (New Brunswick, NJ: Rutgers University Press, 1992), 19–20.

12. Lay, *Ways of the World*, 20. The development of the internal combustion engine necessitated the development of a new kind of "posthouse," the gasoline station, which needed to be established at regular intervals along well-traveled routes. Current opposition to electric vehicles, owing to their short range, rests on historical ignorance of the slow development of regularly spaced gasoline stations, serving a need analogous to charging and/or battery exchange stations, which would perform the same function as posthouses and the gas stations.

13. Lay, *Ways of the World*, 29. The most sophisticated treatment of speed and mobility in modernity is the work of Hartmut Rosa, extensively examined in his book, *Beschleunigung: Die Veränderung der Zeitstrukturen in der Moderne* (Frankfurt am Main: Suhrkamp Verlag, 2005). For shorter works in English, "Social Acceleration: Ethical and Political Consequences of a Desynchronized High-Speed Society," *Constellations* 10.1 (2003): 3–33; "The Speed of Global Flows and the Pace of Democratic Politics," *New Political Science* 27.4 (2005): 445–59; and, most recently, "Full Speed Burnout?: From the Pleasures of the Motorcycle to the Bleakness of the Treadmill: The Dual Face of Social Acceleration," *International Journal of Motorcycle Studies* 6 (Spring 2010), http://ijms.nova.edu/Spring2010/IJMS_Artcl.Rosa.html.

14. Winfried Wolf, *Car Mania: A Critical History of Transport*, trans. Gus Fagan (London: Pluto Press, 1996), 7.

15. Wolf, *Car Mania,* 4. She also notes, "The Stockton-Darlington line in the industrial heart of England, opened in 1825, is generally considered to be the first rail link in the world. But this is only partly true. It was indeed the first public passenger link and it was the first steam-powered locomotive, but horse-drawn rail transport had already been in existence for quite some time. The steam engine was already in use in manufacturing at the beginning of the 19th century" (1).

16. "In the US rail owners made large-scale use of bribery to destroy competition from the canals. The Erie Canal was destroyed by the prominent rail magnate,

Vanderbilt, and the rail owners Garrett and Hopkins were able to bribe the members of the state Legislature of Maryland to close the Chesapeake and Ohio Canal. In both cases these canals had been built on the basis of massive public investment. The Chesapeake and Ohio Canal was run by the state of Maryland. This destruction and waste of public property and public investment, on the one hand, and private enrichment, on the other, is something we will meet many times in the history of railway destruction as well" (Wolf, *Car Mania*, 12). For an engaging account of the creation of the Erie Canal, see Simon Winchester, *The Men Who United the States: America's Explorers, Inventors, Eccentrics, and Mavericks, and the Creation of One Nation, Indivisible* (New York: Harper Perennial, 2014), 231–341.

17. Wolf, *Car Mania*, 47–48.

18. The concept of "freedom" as a signal quality of two-wheeled transport (e.g., freeing nineteenth-century women, the freedom that comes from motorcycle riding) will be addressed in part 3. For a brief discussion of motorcycling freedom as transcendence, see Steven E. Alford and Suzanne Ferriss, *Motorcycle* (London: Reaktion Press, 2008), 135–42.

19. The best account of the Safety bicycle's development can be found in David V. Herlihy, *Bicycle: The History* (New Haven, CT: Yale University Press, 2004), 225–308.

20. Wolf, *Car Mania*, 134–35.

21. For an extensive examination of European and American responses to the presence of bicycles on roads, see Carlton Reid, *Roads Were Not Built for Cars: How Cyclists Were the First to Push for Good Roads & Became the Pioneers of Motoring* (Washington, DC: Island Press, 2015). Reid's book argues that, "Roads were not built for cars. Nor were they built for bicycles. They were not built for sulkies, or steam engines, or any form of wheeled vehicle. Roads were not built for horses, either. Roads were built for pedestrians" (Kindle loc. 2146).

22. Earl Swift, *The Big Roads: The Untold Story of the Engineers, Visionaries, and Trailblazers Who Created the American Superhighways* (New York: Houghton Mifflin Harcourt, 2011), Kindle loc. 1530.

23. Consider, by analogy, the "choices" online consumers have for social media connections: as of this writing one has the choice between Facebook and Facebook, and Twitter and Twitter. These limitations did not arise owing to online consumer demand.

24. Lay, *Ways of the World*, 133.

25. Lay, *Ways of the World*, 135.

26. "If (said he,) I had no duties, and no reference to futurity, I would spend my life in driving briskly in a post-chaise with a pretty woman; but she should be one who could understand me, and would add something to the conversation" (James Boswell, *The Life of Samuel Johnson*, 1791 [New York: Penguin Classics, 1986], 231).

27. Qtd. in Lay, *Ways of the World*, 138.

28. Lay, *Ways of the World*, 141.

29. C. K. Shepherd, *Across America by Motor-Cycle* (1922), in *An Anthology of Early British Motorcycle Travel Literature*, ed. Tim Fransen (Essex: Essex-Dakar Books, 2009), 488.

30. Shepherd, *Across America*, 502–3.

31. Lay, *Ways of the World*, 91, 162.

32. I. B. Holley, Jr., *The Highway Revolution, 1895–1925: How the United States Got Out of the Mud* (Durham, NC: Carolina Academic Press, 2008), 153.

33. Lay, *Ways of the World*, 144. Also see Herlihy, *Bicycle*, 204–5; Stephen B. Goddard, *Colonel Albert Pope and His American Dream Machines: The Life and Times of Bicycle Tycoon Turned Automotive Pioneer* (New York: McFarland, 2008), 78–80; Bruce D. Epperson, *Peddling Bicycles to America: The Rise of an Industry* (New York: McFarland and Company Inc, 2010), Kindle loc. 1629–2088.

34. Lay, *Ways of the World*, 144; 180–81. An entertaining account of parallel developments in France can be found in Eugen Weber, *France, Fin De Siècle* (Cambridge, MA: Belknap Press, 1986), 195–212.

35. The stories of British and American responses to the perceived need for improved roadways can be found in Reid, *Roads Were Not Built for Cars*, chapter 7 (Kindle loc. 3402–3738) and chapter 10 (Kindle loc. 4218–4624), respectively.

36. See Epperson, *Peddling Bicycles to America*, and Stephen B. Goddard, *Colonel Albert Pope*.

37. Godard, *Colonel Albert Pope*, 70.

38. As a snapshot of his success, Epperson notes, "The 1890 Census of Manufacturers, taken in the summer of 1889, found that the entire domestic bicycle industry employed 1,925 employees, who earned wages of $1.1 million, and made $2.56 million in product, or somewhere around 20,500 bicycles. Thus, Pope's employment accounted for about 16 percent of the total industry, although he was making about a third of its bicycles" (Kindle loc. 1749).

39. Goddard, *Colonel Albert Pope*, 76.

40. Goddard, *Colonel Albert Pope*, 74.

41. Epperson, *Peddling Bicycles to America*, Kindle loc. 2537ff.

42. "In April 1895, the company put out the greatest advertising bonanza in the history of cycling, a 42-page spread entitled 'The Marvels of Bicycle Making,' in the March issue of McClure's" (Epperson, *Peddling Bicycles to America*, Kindle loc. 3946). See also Goddard, *Colonel Albert Pope*, 80.

43. Goddard, *Colonel Albert Pope*, 78.

44. Epperson, *Peddling Bicycles to America*, Kindle loc. 1467.

45. For an account of the parallel "sidepath" movement, see James Longhurst, *Bike Battles: A History of Sharing the American Road* (Seattle: University of Washington Press, 2015), 62–79.

46. Lay, *Ways of the World*, 43.

47. Bitumen is "the viscous, 'heavy' component of petroleum," while "asphalt is a mixture of bitumen, sand, and stone" (Lay, *Ways of the World*, 50).

48. Lay, *Ways of the World*, 53. Reid notes the modern problem of locating these roads in Britain for archeological study: "While many of Britain's 'modern' roads—especially the main ones—follow the alignments of known Roman highways, many stretches of Roman road have yet to be discovered. As well as using aerial surveys, ground-penetrating radar or extrapolations from known Roman alignments, there's a sweet-smelling way of spotting a hidden Roman road: follow the flowers. Roman soldiers would accidentally deposit seeds as they trudged. Linear accumulations of

invasive species such as greater celandine, corn cockle, cotton thistle, scarlet pimpernel, white mustard and the field woundwort, all flowers used by Roman soldiers, can suggest the proximity of a long-forgotten Roman road. Blackthorn hedges, too, can hide Roman roads beneath them" (*Roads Were Not Built for Cars*, Kindle loc. 1424).

49. Reid notes that the British were not the first: "British engineers tend to get much of the credit for introducing modernised road-building techniques, but they were anticipated in Italy and France. In 1585, Italian engineer Guido Toglietta wrote a treatise on a road-surfacing system using broken stone and good drainage. France was the first country to apply the new methods. Europe's first civil engineering university, the pre-revolutionary École Nationale des Ponts et Chaussées, the National School of Bridges and Highways, was founded in Paris in 1747. It exists to this day. The first of the great eighteenth-century road engineers was Frenchman Pierre-Marie-Jérôme Trésaguet. In 1775 Trésaguet developed a new type of relatively light road surface, based on the theory that the foundation should support the load and there should be multiple layers, topped with gravel. The newly improved French roads—essential for the later military campaigns of Napoleon—were the best in Europe until the first part of the 20th century and, with their excellent surfaces, attracted pioneer motorists like moths to a flame" (*Roads Were Not Built for Cars,* Kindle loc. 1474).

50. Holley, *Highway Revolution*, 154.

51. Holley, *Highway Revolution*, 51.

52. The first use of macadam in America "was in 1823 between Boonsboro and Hagerstown on Maryland's Boonsboro Turnpike, which is now part of US Highway 40. Perhaps as a precaution, the stone layer was about 60% thicker than McAdam recommended" (Lay, *Ways of the World*, 83).

53. The road toward pneumatic tires was a long one, beginning with the development of vulcanization, or hardening, of rubber by Charles Goodyear in 1844. John Dunlop first invented a pneumatic tire for his son's tricycle in 1887, and received a patent in 1888 (the patent was subsequently challenged). The pneumatic bicycle tire was adapted for motorcycles in the 1890s, but it wasn't until after the turn of the century that inflatable tires were successfully used on automobiles. See the Rubber section in the following chapter.

54. Swift, *Big Roads,* Kindle loc. 200. For another view of how London handled the problem, see Reid: "It's often claimed that it was the motor car which rid cities of manure. This is not the case; cities got rid of manure, and did so before the end of the horse era. Unofficial dung-heaps may have been common in cities in the first half of the 19th century, but from the 1840s onward sanitation campaigners such as Edwin Chadwick, spurred on by epidemics of cholera, typhus and other infectious diseases, were highly successful at cleaning up cities" (*Roads Were Not Built for Cars*, Kindle loc. 3425).

55. T. D. Denham, "California's Cycle Way," *Good Roads Magazine*, November 1901, http://www.fhwa.dot.gov/infrastructure/the_great_cycle_way_.cfm. See also "California Cycleways," http://www.californiacycleways.org/dobbins.htm.

56. Denham, "California's Cycle Way."

57. See "Minuteman Bikeway: America's Revolutionary Rail Trail," http://www.minutemanbikeway.org.

58. Mark H. Rose, *Interstate: Express Highway Politics, 1939–1989* (Knoxville: The University of Tennessee Press, 1979, 1990).

59. Lay, *Ways of the Worlds*, 99.

60. Jim Fitzpatrick, *The Bicycle in Wartime: An Illustrated History* (Kilcoy, Australia: Star Hill Studio, 2011), 2.

61. For a brief discussion, see Alford and Ferriss, *Motorcycle*, 45–48. See also Janusz Piekalkiewicz, *BMW Motorcycles in World War II: R12/R75* (West Chester, PA: Schiffer Military History, 1991).

62. By contrast, Jean Cocteau's *Orphée* (1950) associates wartime motorcycles not with escape but death, as two military surplus American-made Indian motorcycles mow down the protagonist (Jean Marais).

63. "Between 1946 and 1950, Americans replaced older vehicles and added new ones rapidly, forcing up registrations by more than two-thirds. In 1945, about 31 million vehicles of all sorts were registered; in 1946, state officials listed more than 34.3 million; and by 1950, they had registered 49 million, including 8.6 million trucks" (Rose, *Interstate*, 31).

64. For a detailed history of how bicyclists' rights have been treated in the courts and in social policy, see Longhurst, *Bike Battles*.

65. This Balkanization has been vividly described in Robert D. Kaplan's *An Empire Wilderness: Travels into America's Future* (New York: Vintage, 1998).

66. The interests of bicyclists were simply ignored, prompting the creation of bicycle coalitions and associations. Most major urban centers now have local bicycle coalitions, and state-wide associations, such as CABO in California and MassBike in Massachusetts, promote rider rights and safety, advocating for three-foot buffer zones, for instance. The League of American Bicyclists continues to promote a "bicycle-friendly America" (see http://www.bikeleague.org/) and People for Bikes seeks to be the national advocacy organization for riders (see http://www.peopleforbikes.org/pages/our-goals). The Alliance for Biking and Walking seeks to promote the interests of pedestrians and cyclists throughout North America (see http://www.peoplepoweredmovement.org/site/). Similar organizations exist in Britain, including Bike Right (http://www.bikeright.co.uk/) and BikeHub (see http://www.bikehub.co.uk/featured-articles/cycling-and-the-law/). Motorcycle rights organizations (MROs), often portrayed in the media as unwashed libertarians with a single agenda—eliminating mandatory helmet laws—have been a voice in the promotion of motorcyclists' needs and interests in road travel (e.g., national support for motorcycle safety training, health insurance discrimination issues, eliminating prohibition of motorcycles on federally funded roads, elimination of bans on sales of "superbikes," stronger enforcement of penalties for automobile drivers injuring motorcyclists, and promotion of greater public awareness of motorcyclists among the automobile and truck driving public). For examples, see http://www.mrf.org/index.php and http://www.americanmotorcyclist.com. For a comprehensive list of rights organizations, including state ABATE chapters, see http://weaselsusa.org/mro.htm. On British MROS, see Suzanne McDonald-Walker, *Bikers: Culture, Politics and Power* (Oxford: Berg, 2000).

Chapter Three

Rubber and Steel

The "Raw" Materials

Technological utility always occurs within a cultural context. As we have seen in the discussion of roads, while they can be reductively understood as a means toward more efficient movement, they exist within the sphere of mobility, a complex of human values that determines how roads are understood within a particular culture. Correlatively, as we have argued, looking at the inventions of humankind to extend its biological capacities—technology—as a utilitarian response to human needs and desires is also reductive. But where do we turn when we desire to extend our capabilities by transforming elements of nature into products of human use? We look at the "raw" materials of the earth. Speaking generally, we could say that a "raw material" is any component of the earth that can be transformed by human labor into an object of use, an object that extends efforts limited by our biology (e.g., telescopes:sight, ladders:climbing ability, telephones:voice, etc.). But the earth itself isn't a "raw" material. We don't look at, for example, the ocean or a snow-covered mountain as materials, yet hydraulics and mining produce useful extensions of our powers. To put it another way, raw materials have to appear *as* raw materials for them to be understood as useful. In this chapter, we will look at two extremely common technological building blocks of two-wheeled vehicles—rubber and steel—whose paths to being understood as a raw material were quite different. One was simply an uninteresting plant product that could be used as a toy or a component of a game, while the other has been employed for much of human history in warfare. It took until the eighteenth century for one to be even recognized as a raw material, while the other has been used in sword making and other instruments of war for more than 1,500 years. Yet within a scant 125 years, together they have become the commonplace components of two-wheeled lives worldwide.

RUBBER

We tend to take the superficially humble, black substance for granted, but it contains within it the whole buried world of social and ecological relations.

—John Tully, *The Devil's Milk: A Social History of Rubber*

At the 1851 Great Exhibition in London, "it was the exhibition of rubber that grew the greatest crowds. Charles Goodyear spent $30,000 of his own money to create Goodyear's Vulcanite court, a three-room display in which everything was made of rubber: furniture, draperies, rugs, and fixtures–even the walls and a large 'Elizabethan' sideboard. There were rubber inkstands, knife handles, stockings, bandages, hot water bottles, syringes, dolls, and air cushions. Goodyear spoke of air-inflated saddles, inflatable boxing jackets that could absorb a punch, and a rubber dress for ministers performing full-body baptisms. He envisioned the day that rubber life preservers would eliminate drowning as one of the evils of the world. Rubber could be prefabricated into any shape; it was a protean substance, hailing from nature but perfected by science. It was the material of the future, a true gift from God."

—Joe Jackson, *The Thief at the End of the World: Rubber, Power, and the Seeds of Empire*

As noted in our account of the development of roads, the bicycle and motorcycle cannot bc understood in isolation: the rider, vehicle and traversed surface have to be considered as elements of the same focus of study. We can say, for example, that the level of discomfort experienced in traversing a dirt and/or timber road rutted by a combination of weather, horses, and horse-drawn wagons is no picnic for a cyclist and, indeed, in most cases, the poor condition of the road would be enough for most reasonable people to eschew bicycle (or motorcycle) travel altogether. In the absence of a smooth, maintained road surface, could there be another solution for a rough road that didn't involve the expense, politics, and material involvement of resurfacing the road? Less intrepid enthusiasts were presented with a solution that, alongside suspension, transformed the experience of riding bicycles and motorcycles alike into one at least amenable, if not completely comfortable: the pneumatic tire.[1] To produce such a tire, however, one needed a substance virtually unknown until the nineteenth century, one that, like the potato, emerged from the jungles of South America to transform transportation, electrification, and among other things, pencil pushing, for those in the West.

Rubber is one of the most useful natural (and artificial) substances on the planet.[2] But for it to become truly useful, specific technical developments

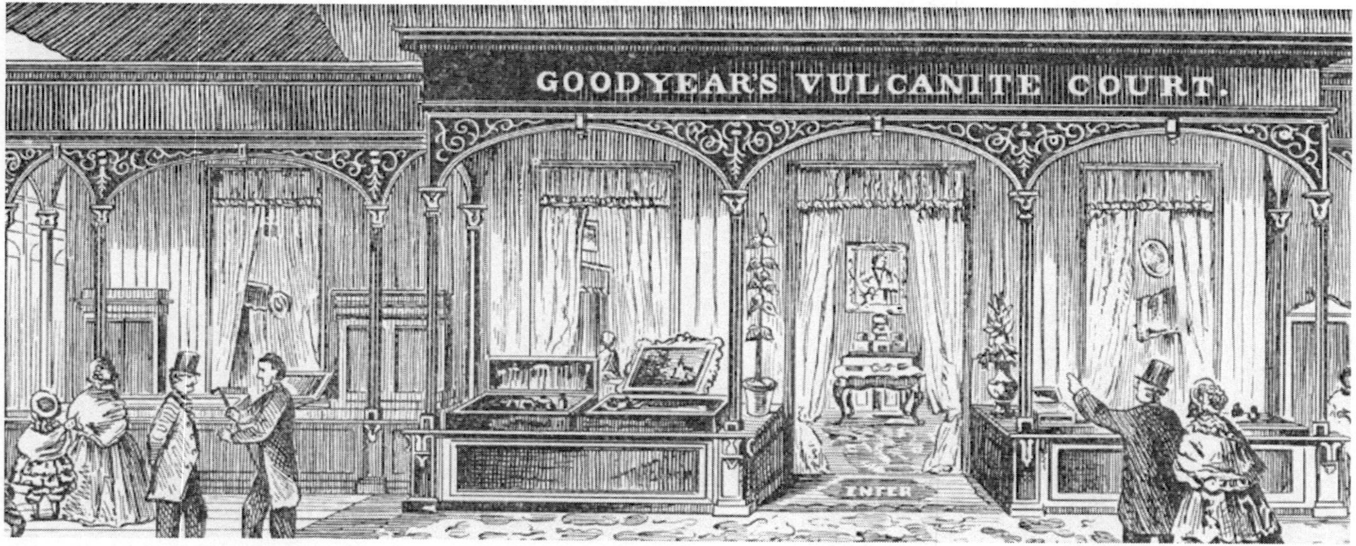

Figure 3.1. **"Charles Goodyear's Exhibition of Hard India Rubber Goods at the Crystal Palace, Sydenham, England," from *Trials of an Inventory: Life and Discoveries of Charles Goodyear* by Bradford K. Pierce, 1866.**

must have occurred. The discovery of various chemicals, namely naphtha and turpentine (first employed in the mid-eighteenth century), made rubber workable, while vulcanization (c. 1840) made it more durable.[3] So even if it existed, and it were seen to be a potential object of use, the technical means of processing it (and the intellectual understanding of what occurred during processing) had to be present as well.

But why are we aware of rubber's existence at all? As a milky substance found inside certain plant species, latex (and a similar and at one time equally important substance, gutta percha[4]) exists in many parts of the world.[5] Plants as diverse as fig trees and dandelions produce the hydrocarbon polymer with elastic properties as well.[6]

However, along the way toward its employment in devices, it was discovered that one plant, the *Hevea brasiliensis*, was far superior to any other plant: when wounded to drain the latex, the tree responded by producing more.[7] How did we learn about this plant's existence? It had long been used in Mesoamerica in varied games employing balls, and Hernán Cortéz had returned to Spain from Mexico with two teams of Indians, along with the rubber balls they used. Other reports circulated in Europe of the conquistadores using rubber for shoes (learning from the Indians how to fashion something like the modern Vibram Five Fingers "barefoot" running shoes) and as protection for their legs against insects.[8]

Still, rubber was treated as something of a curiosity until 1735–1736 when French geographer and adventurer Charles Marie de la Condamine traveled to Brazil and returned with samples, naming the substance "latex" (from the Spanish word for "milk"). Along with François Fresneau, he conducted various experiments on the substance and reported some of their findings to the French Academy of Science.[9]

The French were, of course, not alone in their fascination with Central and South America, following its "discovery" by the Spanish and Portuguese. Inspired by the writings of Charles Darwin, Alfred Russell Wallace, and others, Englishman Henry Wickham began a life of international travel in 1866 at age twenty, sailing from England to Nicaragua. After enduring a number of hardships in Brazil, he made it his business to gather the plants and convey them to England in 1876. Wickham's story has been told in detail in Joe Jackson's *The Thief at the End of the World: Rubber, Power, and the Seeds of Empire.*[10] As Jackson notes, Wickham did not act solely for his own sake, but rather sought to enhance Britain's international economic fortunes by taking seedlings of the native South American tree and importing them to Kew Gardens, where, eventually, the seeds were cultivated with almost accidental success in British tea plantations in the Far East, given the horticultural ignorance regarding the propagation and care of the seedlings, the appropriate cultivation regimen, and how to control pests attracted to the tree.[11]

> Rubber's elastomeric properties are the core of its appeal. In its composition, rubber is . . . elastic because of its atomic organization into long, crumpled, repeating chains. These are interlinked at a few distant points, and between each pair of links the hydrogen and carbon building blocks rotate freely about their neighbors. This results in a wide range of shapes, like a very loose rope attached to a pair of fixed points on a rock wall.[12]

This made early rubber goods pleasingly pliable, but at a cost. They became either brittle in the cold or sticky (and eventually melted) in the heat, resulting in substantial losses for those seeking to market rubber goods, until vulcanization rendered rubber more durable.

> With vulcanization . . . elasticity is compromised. The polymer chains are joined together by sulfur bridges that create a three-dimensional network: now there are more bridges between the chains than in the "uncured" state, making each free section of chain shorter and subject to a quicker tightening under strain. This results in a rubber that is harder, less pliable, and far less likely to deteriorate in extremes of temperature.[13]

The story of how this problem was solved by Charles Goodyear and Nathaniel Hayward has been told many times, first by Goodyear himself and then by numerous biographers.[14] Beginning in 1834, Goodyear first became fascinated by the (disintegrating) retail products of the Roxbury India Rubber Company. He began a lifelong series of experiments (accompanied by recurrent lawsuits and multiple imprisonments for debt) and, largely through accident, discovered that sulfur, combined with heat (and, for other purposes, treated with nitric acid), stabilized the compound, making it resistant to the vagaries of temperature and workable through machine processes. By 1839 he became satisfied with the outcome of his technique, and eventually acquired a patent for his vulcanization procedure in 1844. Thomas Hancock (who coined the term "vulcanize") began creating solid tires in England by 1846, and these were eventually adapted for velocipedes in the 1860s. Initially criticized for being "an impractical luxury" given their tendency to wear out or fall off, advances in affixing them to metal rims made them more secure.[15] As an advance over iron wheels, solid rubber reduced, but did not eliminate the discomfort of riders on roads marred by a combination of horse and wagon traffic and dried mud.

As John Tully notes, "The wheel is rightly reckoned as one of the most significant inventions in human history, but it took the addition of compressed air-filled rubber tires to bring it to perfection."[16] While popular history gives the laurels for the pneumatic tire to J. B. Dunlop, who in 1888 experimented with inner tubes for his son's bicycle, his work was preceded by an 1845 patent approved for another Scotsman, Robert William Thompson, who prevailed in a patent conflict between the two. Subsequent to Dunlop's work, the 1890s are rife with numerous inventors of valves, "clincher" tires, and beaded-edge tires.[17] By 1895—ten years after the Rover and the Einspur—pneumatic tires became a feature of the Paris-Bordeaux motorcar race.[18]

Thus far, our account of the prehistory of the bicycle and the motorcycle has noted the interrelation of first, rubber coated wheels and, happily, the development of the pneumatic tire. However, these developments did not simply spring from a series of talented (and, in the case of Goodyear, indefatigable) tinkerers, but resulted from a set of events and modes of consciousness that cannot, in a linear fashion, be said to point the way to the development, by the 1890s, of one of the economically and socially transformative devices of the nineteenth century, the pneumatic tire.[19]

We might step back and ask, for example, what brought Wickham to Brazil? Two significant factors: Western voyages of discovery resulted in the meeting, for the first time in history, of Europeans with their South American counterparts, and the well-documented violent and destructive path of the Europeans' dominance over the Amerindians.[20]

But the exploitation of natural and human resources that resulted from European imperialism needn't necessarily have followed the two cultures' encounter. An economic system based on individualism, personal enrichment, effective inequality, and a never-ending search for markets accompanied the sailors to their destination. The sense of cultural and individual entitlements spawned by a religion that believed in a particular people being God's chosen and favored ones added to the picture. While the effects of a culture grounded in capitalism and Christianity encountering others who didn't share its beliefs have been extensively documented, it's worth keeping in mind that these cultural assumptions served as the background, motive forces for the transmission of this most useful substance from South America to Europe.[21] In the absence of capitalist and Christian assumptions, in a culture based on, for example, compassion for others, with the primary social value being goodness rather than a devotion to acquiring riches, rubber trees would have stayed where they originated, and not migrated to Malaysia, India, and elsewhere, to say nothing of Kew Gardens. We can remain ambivalent about the significance of rubber while recognizing the necessary preconditions that created its value.

While the importance of South American rubber to European technological progress can hardly be exaggerated, rubber was not the first substance to be spirited out of South America and put at the disposal of European scientists and technologists. Given the distance from Spain, England, and other proto-imperialist European nations (to say nothing of their interest in China and India), Africa would be the first continent to be explored and exploited for materials (leaving out the Arab and African tradition of selling African slaves). However, Africa was literally a graveyard for European explorers, soldiers and missionaries, owing to the prevalence of malaria.[22] Deaths from this disease, felling sixty to eighty percent of explorers, missionaries, and would-be tradespeople, were such that the "Dark Continent" was to remain so until deaths from the disease could be at least reduced and controlled, if not eliminated.

The story of the discovery of quinine as a prophylactic against the disease has been recounted elsewhere, but what's important here is that initially quinine came from a single source, the bark of the cinchona tree, found only in the Andean highlands.[23] Well before the biopiracy of Brazilian rubber plants by the English and other Europeans, the bark of this tree was taken in vast quantities from the Andean forests.[24] Without it, the conquest of Africa could have never occurred. Nor could one have predicted the spread of rubber cultivation and the horrors it visited upon the native populace by King Leopold II of Belgium in the Congo and the Firestone Company in Liberia.[25] Obviously, no European imperial planner determined to sail to South America and grab the bark of an obscure tree in the Andean mountains as a strategy for exploiting the wealth of Africa. Yet, without this confluence of events, African exploration and exploitation would simply not have occurred.[26] One can only speculate how the contemporary picture of a continent riven by political instability and disease—many of its ills attributable to the heritage of colonialism—would have been different absent the discovery of the chemical properties of the bark of an Andean tree.

Of course, the presence of Europeans in South America involved a prior confluence of events in oceanic navigation (e.g., reliable ocean-going clocks that could be used to measure longitude), Captain Cook's implementation of sources of vitamin C to combat scurvy, and the development of superior firepower, leading from muskets to breach-loading rifles of then-astonishing speed and accuracy, among many others.[27] As we will see, the demands of Empire stimulated the need for newer and more sophisticated weapons to physically control markets of desired overseas goods, which in turn stimulated the development of ever more sophisticated armaments once older ones had fallen, inevitably, into the hands of the colonized, which then stimulated developments in metallurgy, and a large scale transition from iron to steel, particularly strong tubular steel to fashion rifle barrels. These steel tubes became, along with rubber, the "raw" materials of the bicycle, a device universally acknowledged to be instrumental in the social, economic, and political progress of European women. When technological development is observed from this perspective, the links among various social and technological forces appear to be not so much causally comprehensible as mysterious in their enormous complexity, and something to inspire humility in those who today render authoritative opinions on the future of our own technology.

STEEL

> By the 1920s the nation's physical infrastructure was built of steel, its economic infrastructure was built upon the making and using of steel, and its social infrastructure was shaped by the producing and consuming of steel. In short, the United States was a nation of steel.
>
> —Thomas J. Misa, *A Nation of Steel: The Making of Modern America, 1865–1925*

As noted, despite rubber's presence in trees and other plant life, it remained unrecognized as a useful material (other than in Amerindian games and toys) until the eighteenth century when Charles Marie de la Condamine first described its scientific properties. Even then, it took the lifelong efforts of Goodyear and many others to develop it into the material it became, a substance of seemingly limitless applications, particularly in the fields of electricity and transportation.

Steel, however, is another matter. Iron has been recognized for its utility following transformation of its ore through heating for most of human history. Steel was developed through various processes from this most ubiquitous and useful metal. The fourth most abundant element, iron, replaced bronze in the Caucasus region around 2000 BCE, being harder, more durable, and capable of holding a sharper edge.[28] Although the basis for steel and, hence, a critical component of the Industrial Revolution in Britain, iron was mined and smelted using coke in China as early as 1100, a process not seen until the 1700s in Europe.[29] The development of steel making is simply another step in iron's long record of human use and, although more modern materials have been employed in the twentieth and twenty-first century, such as titanium and carbon fiber, steel remains a crucial component of bicycle manufacturing. Coincident not only with rubber and other, more elaborate human creations, such as roads, the presence of a steel bicycle frame resulted from social, political, and economic forces unrelated to the bicycle. In fact, its origins are more reliably found in the development of weaponry resulting from European imperialism; railroads, with their attendant complicated interplay of politics and capitalism; the classic American notion of Manifest Destiny that underlay American westward expansion; and the always reliable naked human greed.

The bicycle or the motorcycle, like all forms of transportation, interposes itself between the road surface and the person operating the vehicle. As such, it is subject to stresses from both directions: the weight and unpredictable movements of the operator, as well as the unforeseen hills, declivities, bumps, gouges, rocks, and other debris that strain the tensile strength of the frame and, in general, require the frame's component metal to flex, and then return to its original shape without ongoing deformation. Bicycles can be made from a variety of materials, among them wood, bamboo, iron, steel, aluminum, titanium, and, more recently, carbon fiber and other exotic compounds. One reason for the range of materials available for the bicycle's construction is the diamond-frame design, an innovation that the Rover made an enduring structural element. Based on the engineering principles of the inherent strength of the triangle (a diamond being comprised of two triangles), the diamond-frame structure is internally reinforcing, giving stability and durability missing in other designs.

In addition to the strength of the diamond-frame, another consideration is obviously weight. Increased weight might be an advantage in bicycles devoted to rugged terrain (e.g., mountain bikes where, during the 1970s, for probably the first time in bicycle's development, weight became a secondary consideration), but for most bikes, the lighter the better. Prior to the advent of modern materials, early two-wheelers (draisines and velocipedes) were made of heavy, corruptible wood and iron. Once the problem of excessive weight was recognized, common sense would suggest that, hollow tubular materials (e.g., bamboo or steel) sustain the best balance between structural integrity and weight.[30] However, while bamboo tubes are a gift from nature, hollow steel tubes had to be fabricated, designed to possess tensile strength and a flexible response to varying road conditions.

Modern higher-end bicycles are made from a specific steel alloy, 4130, or chrome-moly (chromium-molybdenum, also known as CroMo) steel, known for its "weldability, formability, strength, ductility and toughness."[31] This tubular steel alloy did not appear overnight. To understand the sources of steel bicycles, we need to understand something of the history of firearms.

As is well known, gunpowder was employed for various uses by the Chinese around the first millennium, principally for rockets. However, using gunpowder as an explosive material to power projectiles through space was preceded by "fire lances" (quite like a modern Roman candle firework) and, by the thirteenth century, brass, bottle-shaped devices that simply produced a loud explosion, something terrifying to opponents of Chinese and Mongol forces. These bottle devices gave rise to a primitive form of cannon (around 1356), which ejected scraps of metal. These brass weapons in China and India (and subsequently in Europe) were later fashioned with cast iron, which required skilled craftsmen to overcome the natural brittleness of such a material to be formed into a barrel and then used to house an explosive charge.[32]

While steel had been produced as early as 600 CE in Iran, it was extremely labor intensive and produced low yields of "Damascus steel," which was fashioned into swords. Smelting, rolling, and boring processes could not, until the eighteenth century, form tubular shapes. However, from the sixteenth century onward, an ingenious Turkish method involved taking a flat steel strip and wrapping it around a metal pole, then welding the edges together as depicted below.[33]

It is significant to note that, unlike other materials such as rubber, the advances in metalworking were almost exclusively at the service of warfare (and only later, transportation). Both periodically insular societies such as the Chinese, as well at more territorially aggressive ones, such as the Mongols, employed their considerable technological energies toward developing deadly weapons to use against perceived enemies. Only as an outgrowth of a devotion to developing war materiel did any practical developments occur that would have enhanced daily life (such as, for example, axles for wheeled carts and other vehicles).

Any discussion of steel must begin by noting the problematic definition of this product: there are "steels," not steel. Historically, categorizing steels proceeded on two bases, either by indicating the process of refining the steel (Bessemer, open hearth, various electrified processes, etc.) or through a chemical analysis of the resultant metal.[34] In the case of the early history of the bicycle, firms producing steel were neither interested nor equipped with the engineering capacity and/or chemical analysis expertise to understand steel on the molecular level. Instead, in the late nineteenth century, producers and consumers both relied on the process of steel production rather than its components to distinguish among the various types of steel.

Most schoolchildren who learn anything about metals hear about the Bessemer process, given that it resulted in a steel that was responsible for transforming the daily existence of the citizens of the steel-producing countries

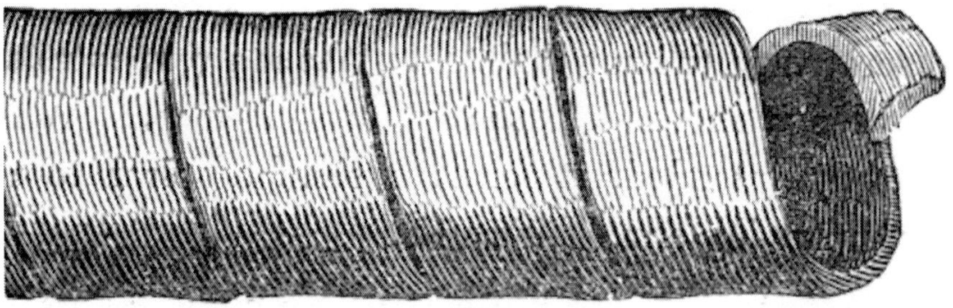

Figure 3.2. An illustration of Damascus steel being rolled into a barrel from *Gunnery in 1858: Being a Treatise on Rifles, Cannon, and Sporting Arms* by William Greener.

through alterations in transportation (railroads and, in the twentieth century, automobiles), housing and business (skyscrapers), as well as warfare (not only improvements in weaponry, but armor to protect weapons of war, such as ships and tanks).

To make steel, one needs to take pig iron (melted and then reconstituted iron) and, through heating, subtract certain elements in it, namely carbon and, as processes improved, phosphorus (the latter can remain in the steel produced, but it makes it brittle and therefore dangerous as a construction material). In the Bessemer process (later modified and improved through the Thomas basic process) the heat of the furnace is increased through blowing forced air into the container containing the molten iron, thus more effectively reducing the carbon content (as well as introducing coke—a product of distilled coal—to remove sulfur as well). The carbon content of the processed metal determines just what kind of metal it is:

> wrought iron has a little carbon (0.02 to 0.08 percent), just enough to make it hard without losing its malleability. Cast iron, in contrast, has a lot of carbon (3 to 4.5 percent), which makes it hard but brittle and nonmalleable. In between these is steel, with 0.2 to 1.5 percent carbon, making it harder than wrought iron, yet malleable and flexible, unlike cast iron.[35]

The popularity of Bessemer process, which, depending on the factory, produced medium- to inferior-grade steel, coincided with a massive, seemingly limitless American demand for steel rails for the railroads, following the unfortunate and untimely breakage of iron rails. "Steel towns" arose in Britain and America, with the American northeast and Chicago dominating the domestic production.

Unlike the somewhat crude specifications of rails (toughness, fatigue strength, etc.), bicycle frames require more refined properties, focused on a balance between steel's innate qualities that allow it to withstand the stresses of carrying an individual over often uneven and rough surfaces, and its weight. In retrospect, it's obvious that steel tubes combine the best of these two properties. One first, however, had to have a source of steel tubes for frame construction.

Factories since the Industrial Revolution contained capital-intensive machines whose continuous fabrication of products determined the company's profitability. Given the periodic upswings and downturns of the manufacturing business, managers were vigilant in developing new ways of employing their machinery. One sees repeatedly that bicycle (and motorcycle) manufacture originated in factories devoted to producing other products, in particular weapons and sewing machines.[36] For example, as early as the 1860s, sewing machine manufacturers in England (such as Singer and Coventry) and America (Weed), produced bicycles as well. In 1901, the Royal Enfield motorcycle was

Cycle & Carriage Co.
FEDERAL STORES, KUALA LUMPUR.
LOOK OUT!
The World-renowned Singer Cycles
Singer Sewing Machines.
SINGER SEWING MACHINES
Singer Cycle with lamp, bell & tools complete
with Gear Case $100.00 ; without Gear Case $90.00
For Cash 20 discount allowed, and for monthly payments
EASY TERMS ALLOWED.
Singer Sewing Machines. Same as above.
Catalogues for Provisions, Spirits & Wine & Cigars etc.,
Cycles, Gramaphones and Sewing Machines.
Free on Application.
CYCLE & CARRIAGE CO.,
GENERAL STOREKEEPERS & REPAIRERS.

Figure 3.3. A 1906 advertisement from Kuala Lumpur for Singer bicycles and sewing machines.

produced by the former Royal Small Arms Factory. Its promotional slogan boasted: "made like a gun, goes like a bullet." Most notable is Birmingham Small Arms (BSA). In 1880, BSA manufactured the Otto dicycle, before turning production to Safety bicycles and eventually motorcycles, becoming for a time in the 1950s the largest motorcycle manufacturer in the world. More commonly, companies manufactured the array of parts that had become fixed components of bicycles, rather than entire vehicles. Some companies specialized in producing the seamless hollow tubes used in constructing both guns and two-wheeled vehicles.[37] Often these connections resulted from a type of technological bricolage, as the example of William Murdoch demonstrates.

In 1815, Englishman William Murdoch developed a lighting system for the city of London involving coal gas. To transport the gas to the lamps, he required some sort of piping, then unavailable. Murdoch solved his transport problem by joining together the barrels of discarded muskets. Once the system gained popularity, demand grew for metal tubes.[38] Combine this type of adaptive demand with the downturn of demand for railroad ties in the late 1880s, and the rise in popularity of bicycles, and a new market for the type of tubes found in rifles and other weapons is discovered.

Pierre Michaux's 1868 bicycle patent called for, but did not result in the production of steel tubes. By 1872, British high-wheelers used "hollow backbones" for their bikes, and, in 1877 a patent was applied for a New Hollow Spoke bicycle. By the mid-1880s German brothers Reinhard and Max Mannesmann developed a process for making seamless steel tubes, and their process was introduced in America by a former employee. However, America was still importing most of its tubing from Britain until the 1890s, when domestic factories were established (including one built by Albert Pope, the Pope-Mannesmann Company). In addition, Chicago companies developed methods of stamping metal, which included methods for making tubing.[39]

The development of novel steel-making processes that superseded the Bessemer model, as well as newfangled and exotic alloys, created new and better "steels" that bicycle manufacturers could take advantage of. However, other than small initiatives, such as Pope's tube factory and his attention to developing faster methods of reliably producing ball bearings, bicycles (and later, motorcycles) benefited from imperatives outside their bailiwick. In America, for example, steel production was driven by the colossal, complex national enterprise of railroad building, what Thomas J. Misa calls, "the reckless mass production of steel rails [that] was much in evidence for three decades beginning in the 1870s."[40] Disgruntlement with the shoddy quality of railroad ties, produced in haste with a secure eye on profit, prompted improvements in steelmaking techniques. As well, urbanization, particularly in America, ultimately a consequence of the Industrial Revolution, was hastened by the replacement of iron for steel in urban dwellings, giving rise to the skyscraper, which greatly increased urban density, as well as demand for quality, durable steel.[41]

In line with the outlook of this study, one can say that any attempt to explain the "cause" of the national adoption of railroads is complex. In comparison to Britain, however, in America we can observe a unique motive, connected to Manifest Destiny. In distinguishing between British and American approaches to technological product, Arnold Pacey notes the British pride in the quality of the "product," while Americans contextualized these products differently:

> So while a suitable analogy for railway building in Britain might be the aqueducts of ancient Rome (some viaducts present a close visual parallel), one analogy that has been used with respect to American railroads is the space race of the 1960s, because the railroads were concerned with a conquest of geographical space rather as the 1960s adventure was a conquest of cosmic space.[42]

We might say then, that one vector of development that led to the steel bicycle frame was the restless American exceptionalist imperative to reach the west coast, or die—as so many settlers did—trying, a form of internal territorial imperialism. Railroads democratized travel westward and the anticipation of increasing numbers of travelers motivated railroad builders in search of profits. The land, inhabited throughout by what were considered expendable Amerindian groups, was acquired at the endpoint of a long, steel, rifled tube. Taken together, guns and railroads, in the "conquest of cosmic space" provided the possibility for the bicycle and, ultimately the steel parts of the internal combustion machine that was eventually strapped to it.

Hence, it is difficult to say how one should understand these methods of transforming raw materials that ultimately resulted in the bicycle, a transportation device with positive transformative effects in many social realms (e.g., gender relations, mobility for poorer citizens). For example, the relentless search for new markets and extractable materials (rubber in South America, iron in the north central United States), which in turn posed economic and political threats to the "markets"—native populations who happened to live there—engendered exploitative violence as a condition for economic progress. Developing technologies aided the supposed natural human desire for aggressive environmental exploration of the wider world. The emerging, globalizing capitalistic economic environment saw the world as a source of extractable materials rather than an ecosystem that should be treated with responsible stewardship. These potential explanatory sources, in their variety, suggest that how one explains the spread of rubber, iron, and steel technology depends a good deal on the national assumptions about human nature and human relations one brings to the argument. Of course, even a brief glance at the notoriously corrupt, wasteful, and culturally aggressive development of the railroads, particularly in America, emphasizes other forms of damage, generally in the speculative pursuit of markets, to the detriment, above all, of native populations.[43] While technological developments in pursuit of national defense and territorial transportation have had unquestionably positive effects (one need cite only the Internet's emergence from DARPA, the Defense Advance Research Projects Agency), the "progress" attendant to these developments must be understood in the larger context of their (sometimes profoundly negative) collateral consequences.

NOTES

1. See Pryor Dodge, *The Bicycle* (Paris and New York: Flammarion, 1996), 139; David Herlihy, *Bicycle: The History* (New Haven, CT: Yale University Press, 2004), 246. Note that Wiebe Bijker argues riders embraced the tire more for speed than

stabilization (*Of Bicycles, Bakelites, and Bulbs: Toward a Theory of Sociotechnical Change* [Cambridge, MA: MIT Press, 1997], 84–85).

2. "Rubber is a naturally occurring hydrocarbon, polymer of the monomer isoprene, described by the chemical formula of CH2: C(CH3)CH:CH2" (John Tully, *The Devil's Milk: A Social History of Rubber* [New York: Monthly Review Press, 2011], 21.

3. "In 1823, [Charles] Macintosh radically improved the quality of rubberized fabric by sandwiching a layer of naphtha-treated rubber between two layers of cloth. Naphtha was a cheap and plentiful byproduct of coal gas production and of little economic value until MacIntosh used it to treat rubber" (Tully, *The Devil's Milk*, 39). For vulcanization, see the discussion of Goodyear below.

4. "Gutta-percha–The name comes from a Malay word for gum or resin, is a natural plastic, sap or gum of certain trees from Southeast Asia, in particular the taban. . . . It is very dense and watertight, more so than rubber; a gum plastic rather than gum elastic" (Tully, *The Devil's Milk*, 124).

5. "There are some 268 native rubber-bearing plants in India alone, around 137 in Africa, and many potential sources in northern Australia" (Tully, *The Devil's Milk*, 21–22).

6. "No one truly understands the function of latex in the wild. While many botanists believe latex has evolved as a defense against herbivores, since it usually gives the plant a bitter taste, others think that lactifers have developed as a conduit for waste, that lactifers are a sewage system of the plants and latex the liquid manure" (Joe Jackson, *The Thief at the End of the World: Rubber, Power, and the Seeds of Empire* [New York: Viking, 2008], 46–47).

7. "With two very small exceptions, [*Hevea Brasiliensis*] is confined to the land south of the River Amazon, dropping from its estuary at Belém to about 15° south, then swinging west to the border between Peru and Bolivia, before swinging round in a great loop taking in about one-third of Peru, before rejoining the Amazon where Brazil, Peru, and Colombia meet. The two exceptions are a small looped incursion to the north-west of Manaos (today known as Manaus) and a triangular excursion north of the estuary delta 1° or so north of the equator" (John Loadman, *The Tears of the Tree: The Story of Rubber* [New York: Oxford University Press, 2014], 81).

8. For a detailed account of the various tribes, including the Olmecs or "rubber people," as well as their games, along with a brief discussion of then-contemporary Spanish accounts of rubber, see Loadman, *The Tears of the Tree*, chapter 1, 1–11.

9. See Jackson, *The Thief at the End of the World,* 22, and Loadman, *The Tears of the Tree*, 14–21.

10. For a revisionist account of what Wickham may or may not have done, see Loadman, *The Tears of the Tree,* 88–97.

11. The Royal Botanic Gardens, Kew, "formed from two adjoining pleasure gardens of the Hanoverian Kings, . . . was given new life in 1841 as a state institution. Funded by Parliament and charged to aid 'the Mother Country in everything that is useful in the vegetable kingdom,' its mandate was to be the nerve center for the many gardens in the British colonies and dependencies, such as Calcutta, Bombay, Saha-

ranpur, Mauritius, Sydney, and Trinidad, as utility is wasted for want of unity and central direction.' Although its beauties were open to the public, its true role was that of research and development, providing scientific age of the Empire's vast plantation economy—a mission considered crucial for 'the founding of new colonies' and the maintenance of their economies" (Jackson, *The Thief at the End of the World*, 40). As Tully notes, Kew Gardens, the Royal Botanic Gardens, was central to the development of agribusiness in Malaya and "without this expertise it is difficult to imagine the rise of the plantation industries, which allowed transplanted crops such as coffee, tea, sisal, cinchona, and rubber to flourish for the benefit of the Mother Country" (*The Devil's Milk*, 186).

12. Jackson, *The Thief at the End of the World,* 25.

13. Jackson, *The Thief at the End of the World,* 25.

14. A useful popular account is Charles Slack, *Noble Obsession: Charles Goodyear, Thomas Hancock, and the Race to Unlock the Greatest Industrial Secret of the Nineteenth Century* (New York: Hyperion, 2002). For a brief account, see Loadman, *The Tears of the Tree*, 29–44.

15. Herlihy, *Bicycle*, 137.

16. For a brief account, see Tully, *The Devil's Milk*, 49–50.

17. According to Carlton Reid, "The first air tyres required special wheels that had to be factory-fitted, couldn't be easily repaired and looked decidedly plump compared to the skinny 'bootlace' solid tyres of the day. The saving grace for 'pudding tyres' was their speed—they turned donkeys into racehorses. Track racers weren't fussed about comfort but when so-so racers on pneumatics beat top riders on solid tyres, the days of the hard tyre were numbered" (*Roads Were Not Built for Cars: How Cyclists Were the First to Push for Good Roads & Became the Pioneers of Motoring* [Washington, DC: Island Press, 2015], Kindle loc. 930).

18. Tony Hadland and Hans-Erhard Lessing, *Bicycle Design: An Illustrated History* (Cambridge, MA: MIT Press, 2014), 189.

19. "The 1890s would be the decade of the bicycle. The 7 million bicycles found worldwide in 1895 used most of the world's rubber, a boom that would not have occurred if not for the invention of the pneumatic rubber tire. Although there had been bicycles previously, they rode on solid rubber tires. These were puncture-resistant, a boon on roads where nails were frequently shed from horseshoes, but they lacked suspension, were hard to steer, and were an unpleasant ride. This changed by the late 1890s. The market was flooded with steel tubes, ball bearings, variable speed gears, and high-quality chains. Above all else, it was flooded with replaceable rubber tires and inner tubes, mass-produced in the factories of Dunlop in Birmingham, England; Michelin in Claremont-Ferrand, France; and Pirelli in Milan, Italy" (Jackson, *The Thief at the End of the World*, 206).

20. We could indeed ask a further question, as to why Europeans showed up on the shores of South America and not Incans at the palaces of Spain, a question posed, and much discussed, in Jared Diamond's *Guns, Germs, and Steel: The Fates of Human Societies* (New York: W. W. Norton, 1999) and elsewhere.

21. Michael Adas sees these and other attitudes informing the subsequent European imperialist campaigns as well: "From early in the 19th century the notion that

it was the Europeans' destiny and duty to develop the resources of the globe was included in the mixture of humanitarian sentiment, cultural arrogance, and self-serving rationalization that advocates of imperial expansion blended into the civilizing-mission ideology" (*Machines as the Measure of Men: Science, Technology, and Ideologies of Western Dominance* [Ithaca, NY: Cornell University Press, 1989], 220).

22. An account of the staggering death toll on Europeans can be found in Daniel R. Headrick, *The Tools of Empire: Technology and European Imperialism in the Nineteenth Century* (New York: Oxford University Press, 1981), 58–79.

23. "The dawn of a breakthrough in treating malaria dates from the year 1820, when two French chemists, Pierre Joseph Pelletier and Joseph Bienaimé Caventou, succeeded in extracting the alkaloid of quinine from cinchona bark. Commercial production of quinine began in 1827, and by 1830 the drug was being manufactured in large enough quantities for general use" (Headrick, *Tools of Empire*, 66).

24. "Biopiracy in its modern sense refers to the appropriation, without payment and usually by patent, of indigenous biomedical knowledge and genes by foreign corporations, institutions, or governments" (Jackson, *The Thief at the End of the World,* 192). "It is worth noting that la Condamine also found and reported on the cinchona tree, another 'white man's miracle tree' which was later 'transplanted' to the east by Sir Clements Markham to provide a source of quinine" (Loadman, *The Tears of the Tree,* 18).

25. For an account of Leopold's terror and megalomania, see Adam Hochschild, *King Leopold's Ghost: A Story of Greed, Terror, and Heroism in Colonial Africa* (New York: Mariner Books, 1998).

26. "Until the 1850s all the world's cinchona bark came from the forests of Peru, Bolivia, Ecuador, and Colombia, where the trees grew wild. As world demand increased, the bark exports of the Andean republics rose from two million pounds in 1860 to twenty million in 1881. At that point the Andean bark was swept from the world market by the competition of Indian and Indonesian bark, the result of deliberate efforts by Dutch and British interests" (Headrick, *Tools of Empire*, 71).

27. "No period in history produced so dramatic a development of infantry weapons as did the 19th century. In terms of effective firepower the disparity between the rifle of World War One and the Napoleonic musket was greater than between the musket and the bow and arrow" (Headrick, *Tools of Empire,* 84).

28. Joseph S. Spoerl, "A Brief History of Iron and Steel Production," http://www.anselm.edu/homepage/dbanach/h-carnegie-steel.htm.

29. Arnold Pacey, *Technology in World Civilization: A Thousand-Year History* (Boston: MIT Press, 1991), 7. Pacey further argues, "The introduction of coke-fired iron-smelting in England is therefore regarded as an important milestone, and the place of its introduction, at Coalbrookdale in Shropshire, has been hailed as 'the birthplace of the industrial revolution'" (111).

30. On the use of bamboo, beginning in the 1890s, see Hadland and Lessing, *Bicycle Design*, 178. Herlihy notes that bamboo proved too flexible and that replacing iron tubes with steel tubes enabled bicycles to "shed nearly half their original bulk" (*Bicycle*, 288, 163).

31. Scot Nicols, "Steel is Real: Metallurgy for Cyclists, Part 2," Ibis Cycles, http://www.ibiscycles.com/support/technical_articles/metallurgy_for_cyclists/steel_is_real/. The author notes that this steel "contains the following alloying agents: 0.28- to 0.33-percent carbon, 0.4- to 0.6-percent manganese, 0.8- to 1.1-percent cromium, 0.15- to 0.25-percent molybdenum, 0.04-percent phosphorous, 0.04-percent sulfur, and 0.2- to 0.35-percent silicon," with the remaining 95 percent being iron.

32. Arnold Pacey, *The Maze of Ingenuity: Ideas and Idealism in the Development of Technology* (Cambridge, MA: MIT Press, 1974, 1992), 47–49.

33. Pacey, *Technology in World Civilization,* 80–81.

34. For an extensive discussion, see Misa, *A Nation of Steel: The Making of Modern America* (Baltimore: Johns Hopkins University Press), 29–39.

35. Joseph Spoerl, "A Brief History of Iron and Steel Production."

36. Herlihy, *Bicycle*, 147, 190, 216. We return to this connection in greater detail in the next chapter.

37. Hadland and Lessing, *Bicycle Design*, 174–75. For more on tubing, see Reid, *Roads Were Not Built for Cars*, Kindle loc. 5827–862.

38. David Howell, "A Brief History of Steel Pipe," http://www.pipelineequities.com/A-Brief-History-of-Steel-Pipe.php.

39. Hadland and Lessing, *Bicycle Design*, 171–75. See also Reid, *Roads Were Not Built for Cars,* Kindle loc. 5827–862.

40. Misa, *Nation of Steel*, 270.

41. See Misa, *Nation of Steel*, 45–90.

42. Pacey, *Maze of Ingenuity*, 214.

43. In this regard, see Richard White, *Railroaded: The Transcontinentals and the Making of Modern America* (New York: W. W. Norton, 2012).

Chapter Four

Textiles

Machines, Fabrics, Fabrication

Society is founded on cloth.

—Thomas Carlyle, 1833

For a two-wheeled vehicle to transport its rider, it had to be able to roll easily over roads. The "bone shaking" ride of wooden wheels was smoothed through the confluence of road improvement, substituting rubber for leather, and swapping steel for wood in wheel construction—each transformation involving a complex, dynamic process, as we have seen, fusing materials and culture. Material—understood in the simple sense as cloth—equally affected the development of the bicycle and the motorcycle. To form the durable outer carcass of the pneumatic tire, for instance, bands of textile cords (canvas) are coated with rubber.[1] However, the technology of the bicycle and motorcycle intersects with textiles in two far more significant ways: as a fundamental component of the wheel design and manufacture, and as the protective and decorative covering of the rider. Textiles are, quite literally, the threads linking human to machine.

Textiles, understood in their complex socio-technological context, form the core of material culture. "Material" is another word for cloth, and, as Jane Schneider argues, "Cloth and clothing constitute the widest imaginable category of material culture, covering a spatial domain that extends from the miles of textiles annually produced by hand or factory to the most intimate apparel of the human body, and a temporal domain whose earliest moments, lost to archaeology because of poor preservation, pre-date the Neolithic."[2] The appearance of the bicycle and motorcycle in the Industrial Age introduces another layer of complexity, for technological innovation was driven by the textile sector. In the words of one historian, "A new machine technology was created by a complex combination of inventions, by the development of mechanical spinning, machine printing and chemical bleaching, by the application of power to drive the wheels of industry and by the shift of production from home and shop to factory."[3]

While it is commonplace to identify technological innovation in textile production as the origin of industrial capitalism, it can equally be argued that consumers, not producers, spurred development owing to their insatiable demand for cheap, colorful cotton goods. England became the undisputed center of textile manufacture, but only to fend off the calico trade from India and only owing to America's cultivation of cotton crops. Certainly the fabrics produced by the textile trade contributed to the construction of tires and other components of the vehicles, but ancillary developments in engine design, global trade, crop cultivation, and labor relations exerted influence—both intended and unintended. This section attempts to unravel the complex web of relations entangling the machines and their riders.

SPINNING WHEELS AND SEWING MACHINES

In Chris Burden's kinetic sculpture, *The Big Wheel* (1979), a motorcycle propels a massive wooden wheel.[4] His artwork neatly encapsulates the connection between big wheels and small, wood and steel, nineteenth-century industry and twentieth-century technology. But, while in Burden's sculpture the engine drives the wheel, the reverse is more accurate.

Obviously, the wheel, fundamental to human history, is central to bicycle and motorcycle design. Less obvious may be the connection of both devices to the spinning wheels that propelled textile production. Both the wheels propelling the bicycle and the engines powering the motorcycle derive, in part, from devices related to textiles. Two-wheeled machines owe their development and production in large part to the sewing machine. And their wheels derive from the spinning wheel that transformed raw fibers into the threads woven into fabrics, which when stitched together, create parts of the machines and the garments covering their riders. The various sources of power attached to the spinning wheel—animals, humans, wind, water, steam—led to the combustion engine that added "motor" to "cycle."

The vehicles' debt to the spinning wheel, rather than to the more common historical examples of chariot or wagon wheels, may be surprising. But the spinning wheel has its own place in history: "The significance of the spinning wheel is as large in the history of mechanical invention as it is in the history of textiles; it was not merely the first machine to transmit power via a belt, but after 1524, when Leonardo (surprise!) put wheel, crank, connecting rod,

Figure 4.1. Chris Burden, *The Big Wheel*, 1979. Iron, cast, motorcycle, wood, and steel. 112 x 175 x 143 in. (284.5 x 444.5 x 363.2 cm). Courtesy of the Museum of Contemporary Art, Los Angeles. Gift of Lannan Foundation

and treadle together, it was the first to do so with various parts of the machine revolving at different speeds."[5] Each of these components—wheel, crank, connecting rod (or chain) and treadle (or pedal)—figures into cycle design.

Understandably, given our discussion of genius and invention in the introduction, the origins of the spinning wheel are murky. Spinning is an ancient process, transforming raw fibers—such as flax, wool or cotton—into yarn by twisting the "fibers into a cohesive structure so that the fibers will bind together and have as much strength as possible" to be woven into goods.[6] For most of human history—from the time of the ancient Egyptians—spinning was done by hand: a distaff held the raw fibers, which were spun onto a spindle.[7] Early attempts to mechanize the process, in China or India in the eleventh century, fixed the spindle horizontally to rotate when attached by a cord to a large wheel turned by a hand crank (sometimes mounted directly on a spoke).[8] This represented an original insight into the transference of power: one turn of the larger wheel sent the spindle turning more quickly. When a flyer was attached around the spindle, the yarn could be spun and simultaneously wound on a bobbin, but this necessitated a more complex system to enable the flyer to rotate at a different speed, accomplished by adding another belt to the larger wheel (which spun at a third speed). By the early sixteenth century, treadles were attached to drive the wheel by a connecting rod, allowing the feet—rather than the hand—to drive the machine.[9]

This same application of human power to drive a wheel featured in early bicycle experimentation—first the arms, then the feet, either as substitute for the hand crank or the pumping of feet on a treadle. In 1821, Lewis Gompertz of Surrey proposed attaching a handle operated by the arms to assist the legs.[10] This does not seem to have caught on.[11] Instead, "the great success of the modern *veloce*" came from the crank application of the feet, when early French designers attached pedals directly to the front wheel.[12] But greater propulsion power comes from the rear wheel. In 1869, both Thomas McCall and Peyton & Peyton devised means of attaching treadles to the rear wheel by connecting rods, just as a connecting rod had attached a treadle to the spinning wheel. These designs were superseded ten years later when Henry J. Lawson attached a chain (another invention credited to Leonardo in 1482) to the rear wheel, a solution not unlike attaching a cord to link a large wheel to the spindle.

His "Bicyclette" (derisively nicknamed the Crocodile for its elongated frame) did not find an eager audience, owing to rider reservations about sitting so low to the ground, having been accustomed to riding high over the front wheel. It also violated existing visual expectations: "It's the queerest machine I ever set eyes on," proclaimed a writer for *The Cyclist*.[13] The device's unusual aesthetics combined with riders' fears of appearing "undignified"

Figure 4.2. Henry Lawson's "Bicyclette" (1879), with chain connecting pedals to rear wheel.

trumped the bike's design advantages.[14] Incorporating the spinning-wheel example of using wheels rotating at different speeds, Lawson's Bicyclette provided greater propulsive power: "he could 'gear up' the driving wheel simply by making the sprocket attached to it of a smaller circumference than that of the chain wheel driven by the pedals, so that the rear wheel completed more than one revolution every time the cyclist brought the pedals around."[15] A *London Daily News* item published decades later, in 1895, proclaimed Lawson a "revolutionizer of cycle construction," marveling that "modern improvements such as the chain gear" enabled humans to achieve astounding feats, such as covering 515 miles in twenty-four hours.[16]

By that time, the Safety bicycle had equalized wheel size, and the wheel had given rise to "the wheel," as the bicycle was then commonly known. In *The Common Sense of Bicycling* (1896), Marie Ward described its enduring two-wheel design simply: "the main idea of the bicycle does not change—a fixed wheel to which motion is imparted, and a movable or guiding wheel, independent of the power wheel, and revolving only because the machine is pushed or pulled forward. This second wheel gives stability, and supports the wheel at a movable point."[17]

Lawson had earlier convinced Singer and Company, the manufacturer of sewing machines, to produce a treadle-driven device in 1878.[18] The connection between manufacture of the two machines, which both use foot power to turn wheels, was ubiquitous in Britain and in America. Britain established primacy in Coventry, when Rowley Turner, the Paris-based agent for Coventry Sewing Machine Company, brought a Michaux cycle to the factory in 1868 and convinced the board of directors, including founder James Starley, to start their own line.[19] In Connecticut, Albert Pope followed the British example, riding his Coventry-made Duplex Excelsior to the Weed Sewing Machine Company in Hartford, convincing them to reproduce his bike.[20] The company produced bicycles for the next seventeen years, making "fewer and fewer sewing machines and more and more bicycles."[21]

This technological convergence of bicycles and sewing machines is more complex still, when one considers that many sewing machine companies in the eastern United States had originally produced firearms.[22] The Weed Sewing Machine Company, for instance, had formerly been the Sharps Rifle Manufacturing Company. Despite the seeming disparities between the two products, they shared manufacturing processes and machine tools.[23] As the Safety bicycle grew in popularity, both arms manufacturers and sewing machine companies ramped up production: "Iver Johnson arms company switched from ordinaries to safeties and soon found John P. Lovell Arms company, Remington Arms Company, Winchester, and the Colt Armory competing with it. The White Sewing Machine Company, the Elgin Sewing

Machine Company, and the American Sewing Machine Company, among others, began to compete with the Weed company."[24] Who could have anticipated that declining demand for firearms and the increased popularity of sewing machines would propel the bicycle craze of the 1890s?

SEWING MACHINES, CYCLES, AND HEALTH

The confluence of the popular pedal-powered machines introduced further gender-related complications, focused on women's sexuality and health. In *A Wheel within a Wheel*, Frances Willard raised a seemingly innocuous question: "The question is often asked if riding a wheel is not the same as running a sewing-machine."[25] But she was alluding to a host of "scientific" studies warning of the deleterious effects of operating bipedal machines. Like the fashion for bicycling itself, such concerns seem to have been imported from France: "French doctors in the 1860s . . . made the sensational claim that bipedal sewing machines have a harmful masturbatory effect on women as the rubbing of their thighs caused genital excitement."[26] One newspaper report had argued that the sewing machine fated seamstresses "to nymphomania" and "sensual madness."[27] Similar claims were made about women operating the other bipedal machine. Dr. Ludovic O'Followell—author of *Bicyclette et organe genitaux* (The Bicycle and the Genital Organs)—opined that cycling could "procure genital satisfactions, voluptuous sensations," and a kind of "sportive masturbation."[28] A leading clinician writing in *La France Médicale* argued that, "no innocent girl could accidentally masturbate by riding a bicycle, . . . but it was possible for a woman to press against the saddle in such a way that she could deliberately sexually stimulate herself."[29] As sports historian Richard Holt argues,

> Men were concerned that women would either lose sex appeal or, conversely, that they as men would lose control of their own wives and daughters. The cycling issue was a kind of prism in which the whole gamut of men's attitudes towards women was put on display. Many men could only conceive of female cyclists as either sexless athletic spinsters or, as was frequently displayed in the posters of the period, half-naked, voluptuous and, by implication, sexually available.[30]

Suspicions about the sensual pleasures of cycling endured into the twentieth century. Popular culture representations of women motorcycle riders in 1960s America pictured them as threatening, hypersexualized menaces to men: in *She-Devils on Wheels* (1968) female riders were advertised as "man-eaters on motorcycles, feared by the men they use as lovers" with "Guts as hard as the steel of their hogs!" and in *The Mini-Skirt Mob* (1968) "They play around with murder like they play around with men! They're hog straddling female animals on the prowl." In Britain, *Girl on a Motorcycle* (1968) featured Marianne Faithfull fantasizing about sex as she rode her Harley-Davidson, naked under her leather suit, to meet her lover.[31]

Nineteenth-century reservations about the bipedal machines, initially focused on sewing machine operators, derived from traditional attitudes about women's fragility and fixated on dangers of using the machines to their reproductive capacities. The seamstress's posture, seated hunched over the machine in a tight corset, provoked concerns that she could damage her reproductive organs by cutting off blood flow and air supply. One doctor explained,

> The woman at the sewing-machine works indoors, stoops over her work, contracting the chest and almost completely checking the flow of blood to and from the lower half of her body, where at the same time she is increasing the demand for it, finally aggravating the whole trouble by the pressure of the lower edge of the corset against the abdomen, so that the customary congestions and displacements have good cause for their existence.[32]

This hyperbolic criticism provoked bicyclists to stress the differences between their posture and the seamstress's. Willard cites a doctor who admits that "Women, at least, sit erect on a wheel, and consequently the thighs never make even a right angle with the trunk, and there is no stasis of blood in the lower limbs and genitalia. Moreover, the work itself makes the rider breathe in oceans of fresh air."[33] Despite his claims about the bicycle facilitating "sportive masturbation," even Dr. O'Followell conceded that cycling "carried no danger to childrearing" and could even enhance reproduction since it discouraged the wearing of corsets. The majority of medical professionals endorsed cycling as a gentle form of exercise and "some even claimed recreational cycling would increase the birthrate by stimulating the body and the sexual drive."[34] In fact, bicycling appealed to riders of both sexes as a form of exercise. One reporter wrote in 1895, "The bicycle has done more to foster love of out-of-door life than any other invention."[35] Another, writing for *Sporting Life*, an influential sporting weekly published in Philadelphia, embraced the health benefits but with some reservations:

> Cycling among women must, up to a certain point, resemble cycling among men; it must be the pastime of the middle class, not merely tolerated, but welcomed and recognized as a health-giver and restorer. But if it is to attain that position the greatest care must be taken to prevent anything which might cause it to degenerate into, or even be regarded as, a mere vulgar amusement.[36]

The emphasis on cycling as health-giving and restorative is clear but the qualifications merit reflection: cycling among women should resemble cycling among men only "up to a certain point," a point, it appears, that falls short of vulgarity—or disgust. Anxieties about the appropriate femininity of wheeling women abound in the discussions.

Female enthusiasts were at pains to allay concerns about impropriety, assuring their readers with evidence from medical authorities. Willard argues that, "Many physicians are now coming to regard the 'wheel' as beneficial to the health of women as well as of men," quoting one unidentified, presumably male, expert:

> It will be a delight to girls to learn that the fact of their sex is, in itself, not a bar to riding a wheel. If the girl is normally constituted and is dressed hygienically, and if she will use judgment and not overtax herself in learning to ride, and in measuring the length of rides after she has learned, she is in no more danger from riding a wheel than is the young man. But if she persists in riding in a tight dress, and uses no judgment in deciding the amount of exercise she is capable of safely taking, it will be quite possible for her to injure herself, and then it is she, and not the wheel, that is to blame.[37]

Even Willard qualifies her health claims, noting that while a woman's sex "in itself" is not a barrier, she needs to exercise within certain bounds (i.e., not too vigorously) and in the proper "hygienic" attire (i.e., without a tight corset). In particular, women were not to emulate the male "scorchers." *Cycling* magazine cautioned in 1893 that "for feats of speed and protracted endurance, she is by nature physically unfit, and bound morally, if she respects her sex, to avoid anything in the nature of deleterious excess of exertion."[38] Willard cites another physician, Dr. Seneca Egbert, who prescribes wheeling a cure for the specifically female ailment of emotionalism: "It gets them out of doors, gives them a form of exercise adapted to their needs, that they may enjoy in company with others or alone, and one that goes to the root of their nervous troubles."[39] Despite advocating cycling as healthy for women, both the doctor and the avid wheelwoman invoke stereotypes about women's fragile physical and emotional state.

As apprehensions about the sewing machine and bicycle's impact on women's sexuality endured long into the twentieth century, affecting female motorcyclists, trepidation about the proper limits of female exertion also persisted. Like their nineteenth-century precursors, early female motorcycle riders defended their two-wheeling as a healthy, feminine practice. Marjorie Cottle, a leading sports rider and probably Britain's best known female motorcyclist, claimed, in 1928, that "It has been conclusively proved that motor-cycling is not harmful to women." Like Willard, she felt compelled to reassure the public by citing medical authorities. And she, too, advocated the opposite case: motorcycling was a healthy activity. She said, "Girls will find that motor-cycling brings health. It will give them honest, fresh-air complexions. It will make them hardy and strong."[40] Twin sisters Betty and Nancy Debenham, both ardent motorcyclists, enthused, "Motor-cycling is an ideal hobby for the tired business girl. She can seek health and pleasure during her precious week-ends by exploring the countryside and the seaside."[41] Still, even male supporters in the 1920s, like the *Sporting Life* columnist in 1895, betrayed persistent biases about women's emotionality and femininity in statements such as this one: "While the motor cycle does give the Amazonian type of female in this modern age a healthy means of self-expression (as the psychologist would say), [it also saves] her from such abnormal means of self-expression as the Charleston and the cocktail."[42] Riding a motorcycle may be an alternative to the flapper's mania for dance and alcohol but only if she is the "Amazonian type," a dig that echoes through the century—and beyond—in popular images of women as "she-devils" on wheels or dykes on bikes.

The motorcycle press in the 1920s promoted women's technical competence as riders in their reports on female racers, such as Cottle and Faye Taylour, but also as mechanics, with female columnists offering practical advice on apparel, suitable models and touring destinations, but also maintenance.[43] Manuals written by female bicyclists, such as Willard's and Ward's, also incorporated mechanical advice. Ward was particularly intent to tell her female readers that "the art of bicycling is purely mechanical attainment," arguing that "the needs of the bicyclist are an intelligent comprehension of the bicycle as a machine, an appreciative knowledge of the human machine that propels it, and a realization of the fact that rider and bicycle should form one combined mechanism."[44] Knowledge of both machines—the vehicle and rider—was not simply practical but necessary to avoid possible censure. She counsels:

> Early learn to use the wrench yourself, and study how to apply that instrument properly. Study the different parts of the bicycle, and note how they are put together; and particularly observe each nut and screw, and determine its purpose. Each nut must be at its proper tension to hold securely. Study the valves of the tires and learn their construction; and be sure you know how to apply the pump-coupling properly. Learn the names and uses of the different parts of the bicycle, and study their construction. This is mechanical geography, if I may use such a term. Learn to care for your health and how to prepare your system to resist fatigue. Then you will find that you have mastered the subject, and are prepared to avail yourself of the many pleasures of the sport.[45]

Ward's advice follows the same given earlier to sewing-machine operators. As Julie Wosk documents, "Nineteenth-century writers also envisioned the sewing machine as a means to transform women into more technologically knowledgeable beings. *Godey's Ladies Book* in 1860 suggested that sewing machines would broaden women's knowledge of "mechanical powers," and, in the following century, their ability to operate a sewing machine "would become a measure of their potential to learn other mechanical skills."[46] Not only would such mechanical mastery allow women to master a bicycle, it granted them superior skill in working on motorcycles. Basil Henry Davies, a Lancashire clergyman writing for *The Motor Cycle* under the pen name *Ixion* in 1926, attributed women's mechanical aptitudes to time at the sewing table, which made them "particularly skilled in delicate works such as setting points or valve clearances."[47] Subsequently, however, attitudes shifted, not, one presumes, owing to women's lack of skill but to sexism. As Steve Koerner has found, "In the late 1930s, . . . a leading manufacturer, Norton Motors, publicly declared that it would not employ women in its Birmingham factory because to do so would, the company believed, compromise existing standards of craftsmanship."[48] Nonetheless, some individuals defied convention: Theresa Wallach served during World War II in the British Army Transport Corps as a mechanic, before becoming a dispatch rider, and then moved to America in 1952, where she made a living as a motorcycle mechanic, eventually opening her own shop.[49] The fictional female mechanic Shane (Monet Mazur) in *Torque* (2004) can not only wrench bikes but vanquish female rivals using her sport bike. But their exceptional status—real and fictional—demonstrates the long reach of gender bias associated with female operators of mechanical devices extending back to the sewing machine.

HUMAN MOTORS AND MECHANICAL ENGINES

Attitudes about power undergird gendered perceptions of mechanics. Human-propelled devices, such as the spinning wheel or sewing machine, were firmly associated with women's work. Even the Safety bicycle—operated within limits of its full power—and early motorcycles—lightweight with small engines—were marketed to and embraced equally by women and men. However, increased applications of power—either by pedal or engine—associated mechanical devices with men. In *The Machine in the Garden*, Leo Marx argues that the machine "invariably is associated with crude, masculine aggressiveness in contrast with the tender, feminine, and submissive attitudes traditionally attached to the landscape."[50]

Ironically, shifting attitudes to power and mechanics came about owing to advances in the textile industry, which employed not only machines associated with women but female workers. The application of power to the spinning jenny—first water, then steam, then electricity—transformed perceptions of work and working bodies—through a "single metaphor—the frequently invoked 'human motor,' a striking image that illuminates an underlying affinity between physiology and technology. The metaphor of the machine underwent a change from that of a clockwork composed of diverse parts to that of modern motor modeled on a steam engine or electric-powered technology."[51]

The modern motor derived from those first applied to spinning, weaving and sewing. At about the same time that James Watt was tinkering with the steam engine, a Lancashire weaver happened on an idea for adding more spindles to the spinning wheel, creating the spinning jenny (not a name but a dialect term for *engine*). "While visiting a friend, [James] Hargreaves observed a spinning wheel that had been knocked down; with the wheel and spindle in a vertical position, rather than their then-traditional horizontal one, they continued to revolve. In a flash, Hargreaves imagined a line of spindles, upright and side by side, spinning multiple threads simultaneously."[52] In 1769, Richard Arkwright developed a roller system (likely taking the idea from John Kay, who probably stole it from Thomas Highs) that could spin "the original thread fivefold before the jennylike bobbin-and-flyer gave it the needed twist, producing a thread that was both longer and stronger than could be produced by either hand or jenny."[53] Establishing a factory on the Derwent River, Arkwright used water to power the rollers. Samuel Crompton combined Hargreaves's jenny with Arkwright's for his mule (so called since it was a hybrid of the two devices before it, like crossbreeding a donkey and horse): combining rollers with the jenny, he could produce finer threads.[54] When steam power replaced water in 1790, "spinners could accomplish in 300 hours what it had taken 50,000 hours to produce."[55]

Crompton's mule, in particular, led to Britain's dominance in the textile industry, but only owing to inexhaustible demand for fabrics produced, not in Britain, but in India. What was to become "the world's first truly international industry, linking together the societies of the inhabited globe," credited with originating the capitalist system of production and consumption, serving as "the supreme model of machine production and as the pattern of a market economy, generating both wealth and power" for Britain,[56] rests not on a fine thread but on a complex web of international trade, colonialism, slavery and fashion. Similar practices of global commerce, from international tariffs, outsourcing, and exploitation of foreign markets, can be traced in the development of the bicycle and motorcycle industries. Ultimately, cycle design, pedal power, and motorized vehicles were driven by consumer demand for cloth and clothing.

COTTON: THE FABRIC OF OUR RIDES

Consumer demand for cloth spurred mechanical production and technological innovation—not just for any cloth, but cloth of one fiber—cotton—and not just any kind of cotton fabric, but one specific type—calico (also known as muslin)—a plain weave of unbleached cotton.[57] Crompton's achievement was to "spin the fine counts of yarn essential for the manufacture of Indian-style muslins."[58] That enabled the British to reproduce the inexpensive colorfully printed calico fabrics originally produced in India that had inspired a feverish demand among consumers beginning in the seventeenth century.

Scholars note that, in fact, the textile revolution could just as readily have occurred in South Asia as in Britain, for reasons related to the spice trade centuries before. As Daniel Miller explains, Southeast Asian spice producers had no interest in European goods, including British textiles. Calicoes were superior in quality and South Asian dyeing technology far surpassed Europe's. So to purchase the spices so prized in Europe, traders of the East India Company instead took cotton cloth from South Asia, sold it in Britain and took the profits to purchase spices from the East Indies.[59]

As we have seen in the case of rubber, entirely unintended consequences arose owing to European colonial trade: rubber plants were transported from Brazil to Kew Gardens, where owing to ongoing British imperialistic seafaring, plantations were established, also in coastal Asia, far from the native pests that plagued South American rubber growers.[60] For cotton, British consumers' appetite for cinnamon, cardamom, ginger, and other spices led to the importation of South Asian calicoes, fulfilling and fueling another consumer demand. As Chandra Mukerji and others have argued, the fashion for painted floral chintz fabric in the late seventeenth and early eighteenth centuries meant that brightly colored South Asian calicoes found a ready market. They were not only lighter and softer than British woolen goods, they were also less expensive than the silks and brocades produced in France and Italy. These fabrics had a "breadth of appeal and use that were unprecedented."[61]

Initially, Britain responded by trying to block Indian exports, passing the Calico Acts in 1700 and 1720, prohibiting both the import and ownership of Indian printed cottons, as woolen textile artisans took to the streets of London, "tearing calicoes off the women's backs."[62] Such efforts had little impact on consumer demand. Similar protectionist interventions were later launched by American bicycle manufacturers in 1891 to fend off British imports[63] and by Harley-Davidson in 1983 to restrict Japanese imports.[64] Like the British Calico Acts, these had only temporary benefits at best, suggesting that consumer demand for quality goods may trump government obstruction of international trade.

Instead, pressured by unchecked domestic demand, Britain developed its own textile industry to satisfy it, again with unexpected consequences: not simply did it propel technological innovation in spinning, sewing, and weaving, but unprecedented trade in cotton goods, all at the expense of the same competitor it had initially sought to fend off. The impact on South Asian countries was entirely negative: once Britain's mechanized industry could produce sufficient quantities, high import duties on South Asian calicoes began to take effect. European demand for the more expensive South Asian goods decreased and eventually "Britain was able to turn the tide against India, and later to flood that area with cheap cotton goods."[65] India had become Britain's market. Not only did Britain meet its domestic demand, it exceeded it, and by the nineteenth century it had secured 80 percent of world trade, which it sustained until 1933, with India its main market from 1843 to 1939.[66] In 1842, Sydney Smith proclaimed, "the great object for which the Anglo-Saxon race appears to have been created" was "the making of calico," apparently oblivious to the fact that South Asia had pioneered its creation.[67] (Indians were not, and reviving the cotton industry became a cornerstone of resistance to British imperialism. In 1921, Mahatma Gandhi sought to revive use of the spinning wheel as a mark of India's independence.[68])

Smith's imperialist rhetoric demonstrates that the vaunted Anglo-Saxon supremacy in calico, like rubber, rested on a history of war and colonial possession. Since cotton could not be grown in Britain, it initially imported raw cotton from South Asia instead, a natural consequence owing not simply to India's primacy in the cultivation of "White Gold" over three millennia but because the East India Company had established trading posts there in the seventeenth century, and successions of military incursions in the eighteenth culminated in its becoming "the jewel in the British Crown."

Britain not only exploited its trade with South Asia but with America—and its technological advances in producing cotton textiles were equally dependent on "the distinctive achievement of the United States. The saw-gin, devised in 1793 by the Yale graduate Eli Whitney, must be ranked with Arkwright's roller spinning frame as one of the two great inventions in the history of the cotton industry."[69] The gin was rapidly adopted in the American south, making possible the large-scale production of raw cotton. So rapidly did its exports grow that by 1795 U.S. production was second only to India's. Within a century, it had driven all competitors out of the market, prompting South Carolina senator J. H. Hammond to proclaim, "Cotton is king."[70]

But just as British dominance in manufacture and trade resulted from colonialism, America's claim as the "Cotton Kingdom" rested on slavery. The practice of picking cotton, from its ancient origins in Egypt, was intensely laborious. Since the bolls of the plant ripen at varying rates, harvesting was typically done by hand, as was the equally tedious and laborious process of pulling the fibers (the lint) from the seed, a process Columbus and other European explorers had likely seen in the West Indies, Mexico, and Peru. As in the production of calico, South Asia is cited as a pioneer in mechanizing the processing of the raw material. In the hand-powered Churka gin two wooden rollers pinched the fiber and pulled it away from the seed. In Whitney's gin, a cylinder covered in spikes pulled the fibers from the seeds through the bars of a grid. Eventually, saw blades cut the fibers from the seeds, which fell to the bottom.[71] While it mechanized processing of the fibers, the gin did not eliminate hand picking and the work fell to slaves, as it had in Egypt. In the words of William Rosen, "Abusive labor practices and cotton appear together pretty much everywhere."[72] Increased demand for cotton actually increased use of slave labor in growing and picking the crop. Thus, while cotton production transformed manufacturing and spurred innovations that revolutionized personal transport, the beneficiaries of these advances—from those who profited financially to those who gained mobility—relied on the misery of others, from slaves in America and the Caribbean, to displaced artisans in Europe and South Asia, not to mention the factory workers employed by the textile industry.[73]

FASHIONING CYCLES AND DRESSING RIDERS

The demand for cotton derived from the demand for cotton cloth, which was derived, in its turn, from "the ultimate demand for clothing."[74] In other words, "textiles are admirably suited to the dictates of fashion."[75] In a very real sense, then, the wheels of the textile industry that in part inspired two-wheeled vehicle design were propelled by desires for increasingly differentiated dress, desires that were stoked, and in some cases created, by sophisticated systems of distribution and marketing that actually occurred before the rise of machinery.[76] The proliferation of fashion magazines, pattern books, catalogs, specialty stores, and eventually department stores presented an ever-widening number of options to an emerging market of middle-class consumers.[77] The turn of the nineteenth century witnessed a proliferating array of choices, as Victorian social mores dictated a range of appropriate attire for "work and leisure, day and night, worship and school, summer and winter, youth and adulthood, not to mention women and men."[78] Men's dress experienced a radical shift toward sportswear and casual clothing prompted by "the emergence of a widespread mania for sports and recreation—what historian Hugh Cunningham calls 'a national leisure culture.'"[79] In the second half of the century, demand for sportswear created further variation, with popular sports such as croquet, tennis, golf, and even walking necessitating specific costumes. The popularity of the high wheeler in the 1870s, for instance, made tails and unfitted trousers dangerous. Note the short coat and knickerbockers stuffed into gaiters on the trim male figure in this image from a Columbia bicycle ad of 1879 (thought to depict bicycle and motorcycle manufacturer Albert A. Pope).

Figure 4.3. Advertisement for the Columbia bicycle, 1879.

Cycling is cited as one influence in revising not only the aesthetics of men's fashion but bodily form. Mrs. Burton Kingsland wrote in *Etiquette for All Occasions* (1901) that, "the figure of the man of to-day is slim, athletic, but not burly. . . . It is a period of aesthetic athletes."[80] And men's clothing facilitated their athletic performance. Mrs. Kingsland explained, "For cycling and general country sports, men wear knickerbocker suits of tweed, Norfolk or short jackets, heavy ribbed golf stockings, stout russet laced shoes and cloth caps."[81] The Norfolk jacket, a loose, belted jacket with box pleats on the back and front, became the popular choice.

Note the convergence of economic and technological innovation: as the dangerous high wheel bicycle gave way to the more manageable Safety bicycle, increased numbers embraced the device, encouraged by falling prices. Sports and sporting dress, once associated with the leisured elite, became affordable to the middle class. Mass participation in cycling and mass production of goods combined, as "nearly everyone could afford to adopt the leisure clothing and consumable recreational pursuits once exclusive to the elite."[82] By the 1890s, 90 percent of American men wore ready-made clothing.[83] Unsurprisingly, "tailors complained that men who wore cheap cycling suits were not wearing out their good clothes. A bicycle, costing about the same price as a good suit, supposedly put forty percent of the twenty thousand tailors in New York out of work."[84]

The bicycle craze of the late 1890s produced a concomitant revolution in culture and dress for women. Much has already been written about how bicycling eventually became *the* vehicle for feminist reform, first in fashion, as women traded their skirts for bloomers, and then in politics, as temperance leaguers and suffragettes advocated cycling as a means of independence. Susan B. Anthony's comment to a reporter in 1895 equates dress reform with freedom of movement: "Why, pray tell me, hasn't a woman as much right to suit herself as a man? The stand she is taking in the matter of dress is no small indication that she has realized that she has an equal right with a man to control her own movements."[85]

But, as with narratives of technological progress, the story is more complicated. Transformations in women's dress emerged from a confluence of factors: reformist zeal, spurred by concerns for hygiene and aesthetics, and practicalities introduced by the bicycle. Tightly laced corsets were discouraged for distorting the natural female form, as well, as we have seen, for restricting breathing and constricting vital organs. Similar anxieties were directed at men, whose trousers could let in draughts, making knee breeches and stockings the healthier alternative.[86] Above all, practicality prevailed: the Rational Dress Society was founded in London in 1881 to protest "against the introduction of any fashion in dress that either deforms the figure, impedes the movements of the body, or in any way tends to injure the health. It protests against the wearing of tightly-fitting corsets; of high-heeled shoes; of heavily-weighted skirts, as rendering healthy exercise almost impossible."[87] The bicycle enabled "healthy exercise," thus it necessitated abandoning skirts: the logic was impeccable.

No wonder, then, that Ward's book was titled *The Common Sense of Bicycling: Bicycling for Ladies* and, in its subtitle, sandwiches "dress" between more technical considerations: "With Hints as to the Art of Wheeling—Advice to Beginners—Dress—Care of the Bicycle—Mechanics—Training—Exercise, etc., etc." She devotes entire chapters to the construction, mechanics and physics of the bicycle, as well as detailed instructions about rider position and cycling technique, and in a separate chapter turns her "scientific" lens on dress. Surprisingly, despite comparisons of the bicycle to the horse, there is no mention of adapting equestrian gear. While cognizant of being visible as a rider and hence fashioning an outfit, Ward's preeminent concern is practicality. Rather than engage in debates about skirts (or the absence thereof), Ward states simply, "It is an accepted fact that bicycling cannot be properly enjoyed unless the clothing is suitable." In her mind, "The essentials are knickerbockers, shirt-waist, stockings, shoes, gaiters, sweater, coat, no skirt, or skirt with length decided by individual preference, hat and gloves."[88] Willard echoes Ward's practical language in recounting her first forays into bicycling:

> It is needless to say that a bicycling costume was a prerequisite. This consisted of a skirt and blouse of tweed, with belt, rolling collar, and loose cravat, the skirt three inches from the ground; a round straw hat, and walking-shoes with gaiters. It was a simple, modest suit, to which no person of common sense could take exception.[89]

Common sense prevailed equally in Marguerite Merington's article "Woman and the Bicycle" published in *Scribner*'s the same year. She argued:

> Short rides on level roads can be accomplished with but slight modification of ordinary attire, and the sailor hat, shirt waist, serge skirt uniform is as much at home on the bicycle as it is anywhere else the world over. The armies of women clerks in Chicago and Washington who go by wheel to business, show that the exercise within bounds need not impair the spick-and-spandy neatness that marks the bread-winning American girl.[90]

The practical demands of riding the machine, rather than any feminist zeal, led to their detailed suggestions for dress "reform." The term "adaptation" is more appropriate, since none of the writers advocates new designs or specific purchases. Merington justifies one special adaption for excursions as absolutely necessary, arguing that "skirts, while they have not hindered women from climbing to the topmost branches of the higher education, may prove fatal in down-hill coasting; and skirts, unless frankly shortened or discarded, must be fashioned so as to minimize the danger of entanglement with the flying wheel."[91]

While the women refer to their "outfit" or "costume," they eschew references to fashion. Merington pointedly argues:

> The pastime does not lend itself to personal display, and in criticism the costume must be referred, not to the standards of the domestic hearthrug, but to the exigencies of the wheel, the rider's positions to the mechanical demands of the motion; accordingly, the cyclist is to be thought of only as mounted and in flight, belonging not to a picture, but to a moving panorama. If she rides well, the chances are she looks well, for she will have reconciled grace, comfort, and the temporary fitness of things.[92]

Like Ward, Merington emphasizes the "exigencies of the wheel" and the "mechanical demands of the motion." As it had previously for male riders, the device dictated the choice of garments. Defending women's adaptations of clothing, Elizabeth Cady Stanton proffered this comparison: "Men found that flying coat tails were ungainly and that baggy trousers were in the way so they changed their dress to suit themselves. They have taken in every reef and sail and appear in skin tight garments."[93]

Contrast the cyclists' emphasis on practicality to the fashionable set of nonriders who embraced the cycling outfit as a costume. In *Fancy Dresses Described; or, What to Wear at Fancy Balls* (1887), Arden Holt recommends dressing as "The New Woman," pictured in figure 4.4.

The image was accompanied by this caption:

> She wears a cloth tailor-made gown, and her bicycle is pourtrayed [sic] in front of it, together with the *Sporting Times* and her golf club; she carries her betting book and her latch-key at her side, her gun is slung across her shoulder, and her pretty Tam o'Shanter is surmounted by a bicycle lamp. She has spats to her patent leather shoes, and is armed at all points for conquest.

Both cycling fashion and cycling dress become "sport" for the upper classes, for ball goers in "tailor-made" gowns who wear, rather than engage in, sporting activities.[94] The condescending mockery visible here extended to the popular press. The satirical magazine *Punch* initially mocked the "New Woman" of the 1890s in her bloomers, but was shortly directing its barbs at those who sported cycling costumes without any pretense to actually sporting.

These cartoons mock upper-class pretensions and frivolity in dress, not the garments adopted for riding, garments that, on the bodies of actual riders, bore little resemblance to the costumes in fashion magazines.

Early magazines devoted to motorcycling followed the example of cycling, stressing practicality as well as nineteenth-century etiquette for dress. In

Figure 4.4. The "New Woman" in *Fancy Dresses Described; or, What to Wear at Fancy Balls*, 1887.

Figure 4.5. "The Bicycle Suit," cartoon from *Punch*, 1895.
Gertrude: "My dear Jessie, what on earth is that bicycle suit for?"
Jessie: "Why, to wear, of course."
Gertrude: "But you haven't got a bicycle!"
Jessie: "No, but I've got a sewing machine."

pointed contrast to the current practice of manufacturers to promote apparel as aggressively—if not more so—than their machines, early periodicals devoted to motorcycling feature virtually no ads for clothing tailored to riders. The 1908 issue of *Motorcycle Illustrated*, for example, features ads for grips, lights, saddles, tires, and Mennen's Borated Talcum Toilet Powder, but no clothing. Early issues contained a regular ad for Bull Dog suspenders but it disappeared by mid-year. Instead, the magazine patently emphasizes the machine and its manufacturers—a list that included Harley-Davidson, Indian and the other early companies that would later fail: Merkel, Thor, Thiem, Minerva, Royal, MM, Curtiss. The magazine does work hard to promote the motorcycle as its own unique device, neither the poor man's auto or a bicycle with a motor. But images of riders show that cycling dress remained relatively unchanged for both men and women, that mass-produced, inexpensive garments were still the preferred gear. Mrs. Kingsland stressed that expense didn't matter: "Whatever be one's fortune, if one has not learned habits of neatness and order, one will never be well dressed."[95]

Neatness and order were apparently paramount to early motorcycle riders, who faced not only the dirt and mud from undeveloped roads but discharge from the motor. Mrs. Kingland's advice to her sporting readers in 1901 echoes in an item from *Motorcycle Illustrated* published in 1908, praising riders in an endurance race from New York to Chicago, for their "ability to dress like a gentleman and appear like a civilized being": "there was an object for the riders to keep both themselves and their machines as neat as possible. Most of them wore khaki suits on the road, always had changes of raiment awaiting at the night controls and subjected their day wear to a gasoline bath each night."[96]

The author's reference to "khaki" jackets introduces another basic material, which, like cotton, involves Britain's involvement in India. The term *khaki* derives from both Hindustani and Urdu and means simply "soil-colored." The term—which refers to both the color and the fabric, a tightly twilled cloth of cotton or linen—derives from Britain's colonial past, specifically the army's adaptations of traditional Indian fabrics for camouflage. In 1846, Sir Harry Lumsden raised a Corps of Guides for frontier service from British Indian recruits at Peshawar and, noting the practicality of their outfits, had uniforms dyed to match them. Khaki-colored uniforms were used officially by British troops for the first time during the Abyssinian campaign of 1867–68, when Indian troops traveled to Ethiopia. The British Army subsequently adopted the material for campaign dress in 1884 (the same year the dye was patented), the American Army during the Spanish Civil War in 1898. But not until World War II did it become popular as U.S. military wear, suggesting that like Sir Lumsden, early motorcycle riders were attracted to the fabric for its use as camouflage—not to blend into dusty terrain but to disguise road dirt.

Figure 4.6. Riders in khaki, *Motorcycle Illustrated*, 1908.

This snapshot of the materials that formed cycle gear in the transition from the bicycle to the motorcycle places primacy on practicality and neatness, revealing in turn, fascinating assumptions about both machines and riders. The machine itself—first the bicycle—dictated styles and fabrics that allowed ease and freedom of movement, which prompted revolutions in men's and women's attire. And the rapid pace of change in dress reform depended in its turn on processes of mass production (for both textiles and two-wheeled vehicles), advertising and consumerism that were equally egalitarian. (It's worth emphasizing again that the bicycle and advertising emerged simultaneously, with Albert Pope generally credited with creating modern advertising strategies.[97]) The materials themselves—wool, cotton and khaki—were cheaply available and consistent with everyday wear. This suggests, ultimately, that the bicyclist and the motorcyclist were part of the turn-of-the-century social fabric, not the outcasts and outlaws that would prevail post–World War II.

The prevalent postwar image that prevails globally to this day is of the leather-jacketed "outlaw." While the black leather jacket has dominated discussions of motorcycle fashion, other garments and materials essential to rider protection and style have been overlooked.[98] Instead, riders in the 1950s and '60s were as likely to sport cotton—in the form of waxed-cotton jackets, t-shirts or denim. The iconic image of Marlon Brando posing in his Perfecto "One Star" jacket from Schott as Johnny Strabler from *The Wild One* (1953) is often cited as establishing the fashion for motorcycle riders. However, riders at the time were more likely to sport the attire of his nemesis in the film Chino (Lee Marvin). The president of the San Francisco chapter of the Hells Angels found it so authentic that he bought the same blue-and-yellow striped shirt Marvin wore in the film.[99] The more authentic elements of Brando's ensemble were his simple white T-shirt and denim jeans, both made of cotton. Initially produced by Levi Strauss a century earlier, denim exerted a global influence starting in the 1950s.[100] Yet, on the basis of the film and others produced in 1950s America, the black-leather-jacketed rebel became an image divorced from the act of riding, exported worldwide.[101]

The actual motorcyclists' jacket was more likely to have been cotton—either denim or waxed cotton—than leather, particularly in Britain where leather provided inadequate protection from wind and rain.[102] Most British manufacturers who went on to meet the fashionable, popular demand for leather jackets, such as Belstaff and Lewis Leathers, originally produced waterproof garments designed more for protection than style. D. Lewis opened in 1892, selling tailored suits and raincoats; Belstaff began offering jackets made of Egyptian cotton treated with oil in the 1920s. (Later techniques substituted paraffin wax for oil, hence the term "waxed cotton.") Originally employed by the navy and designed by Barbour for use in World War II, the Ursula Suit made its way to surplus stores after the war, snapped up by young riders as cheap, protective gear. According to then contemporary riders, leather jackets were prohibitively expensive, as well as impractical.[103] Though Barbour has since become so well known that any waxed-cotton jacket is referred to as a Barbour jacket, other manufacturers soon made garments designed for and marketed specifically to riders.

The black-leather-jacketed Rockers were then emulating an image imported from America, tied to rock 'n' roll musicians like Elvis and cinematic rebels like James Dean rather than motorcycling—especially considering that *The Wild One* was not released in Britain until 1968.[104] Their choice of leather jacket and jeans had more to do with oppositional styling, a defiantly tough alternative to the sleek Continental "modern" look of their rival Mods. The Mods' slim suits and ties dictated their preference for the scooter, for its fairings could offer protection for their clothing, as did their green parkas.[105] The scooter, impractically decorated with excess mirrors, became a fashion accessory as much as a means of transport.

In America, the introduction of Japanese bikes did the opposite, with manufacturers marketing its riders as "the nicest people," in defiance of the leather-jacketed outlaw or Rocker image, and its devices as practical machines rather than fashion accessories. Advertisements pictured riders of both sexes in slacks and cardigans, astride small, utilitarian vehicles. While Suzuki did manufacture looms before motorcycles,[106] Japanese manufacturers did not exploit the connection between their vehicles and rider fashion.

By contrast, for the American manufacturer Harley-Davidson fashion has trumped practicality, at least in its contemporary history. Jackets and boots branded with the H-D logo are marketed to riders—and nonriders—as iconic motorcycle gear in advertising suffused with nostalgia for the company's—and the country's—past. The primacy of clothing and accessories to the brand is evident in its creation of a separate Motor Clothes division.[107] Consumers of H-D clothing are purchasing a look that itself harkens back to a popular culture image of rider rebellion rooted in film, not motorcycling, one that appeals equally, if not more, to nonriders than riders. In 1991, the Council of Fashion Designers of America recognized Harley-Davidson for influencing ready-wear fashion, as the motorcycle jacket, designed by fashion houses such as Calvin Klein, Dolce & Gabbana, and Chanel, began appearing on supermodels in the pages of *Vogue*. Now ubiquitous, the jacket, like designer jeans, is a fashion staple with designs by Saint Laurent priced at more than $5,000—the cost of a small motorcycle. As with nineteenth-century cycling costumes, the garments have been appropriated by fashionistas to signal stylishness off the bike.

By logical extension, the motorcycle—inevitably a make popular in the 1950s and '60s when the image of the rebellious rider was born—has been exploited by luxury brands to sell their expensive products, from leather goods to perfume.[108] As Caryn Simonson has pointed out, Belstaff's Fall 2012 campaign, "Legends of Belstaff," featured Ewan McGregor and a black Velocette, capitalizing on the actor's star status, but also his riding skill as evidenced in the travel documentaries *Long Way Round* (2004) and *Long Way Down* (2007), to sell the company's leather riding gear, but also its purses and boots. Shot at Goodwood, home of the Dukes of Richmond & Lennox and site of the Festival of Speed, an annual motor sports extravaganza, the campaign positioned Belstaff as an iconic British brand, its invocation of motorcycle history central to its establishing its pedigree in the minds of global consumers of its high-end goods.[109] Chanel's elaborate campaign for its perfume Coco Mademoiselle included a video directed by Joe Wright featuring Keira Knightley in a cream-colored one-piece leather suit designed by Karl Lagerfeld with matching boots, Ruby "Belvedere" helmet and 1970s Ducati Sport.[110] Both the bike and the suit are secondary to the film's tale of romance. The perfumed Knightley rides her Ducati to a photo shoot, where she seductively poses for a photographer, unzipping her leather suit (an obvious allusion to the 1968 film *Girl on a Motorcycle*). Before he can act on his desire for her, she disappears, hopping on her bike and roaring off. The lyrics to the soundtrack—"This is a man's world but it would be nothing without a woman or a girl"—enforce its narrative of female empowerment. The motorcycle becomes a symbol for independence and sexual possibility, just as the bicycle had for the new woman of the 1890s, but only to sell perfume.

Why revive only the *image* of motorcycling when you can revive the motorcycle itself and thus sell both clothing and vehicles as fashionable? The contemporary revival of Matchless is a case in point. In complexly circular fashion, Italian brothers Manuele and Michele Malenotti, the former owners of Belstaff, have extended their advertising strategy to imbue their new version of the classic café racer with the cachet attached to the luxury goods granted by their association with motorcycling's fashionable past—and to sell clothes to riders (and rider wannabes) simultaneously. Ad campaigns launched in 2013 featured Kate Moss in a Matchless leather jacket draped over the new Matchless Model X Reloaded. As vintage bike enthusiast Paul d'Orléans said, it can appear to be a "fantastically cynical" strategy: "When aging supermodels are draped across a stupendously ugly motorbike wearing logo clothing, it's clear what's the real business at hand."[111] Bike and clothing—both branded (literally) with the iconic Matchless flying "M" logo—sell the brand itself. Even more cynical perhaps, the revived

Matchless brand identity rests not simply on contemporary refashioning of motorcycling's past but a fabricated history of Matchless's own past. The ad campaign featuring Moss associates Matchless's jacket with the one sported by Marlon Brando in *The Wild One*, which was manufactured by rival leather goods producer Schott. The original Matchless company never manufactured clothing.[112] While the ad copy states model Kate Moss is pictured on Brando's bike, in the film the actor was not riding a Matchless but a Triumph (though Brando did own a Matchless, as a photo on the company's website proves). Matchless rebrands itself as "the pioneer of luxury mobility"[113]: while motorcycling's fashionable past was previously used by luxury brands to sell clothing and perfume, now luxury sells contemporary motorcycles revived from the past.

Fashion, itself cyclical and perpetually in motion, offers potent alternatives to evolutionary explanations for technological innovation and linear accounts of its influence on social change. Consider the unlikelihood of predicting that the spice trade provoked an insatiable desire not simply for food but for fabric and that meeting that demand would result in wheeled, textile-manufacturing devices that revolutionized not only textile production but bicycle design. Or that bicycle design would encourage changes in clothing that, in the popular imagination, became divorced from actual cycle gear and even the vehicle itself. It would be simple enough to identify these complex social and technical processes as, for example, the consequence of capitalism's insatiable quest for new markets, whether these be the Asian continent or the nonriders dispersed globally. Or, it could be argued that technical advances spurred both new devices and cost reductions, resulting in the democratization of consumption of novel technical devices (such as the bicycle). Such a progressivist explanation would necessitate tracing the developmental timeline back to British mastery of longitude in navigation (through the invention of a reliable timepiece), for without it the nation would not have developed both its empire and ready markets. But these explanations, whether ideological or technological, imply a type of evolutionary determinism that has lost its explanatory luster. Instead, multiple, concurrent forces converge—along with the occasional inspired tinkerer—and the world is gradually transformed.

Thus, following one thread—textiles—only reveals the complexity of the fabric—material and social. Technological and social changes in Britain and America originated in South Asia and were diffused globally. Positive advances in mobility and social attitudes derived from inhumane practices, such as colonialism and slavery. The wheel—from the spinning wheel to the motorcycle tire—is the hub, spinning in place on its own axle but putting both the machine and its rider in motion. We move on to the concomitant revolutions the wheel impels in riders—social, political, biological, psychological, and metaphysical—in part 3.

NOTES

1. Tony Hadland and Hans-Erhard Lessing, *Bicycle Design: An Illustrated History* (Cambridge, MA: MIT Press, 2014), 193. The rubber-coated canvas is called a ply; early tires used a radial-ply design (cords running transversely), but bias-ply (with cords crossed diagonally) proved more durable.

2. Jane Schneider, "Cloth and Clothing," in *Handbook of Material Culture*, ed. Christopher Tilley, Webb Keane, Susanne Küchler, Michael Rowlands, and Patricia Spyer (London: Sage, 2006), 202.

3. Douglas Farnie, "Cotton, 1780–1914," in *The Cambridge History of Western Textiles*, part II, ed. David Jenkins (Cambridge: Cambridge University Press, 2003), 723.

4. The sculpture consists of a 1968 Benelli motorcycle mounted to a wooden frame and attached to an antique metal flywheel (an eight-foot in diameter, six-thousand-pound scrap from a nineteenth-century factory). The work is part of the collection of the Museum of Contemporary Art, Los Angeles, California: http://moca.org/pc/viewArtWork.php?id=4.

5. William Rosen, *The Most Powerful Idea in the World: A Story of Steam, Industry, and Invention* (New York: Random House, 2010), 224.

6. Harvin Smith and Reiya Zhu, "The Spinning Process," in *Cotton: Origin, History, Technology, and Production*, ed. C. Wayne Smith and J. Tom Cothren (New York: John Wiley & Sons, Inc., 1999), 740.

7. Inevitably women's work, spinning had a linguistic impact as well: the distaff tool gave rise in the seventeenth century to the term's secondary meaning to denote the female branch of the family, and a solitary lifetime of spinning itself to the pejorative *spinster*.

8. Lynn Townsend White, *Medieval Technology and Social Change* (Oxford: Clarendon Press, 1962), 119. Gandhi later revived the *charkha* (the Indian type) during the Indian independence movement in the early twentieth century and a model for self-sufficiency. See Mahatma Gandhi, *The Wheel of Fortune* (Madras: Cambridge University Press, 1922).

9. White, *Medieval Technology*.

10. J. T. Goddard, *The Velocipede: Its History, Variety and Practices* (Cambridge: Riverside Press, 1869), 11.

11. Hand-crank bicycles—or handcycles—remain popular, however, among riders unable to use their legs for propulsion.

12. Historians differ as to which Frenchman is responsible. David Herlihy credits Pierre Lallement in *Bicycle: The History* (New Haven, CT: Yale University Press, 2004). Hadland and Lessing argue, "the origin of attaching cranks to the front axle of a velocipede is the most fiercely debated topic in cycle historiography" and devote an entire chapter to the evidence. See *Bicycle Design*, 37–60.

13. Qtd. in Pryor Dodge, *The Bicycle* (Paris: Flammarion, 1996), 99. The same writer, however, admitted, "here, indeed, is safety guaranteed."

14. This is an example of the role played by "social sentiment," including biased expectations defined by tradition and aesthetics. See part 1.

15. Herlihy, *Bicycle*, 217. Only when the Safety bicycle equalized the size of the wheels did the chain-driven bicycle fully come into its own.

16. Reprinted in the *New York Times*, August 4, 1895, 21.

17. Marie E. Ward, *The Common Sense of Bicycling: Bicycling for Ladies* (New York: Brentano's, 1896), 19.

18. Lawson, like McCall, originally used a treadle design for his "Safety" bicycle in 1876, with a rider sitting over a smaller front wheel. See Herlihy, *Bicycle*, 216. Not only did the design not find consumers, its name did not catch on, until it became synonymous with the Rover in 1885. Hagland and Lessing argue "the ubiquitous treadle sewing machine, especially the variant with two treadles turning a crankshaft by means of rods, served as a model" (*Bicycle Design*, 73).

19. Herlihy, *Bicycle*, 147. In 1896, the company became the Swift Cycle Company.

20. Herlihy, *Bicycle*, 190. Also see Stephen B. Goddard, *Colonel Albert Pope and His American Dream Machines: The Life and Times of Bicycle Tycoon Turned Automotive Pion*eer (New York: McFarland, 2008), 70.

21. Goddard, *Colonel Albert Pope*, 6, 71.

22. David A. Hounshell, *From the American System to Mass Production, 1800–1932* (Baltimore, MD: Johns Hopkins University Press, 1984), 194. "By contrast, Western bicycle builders emerged primarily from the ranks of carriage- and wagon makers, wooden toys and novelties specialists, agricultural implement makers, or as totally new enterprises" (208). According to Nathan Rosenberg, the sewing machine is itself an example of technological convergence: "Although sewing-machine production was virtually nonexistent in 1850, it constituted a flourishing industry in 1860, and grew with remarkably swift strides, nationally and internationally, in the following decade. Out of the innumerable modifications of the sewing machine grew the vast boot-and-shoe and men's and women's ready-to-wear clothing industries; and the machine, by 1890, was used extensively in the production of such items as awnings, tents and sails, pocketbooks, rubber and elastic goods, saddlery and harnesses, etc., and in bookbinding. The rapid diffusion of the sewing machine after 1860 was due to the fact that it provided a highly effective mechanical device for performing an operation common to many industries" ("Technological Change in the Machine Tool Industry, 1840–1910," *The Journal of Economic History*, 23.4 [December 1963], 430).

23. See Hounshell, *American System*, 194.

24. Hounshell, *American System*, 202.

25. Frances E. Willard, *A Wheel within a Wheel: How I Learned to Ride the Bicycle with Some Reflections by the Way* (Chicago,: Woman's Temperance Publishing Association, 1895), 56.

26. Julie Wosk, *Women and the Machine: Representations from the Spinning Wheel to the Electronic Age* (Baltimore, MD: Johns Hopkins University Press, 2001), 31.

27. Eugen Weber, *France: Fin de Siècle* (Cambridge, MA: Harvard University Press, 1986), 201.

28. Weber, *France*, 201–2.

29. Richard Holt, "Women, Men and Sport in France, c. 1870–1914: An Introductory Survey," *Journal of Sport History* 18 (Spring 1991): 124.

30. Holt, "Women, Men and Sport in France," 124. For a detailed account of similar fears in America, see Ellen Gruber Garvey, "Reframing the Bicycle: Advertising-Supported Magazines and Scorching Women," *American Quarterly*, 47.1 (March 1995): 66–101.

31. See Steven E. Alford and Suzanne Ferriss, *Motorcycle* (London: Reaktion, 2008), 142–43.

32. Qtd. in Willard, *Wheel within a Wheel*, 56–57.

33. Qtd. in Willard, *Wheel within a Wheel*, 56–57.

34. Holt, "Women, Men and Sport in France," 125.

35. Herlihy, *Bicycle*, 264.

36. "Here, There, and Everywhere." *Sporting Life* (September 16, 1893): 8.

37. Willard, *Wheel within a Wheel*, 54–55.

38. Garvey, "Reframing the Bicycle," 76–77; Wosk, *Women and the Machine*, 102–3.

39. Willard, *Wheel within a Wheel*, 54–55; Wosk, *Women and the Machine*, 56.

40. Marjorie Cottle, "Motor Cycling for Beauty," *Evening Standard*, September 25, 1928.

41. Betty and Nancy Debenham, "Motor Cycling for Health," *Daily News*, March 16, 1926.

42. Steve Koerner, "Whatever Happened to the Girl on a Motorbike?: British Women and Motorcycling, 1919–1939," *International Journal of Motorcycle Studies* 3 (March 2007), http://ijms.nova.edu/March2007/IJMS_Artcl.Koerner.html.

43. Koerner, "Whatever Happened to the Girl on a Motorbike?"

44. Ward, *Common Sense of Bicycling*, 36, x.

45. Ward, *Common Sense of Bicycling*, 35–36.

46. Wosk, *Women and the Machine*, 28.

47. Christopher Thomas Potter, "Motorcycling 'Types': An Exploration of Some Motorcyclists in 1920s Britain," *International Journal of Motorcycle Studies* 6.2 (Fall 2010), http://ijms.nova.edu/Fall2010/IJMS_Artcl.Potter.html.

48. Koerner, "Whatever Happened to the Girl on a Motorbike?" Kathleen Franz has documented a similar shift in early automotive history: popular culture in the 1910s presented women as mechanically capable, but by the 1920s and 1930s men began to assert "their exclusive authority over the automobile" ("Women's Ingenuity," in *Tinkering: Consumers Reinvent the Early Automobile* [Philadelphia: University of Pennsylvania Press, 2005], 44).

49. "Theresa Wallach," AMA Motorcycle Hall of Fame, http://www.motorcyclemuseum.org/halloffame/detail.aspx?RacerID=309.

50. Leo Marx, *The Machine in the Garden: Technology and the Pastoral Ideal in America* (New York: Oxford University Press, 1964), Kindle loc. 272–84.

51. Anson Rabinbach, *The Human Motor: Energy, Fatigue, and the Origins of Modernity* (Berkeley: University of California Press, 1990), 24, 66.

52. Rosen, *The Most Powerful Idea in the World*, 225.
53. Rosen, *The Most Powerful Idea in the World*, 229.
54. Farnie, "Cotton," 723.
55. Schneider, "Cloth and Clothing," 208.
56. Farnie, "Cotton," 722, 735.
57. "Calico" is named not for Calcutta, the spot chosen for the British East India's trading post in 1690, but for the Malabar Coast entrepôt known as Calicut (see Rosen, *The Most Powerful Idea in the World*, 218). The term, in British English, refers to the plain woven fabric in white, cream or unbleached cotton. In American English, it refers to the typical pattern printed on the fabric: a small, repeated floral pattern. (This meaning led to descriptions of a multi-colored cat as a "calico cat.") Americans use the term "muslin" to refer to the plain cotton fabric. "Chintz" refers to a particular kind of floral pattern—large floral patterns—that can be printed on either silk or cotton.
58. Farnie, "Cotton," 723.
59. Daniel Miller, *Material Culture and Mass Consumption* (Oxford: Blackwell, 1987), 137.
60. For an account of Henry Ford's disastrous attempt to "rationalize" rubber growing and harvesting, see Greg Grandin, *Fordlandia: The Rise and Fall of Henry Ford's Forgotten Jungle City* (New York: Henry Holt, 2010).
61. Chandra Mukerji, *Graven Images: Patterns of Modern Materialism* (New York: Columbia University Press, 1983), 185–92. The fabrics were used not simply for clothing but also for home furnishing and decoration.
62. Rosen, *The Most Powerful Idea in the World*, 219; Schneider, "Cloth and Clothing," 209.
63. Bruce D. Epperson, *Peddling Bicycles to America: The Rise of an Industry* (Jefferson, NC: McFarland & Company, Inc., 2010), Kindle loc. 2537ff.
64. Randy McBee, *Born to Be Wild: The Rise of the American Motorcyclist* (Chapel Hill: The University of North Carolina Press, 2015), 181.
65. Miller, *Material Culture and Mass Consumption*, 137–38.
66. Farnie, "Cotton," 743.
67. Qtd. in Farnie, "Cotton," 733.
68. On the historical origins of this resistance and cloth's position in Indian culture, see C. A. Bayly, "The Origins of Swadeshi (Home Industry): Cloth and Indian Society, 1700–1930," in *The Social Life of Things: Commodities in Cultural Perspective*, ed. Arjun Appadurai (Cambridge: Cambridge University Press, 1986): 285–321.
69. Farnie, "Cotton," 726.
70. Farnie, "Cotton," 728.
71. Mayfield, William, W. Stanley Anthony, Roy V. Baker, Sidney E. Hughs, William E. Lalor, "Ginning," *Cotton: Origin, History, Technology, and Production*, ed. C. Wayne Smith and J. Tom Cothren (New York: John Wiley & Sons, Inc., 1999), 685.
72. Rosen, *The Most Powerful Idea in the World,* 217. A number of recent books document cotton's reliance on slave labor, particularly in America: see Walter Johnson, *River of Dark Dreams: Slavery and Empire in the Cotton Kingdom* (Cambridge, MA: Belknap Press, 2013), Sven Beckert, *Empire of Cotton: A Global History* (New York: Alfred A. Knopf, 2014), Edward E. Baptist, *The Half Has Never Been Told:*

Slavery and the Making of American Capitalism (New York: Basic Books, 2014), and Greg Grandin, *The Empire of Necessity: Slavery, Freedom, and Deception in the New World* (New York: Metropolitan Books, 2014).

73. The exploitation of workers has been extensively discussed elsewhere and, thus, lies outside the bounds of our discussion. Labor in the textile industry was the object and source of Karl Marx's critique of capitalism and exploitative working conditions have aroused global concern, particularly for workers in Bangladesh following the April 2013 collapse of the Rana Plaza factory complex that killed more than 1,100 garment workers and a November 2012 fire at the Tazreen factory that killed 112 workers.

74. Farnie, "Cotton," 743.

75. Miller, *Material Culture and Mass Consumption*, 138.

76. Miller, *Material Culture and Mass Consumption,* 139. Neil McKendrick argues that commerce increasingly directed the course of fashion in the early eighteenth century ("The Commercialization of Fashion," in *The Birth of a Consumer Society: The Commercialization of Eighteenth-Century England*, ed. Neil McKendrick, John Brewer, and J. H. Plumb [London: Hutchinson, 1982], 40–41).

77. See Penelope Byrde, "Dress: The Industrial Revolution and After," in *The Cambridge History of Western Textiles*, part II, ed. David Jenkins (Cambridge: Cambridge University Press, 2003), 884.

78. Schneider, "Cloth and Clothing," 209.

79. Brent Shannon, *The Cut of His Coat: Men, Dress, and Consumer Culture in Britain, 1860–1914* (Athens: Ohio University Press, 2006), 184.

80. Florence Kingsland, *Etiquette for All Occasions* (New York: Doubleday, 1901), 347.

81. Kingsland, *Etiquette for All Occasions*, 344. On the Norfolk jacket, also see Byrde, "Dress: The Industrial Revolution and After," 888.

82. Shannon, *The Cut of His Coat*, 187.

83. Rob Schorman, *Selling Style: Clothing and Social Change at the Turn of the Century* (Philadelphia: University of Pennsylvania Press, 2003), 5. In the United States, production at the turn of the century was geared more toward lighter cloth: "Woollen dress goods and outdoor sporting wear were the most buoyant sections of the industry before the war" (David Jenkins, "The Western Wool Textile Industry in the Nineteenth Century," in *The Cambridge History of Western Textiles*, Part II, ed. David Jenkins [Cambridge: Cambridge University Press, 2003], 787).

84. Dodge, *The Bicycle*, 116–20.

85. Qtd. in Peter Zheutlin, *Around the World on Two Wheels: Annie Londonderry's Extraordinary Ride* (New York: Citadel, 2007). Pryor Dodge notes, "There is a certain irony in the fact that the factories of the sewing machine industry which had burdened women with corsets and skirts eventually produced the machines that freed them from oppressive clothing" (*The Bicycle*, 129).

86. Byrde, "Dress: The Industrial Revolution and After," 908. The movement for aesthetic dress was embraced by Oscar Wilde in "The Philosophy of Dress" (1892).

87. See Patricia A. Cunningham, *Reforming Women's Fashion, 1850–1920: Politics, Health, and Art* (Kent, OH: Kent State University Press, 2003). Professor Hoffman proclaimed in *Tips for Tricyclists* (1887) that "cycling indeed has done more

than any other sport to spread sound notions as to rational principles of dress" (qtd. in Phillis Cunnington and Alan Mansfield, *English Costume for Sports and Outdoor Recreation: From the 16th to 19th Centuries* [London: Adam and Charles Black, 1963], 229).

88. Ward, *Common Sense of Bicycling*, 99, 93.

89. Willard, *Wheel within a Wheel*, 74.

90. Marguerite Merington, "Woman and the Bicycle." *Scribner's* 17 (June 1895): 702–4. Reprinted in *The American 1890s: A Cultural Reader,* eds. Susan Harris Smith and Melanie Dawson (Durham, NC: Duke University Press, 2000), 290.

91. Merington, "Woman and the Bicycle," 290.

92. Merington, "Woman and the Bicycle," 290.

93. Qtd. in Zheutlin, *Around the World on Two Wheels*, 31.

94. Certainly, the same could be said about contemporary outdoor apparel, such as North Face jackets (see Alina Tugeno, "In North Face Jacket, A Reversible Appeal," *New York Times*, November 16, 2013, http://www.nytimes.com/2013/11/17/business/in-a-north-face-jacket-a-reversible-appeal.html?_r=0) or the Marmot Mammoth parka, the "biggie," that has become a status symbol worth killing to acquire (see Tim Teeman, "The 'Biggie': A Tainted Status Symbol," *New York Times*, November 15, 2013, http://www.nytimes.com/2013/11/17/fashion/Marmot-Mammoth-parka-aka-biggie-a-tainted-status-symbol.html).

95. Kingsland, *Etiquette for All Occasions*, 347.

96. "One Team Made Perfect Score," *The Motorcycle Illustrated*, August 1, 1908, 3.

97. Refer to the works of Pope experts Epperson, *Peddling Bicycles to America*, and Goddard, *Colonel Albert Pope*, but also see Carlton Reid, *Roads Were Not Built for Cars: How Cyclists Were the First to Push for Good Roads & Became the Pioneers of Motoring* (Washington, DC: Island Press, 2015), 712–14; Ross D. Petty, "Peddling the Bicycle in the 1890s: Mass Marketing Shifts into High Gear," *Journal of Macromarketing,* 15 (Spring 1995), 32–46; Robert J. Turpin, "'Our Best Bet Is The Boy': A Cultural History of Bicycle Marketing and Consumption in the United States, 1880–1960" (PhD diss., University of Kentucky, 2013), 39, 43; and Thomas Cameron Burr, "Markets As Producers and Consumers: The French and U.S. National Bicycle Markets, 1875–1910" (PhD diss., University of California, Davis, 2005). See part 1 and the chapter on roads in part 2.

98. See Mick Farren, *The Black Leather Jacket* (New York: Plexus Publishing, 1985). Also see Alford and Ferriss, *Motorcycle*, 181–85.

99. Alford and Ferriss, *Motorcycle*, 92–93.

100. Farnie enthuses, "It revolutionised the clothing of the world from the 1950s and justified Hegel's vision of America in 1822 as 'the land of the future'" ("Cotton," 735). For denim's significance in the 1950s and beyond, see James Sullivan, *Jeans: A Cultural History of an American Icon* (New York: Gotham Books, 2006); Rachel Louise Snyder, *Fugitive Denim: A Moving Story of People and Pants in the Borderless World of Global Trade* (New York: W. W. Norton & Co., 2008); and Daniel Miller and Sophie Woodward, *Global Denim* (London: Bloomsbury Academic, 2011).

101. See Lily Phillips, "Blue Jeans, Black Leather Jackets and a Sneer: The Iconography of the 1950s Biker and its Translation Abroad," *International Journal of*

Motorcycle Studies 1 (March 2005), http://ijms.nova.edu/March2005/IJMS_Artcl Philips0305.html.

102. Leather was, by contrast, the material favored by racers, starting in 1951 when Geoff Duke is credited with sporting the first one-piece racing suit, earning him the nickname "The Stylish Champion." See Mick Walker, *Geoff Duke: The Stylish Champion* (London: Breedon Books, 2007).

103. Tim Arrowsmith, "Decoding Black Leather: Building a Biography of British Motorcycle Subcultures before 1965" (paper presented at the IJMS Conference + Exhibition, London, July 2013). The leather jacket followed the same trajectory in motorcycling, originally repurposed by returning servicemen. See Alford and Ferriss, *Motorcycle*, 181–84, and Mick Farren, *The Black Leather Jacket* (New York: Plexus, 1985).

104. In fact, Arrowsmith contends the leather jacket exerted more influence on the punk scene.

105. See Dick Hebdige, *Subculture: The Meaning of Style* (London: Methuen, 1979) and "Object as Image: The Italian Scooter Cycle," *Block*, 5 (1981): 44–64. For an overview of the Mods-Rockers contrasts, see Alford and Ferriss, *Motorcycle*, 78–83.

106. Jeffrey W. Alexander, *Japan's Motorcycle Wars: An Industry History* (Vancouver: University of British Columbia Press, 2008).

107. In 2008, H-D's merchandise sales brought in almost $314 million of the company's overall sales ($5.59 billion), putting its apparel division "on par with some pure-play apparel companies." Licensing revenues for leather, apparel, jewelry and toys accounted for an additional $45 million in 2008 (Padma Nagappan, "Harley-Davidson Apparel Riding High," *Apparel*, January 6, 2010, http://apparel.edgl.com/case-studies/Harley-Davidson-Apparel--Riding-High64294). VF, a global apparel company, which also produces licensed apparel for the Major League Baseball, the National Football League, the National Basketball Association, and the National Hockey League, includes Harley-Davidson in its Licensed Sports division.

108. Caryn Simonson, "'Fashionable' Bikers and 'Biker' Fashion: From Motorcycle Clothing to Luxury Brands—Motor-cycle/Fashion-cycle" (paper presented at the *International Journal of Motorcycle Studies* Conference, Colorado Springs, June 2012). She analyzed both the Belstaff and Chanel campaigns, as well as others by Longchamp.

109. The photographer was Craig McDean. A promotional video can be viewed here: https://www.youtube.com/watch?v=E0YE4NnakNQ.

110. The film can be viewed here: http://www.youtube.com/watch?v=aRV-2_Un-kk&noredirect=1.

111. Paul d'Orléans, "The Rise of the Zombies," *Classic Bike Guide*, August 2015, 50.

112. Caryn Simonson, "Telling Stories: Brand Revival," paper presented at the *International Journal of Motorcycle Studies* Conference, Barber Motorsports Museum, Birmingham, Alabama, July 2015.

113. See "Matchless History At A Glance: The Pioneer Of Luxury Urban Mobility," *Matchless*, http://www.matchlesslondon.com/en/heritage/.

Part III

MACHINES AND RIDERS

Chapter Five

The Paradoxes of Class and Gender among Bicyclists and Motorcyclists

> Socialism can only be achieved on a bicycle.
>
> —Salvador Allende

While grand historical narratives paint the pattern of Western development as a relentless, progressive march, with technological developments leading to the emancipation of people from tedious work to an affluent devotion to more cerebral pursuits, we need to remind ourselves that any unilateral discourse on historical change is without doubt leaving something out.[1] As history has too often demonstrated, *progress* is a word best employed by ironists.

The cases of the bicycle and the motorcycle offer a series of contrasts and comparisons that, when considered together, suggest that technology does not promote (or impede) the interests of any group *simpliciter*, but rather technological devices help only when they occur in a certain context, a context shaped by forces independent of technological innovation. Our attention should not be directed toward the devices themselves, as has often been the case, but rather the social, political, and economic forces that led to the possibility for their existence.[2] Invariably, we will discover that while technological devices do indeed improve lives, those benefits are not only not evenly distributed, but an advance in one area can, and usually does, have negative outcomes for others. This scenario, wherein some benefit while others suffer, cannot be considered simply as the zero-sum result of an advance. Instead, every so-called advance must be considered in the social, economic, and cultural context in which it occurs. For our purposes, one of the most significant areas of concern should be economics, as the powerful forces of capitalism, intersecting with the supposedly neutral arena of technological developments, shape how technology is understood and what effects it has. As an exemplary case, the bicycle and the motorcycle offer a series of interesting paradoxes with respect to how they have, as claimed by many, supported women's rights. These paradoxes have, at their root, issues of economic class. While nineteenth-century crusaders for women's rights saw the bicycle as a means toward women's liberation, one cannot properly understand this phenomenon without examining the parallel issue of economic class. One of the consequences of this exploration is that technological devices (such as bicycles and motorcycles) are not, in themselves, gendered.

As Daniel Headrick claims in his book *The Tools of Empire: Technology and European Imperialism in the Nineteenth Century*, one of the peculiarities of European imperialists, and one that granted them a sense of license in the exploitation of other cultures, was the assumption that "civilization" could be measured by how advanced technology was in the target culture. Other, radical measures of human advancement—let's say compassion for others, social justice, universal health care, or general happiness—could be employed, but "backwardness" itself in the nineteenth century was measured by the sophistication of one's mechanical devices.[3] The bicycle, the typewriter, the telephone, the airplane, the motion picture, the motorcycle: all were developed in an astonishingly short time by a remarkably small number of people living in damp, cold, forested climates. These remarkable achievements led the countries of their origin to assume their superiority over others.

In addition to technological developments and their effects on national and international social justice, another phenomenon occupying thinkers of the nineteenth century was class. While governments sponsored imperial exploits, Proudhon, Bakunin, Kropotkin, Marx, and others analyzed both causes of class inequality and strategies for freeing humankind from the strictures of an inflexible class system. In the ordinary leftist nineteenth-century narratives of class, technology plays a central role as the means of production, and this means of production sets up a dialectical pattern of class conflict that, while naturally ever-evolving toward its own elimination, must be set upon by the underclass and destroyed. As Nietzsche says, if something is falling, give it a push.[4]

How are we to understand this relation of technology to class in less rigidly dialectical, deterministic terms? For good or ill, over time the generally accepted meaning for class has changed from "relationship to the means of production" to "income level." While Marx and other leftists were focused on capital, which equates to static, but ever-increasing income for those who own the means of production, they failed to foresee, among other things, the growth of the middle class and the welfare state, the latter resulting from a government who, in Marx's eyes, was nothing more than the errand boy of the rich. While America currently has the dubious distinction of the greatest inequality of wealth among developed countries, efforts continue to mitigate the unfortunate consequences of our seemingly inevitable move away from democracy and toward plutocracy.[5]

Along with the creation of the welfare state, political, economic, and social forces have, over a century and a half, helped ameliorate the differences between two other groups—men and women—such that, while women in America still earn, as of this writing, seventy-seven cents for every dollar a man earns in comparable work, progress is being made in leveling the salary playing field. How are we to understand the relations between class and gender, and how do developing technologies affect this relation? Examining the bicycle and the motorcycle in economic context can assist us in demonstrating the peculiarly paradoxical relation of class and gender relations to technology.

BICYCLES

In 1896 Susan B. Anthony claimed that, "I think [the bicycle] has done more to emancipate women than anything else in the world."[6] As scholar Robert A. Smith noted, "The *Detroit Tribune* called the perfection of the bicycle the greatest event of the 19th century. In Washington, DC, the Bureau of the Census stated solemnly that 'few articles ever used by man created so great a revolution in social conditions as the bicycle.'"[7] Frances E. Willard, a leader of the temperance movement, who later penned a memoir extolling the virtues of riding, enthused, "We saw that the physical development of humanity's mother-half would be wonderfully advanced by that universal introduction of the bicycle."[8] Even a (presumably male) columnist in *Sporting Life* magazine proclaimed in 1893, "Verily the day of woman's emancipation is at hand."[9]

Young nineteenth-century women found themselves housebound, deprived of autonomy and overseen by a patriarchy that stretched from legislative houses to their own—the latter populated by watchful fathers, brothers, and assorted mature female relations, all of whom shared a single-minded devotion: to prevent the young women from having the slightest bit of heterosexual fun. Then, from the sheds of Scotland and elsewhere, after a couple of decades of development from the Ordinary, came the Safety bicycle in 1885, allowing women the chance to escape their homes, and, accompanied by a young man, to engage in social intercourse far from their relatives' watchful eyes, giving them a sense of individuality, self-awareness and, in a word, freedom. It's a beautiful idea: Pierre Lallement, John Kemp Starley, and a few British tinkerers inadvertently did more to advance women's independence than a hundred of Ms. Wollstonecraft's jeremiads.

Well, yes and no. As Eileen Leonard has argued, "Although technology is often viewed as freeing women, implying that it is a powerful agent of change," not only has the reverse often been true, any consideration of gender necessitates attention to class. "When technology is developed in a capitalist society, it necessarily reflects class interests because only certain groups have the power to determine what is designed and how it is implemented. Capitalists are not neutral agents of progress, but instead have clearly situated political and economic interests."[10] This is clearly the case with the bicycle.

It has been estimated that a bicycle—e.g., American Albert Pope's 1876 high-wheeler Columbia bicycle, pegged at $125 when a sewing machine sold for $13—cost half a year's wages for a worker. If a contemporary worker's average wage is $42,000,[11] then a contemporary bicycle would cost $21,000 today, or the amount of a modest automobile. Elsewhere, prices were no kinder and fell no more quickly. James McGurn notes that even by the mid-1890s in France, "Bicycle prices were dauntingly high. A young primary schoolteacher working in the Normandy countryside recalled that he needed to borrow money from his father, a farmer, and his uncle, a mason, in order to buy a secondhand bicycle in 1898. Even though prices had begun to fall by this date the retail cost of the bicycle would represent three months of a primary schoolteacher's pay. It took five years to repay the loans."[12] In short, the bicycle was "a prohibitively expensive and exclusive technology."[13] We might then ask: exactly which women were liberated by the bicycle, especially prior to the craze of 1896–1898?

Clearly, when we talk about gender, we're also talking about two other issues: class and time. For example, from the introduction of Pope's rear-drive Safety, the Veloce Columbia, in 1886, until 1898, with the general collapse of bicycle prices, rarely did owning a machine even enter the horizon of possibility for a working man, much less a woman.

The nineteenth-century British legislature is to be celebrated for enacting divorce (1857) and property laws (1870; 1882) that, while not exactly legislating gender equality, did grant female citizens some universal, and quite ordinary rights. These rights were granted by virtue of one's citizenship, not one's wherewithal. So, hermeneutically, one has to be careful with the pronouncements by women's advocates on both sides of the pond about the socio-political consequences of the bicycle. Possessing the right to divorce came with one's citizenship; owning a bicycle—and experiencing its attendant social and political freedoms—meant, for the longest time, having sufficient funds to purchase one. The development of the Safety did indeed foster women's independence, but only for those who could own one.[14]

As we noted in chapter 1, prior to the development of the Safety bicycle, in 1884, high-wheelers were ridden by impetuous, well-heeled young men, whose passion for "scorching" aligns them with our beloved contemporary sport bike riders. Bruce Epperson identifies a distinct class identification of the cyclist:

> Another form of abuse faced by the early cyclists was harassment and assault from teamsters and footmen who claimed that the sight and sound of bicycles frightened their horses. While this may have been true in isolated rural areas, urban horses were acclimatized to the noise and congestion of city street life. Urban clashes were more frequently real or perceived class conflicts. The pioneering cyclists were generally affluent and native-born, while teamsters were working-class first- or second-generation immigrants. A successful teamster was not a timid man; road, loading dock and parking space were all limited in the crowded city, and strong vocal chords and quick fists made the difference between a quick heave onto a dock or a long and exhausting portage down the street. Cyclists expected to be deferred to by their social inferiors on the street as they were in everyday life, while teamsters saw cyclists as effete dandies trying to dance around the edges of a street fight they didn't understand and couldn't protect themselves from.[15]

With the advent of the Safety bicycle, little had changed regarding the class identification of the cyclist. What *had* changed, of course, was that the Safety bicycle's novel design introduced a new demographic: adventurous young women who discovered they now had a bicycle they could handle, but only those women with the means to afford them.[16] The equally high-priced Safeties engendered the same class-based hostility toward men and women as did the young men on their flying Ordinaries.

While impecunious pedestrians and equestrians shared the road with the well-heeled bicyclists, the public space of the road provided opportunities for the hostile and envious to express their views verbally as the bicyclists glided by. American Albert Pope's sponsorship of bicycle trade shows, first occurring in 1883 in Springfield, Massachusetts, provided another arena for bicyclists and non-bicyclists to interact. As Smith notes, "Bicycle shows, not bicycles brought Americans together."[17] As in auto shows today, a ticket can allow the most indigent of citizens to kick the tires of cars they will never be able to afford, and simultaneously rub shoulders with those who could pay cash for one without a second thought. Similarly, the experience of bicycling was not open to the general public, but for the price of a bicycle show ticket, one could encounter bicyclists and their magnificent machines.

Cycling clubs' membership was confined to the wealthy as well. "A cycle boom affected the upper classes of the United States in the mid-1890s. New York City's 'Four Hundred,' the self-defining social elite, formed the Michaux Cycle Club in 1895, with headquarters on upper Broadway."[18] Correlatively, the women who sought liberation through bicycling were those who already had the economic means to purchase a bike as a leisure toy.

What eventually produced a more egalitarian demographic of American bicycle owners had nothing to do with sociology or politics, but with economics and the collapse of the bicycle market. The American story is a reasonably complex one, with the formation of a cartel in 1898 contributing to the industry's eventual collapse. The cartel, formed to keep prices up, prevented poorer customers from purchasing bicycles by maintaining large profit margins for the bicycle producers, a business model that, by 1902, was ultimately unsustainable.[19] Additional factors that led to a fall in bicycle prices (and thus undermined the cartel's power) included the batch production method of bicycle construction, which involved making a certain number of bicycles for the upcoming "season," irrespective of any information about demand (creating, over time, excess inventory, which in turn pressured manufacturers to sell at a lower cost); the introduction each year of a "new" model (generally with minor cosmetic modifications), which created a brisk trade in cheaper used bikes; and technological developments, such as the movement away from forged steel tubing to stamped steel. And, as P. J. Parry notes, in Britain, by the turn of the century, the opportunities for rural Britons improved with the availability of the bicycle, but this availability did not result simply from a fall in prices. "In 1901 a standard bicycle would cost around 9 pounds, when the best paid manual workers earned about a pound per week. Even when the average price fell to 4 pounds, in 1909, working-class buyers needed hire purchase schemes, and sometimes formed clubs to buy cycles on contract or by mutual guarantee."[20]

Taken together, these disparate causal factors resulted in the industry's collapse, with the consequent dramatic lowering of bicycle prices. Following the dawn of the twentieth century, it became feasible for the working class to enter the ranks of bicycle buyers and riders. Those ranks included women, who had their way paved for social acceptance by their economic "betters," both men and women who preceded them. (Lacking an American cartel, whose failure had widespread consequences, prices in Britain did not fall uniformly for everyone, even after the turn of the century.[21]) Hence, doing the math, we can say that, from the introduction of the Safety bicycle in 1885 until the collapse of the American cartel, roughly seventeen years (including the bicycle craze of 1896–1898), bicycles were virtually the sole purview of the well-to-do, both male and female, keeping in mind differences among, for example, America, Britain, and France.[22]

Images in the popular press confirm this. The British satirical magazine *Punch,* for instance, regularly skewered the upper-class pretensions of the leisured gentry. One cartoon, published in 1896, pictures a working-class mother and her children looking at a "lady" on a bicycle.

The mother asks, "Wouldn't yer like ter 'ave one o' them things, Liza Ann?" To which her daughter responds, "No. I wouldn't be seen on one. I

Figure 5.1. ***Mr. Punch Awheel: The Humours of Motoring and Cycling,*** **ed. J. A. Hammerton, Project Gutenberg.**

don't think they're nice for lidies!" They mock bicycling as an aristocratic diversion, particularly for women.[23]

Hence, the bicycle was not, through its sheer existence, the political and sociological juggernaut it has been made out to be. For it to function as a vector of social change, other, more obscure events must have occurred as well. Had bicycle prices not fallen, the class-based prevalence of bicycles would have remained like that, for example, of small Cessna airplanes, larger yachts, Tesla automobiles, and other mechanical markers of economic class today. To understand the bicycle's role in our social and political lives, we need to observe, for example, how the process of stamped steel developed in the American Midwest, reducing the reliance of East coast bicycle makers on British tubular steel from Birmingham.[24] We need to distinguish batch methods of production from assembly line production (and the differing economic structures of each), with which they are often confused. We need to understand the transformation of the Western political social contract, to include road building as part of a government's responsibility.[25] Not just the existence of the bicycle, but its cost; not just the lowered cost of the bicycle, but a series of external, seemingly unrelated events in technology, sociology, and politics should be taken into consideration when tracing the role of the bicycle in advancing women's social and political interests. And even then, the term "women" refers almost exclusively to white females and, at beginning of the twentieth century, does not attend to economic and social discrimination against American immigrants (who would themselves certainly be considered white, for instance, Irish and Italian women) as well as women of color that may have prevented them from availing themselves of the advantages of bicycle transportation.

It should also be observed that, as Glen Norcliffe notes, "Modernizing effects of the bicycle on society are also somewhat ambiguous."[26] Wages, working conditions, environmental damage, and other consequences of bicycle factory conditions could not be seen as socially or economically progressive. Even accepting the positive effects on women created by the bicycle, one needs to balance that advance with the conditions at the factories that created them, much like the current manufacturing and consumption trajectory of the iPhone and other high-priced, disposable electronic devices.

In the nineteenth century, the preponderant origin of inventions understood as world-changing technologies was the tinkerer. While Britain has a long tradition of upper-class support of technological development (for example, the establishment of the Board of Longitude in 1714, and its sporadic support of John Harrison, whose invention of the marine chronometer forever changed seafaring), most developments, like those of the early microcomputer era, came from individuals' sheds (given the complex social conditions that engendered the possibility for their creations). Bell's telephone, Karl von Drais's draisine, Lallement's velocipede, Starley's Safety bicycle, Goodyear's vulcanized rubber, Otto's Otto-cycle engine, Daimler's Einspur, the Wright Brothers' airplane, Marconi's telegraph, Tesla's coil: these tinkerer-inventors' mechanical talent and, perhaps more important, persistence, resulted in technological devices we use today. Few among them were entrepreneurs, with figures like Edison being a notable exception. When these devices successfully entered into an economic system geared toward mass production of consumer goods, they became the end product of a system that, in its ceaseless desire to reduce prices through reducing wages and the cost of materials, and the valuation of speed and ease of production over environmental concerns, resulted in widespread damage to worker's health, the environment, and social relations. Consider, for example, Akron, Ohio, "Rubber City," whose working conditions, as John Tully notes, left workers vulnerable to "exposure to high concentrations of aromatic hydrocarbons [which] destroy bone marrow, induce leukemia and other cancers, and damage chromosomes and genetic material."[27] Once rubber demand became powerful, stoked by the need for tires, both for civilian and wartime use, Brazil became a site of horrible abuse and exploitation of native workers, to say nothing of the economic and social catastrophes spawned by Henry Ford's desire to establish his own "jungle city."[28]

In short, the "progress" for women brought about by the bicycle, laudable as it is on its own terms, must be understood in the context of ongoing depredations to worker health, safety, and livelihood as manufacturers competed to produce the most profitable machines at the lowest price. While this does not diminish the benefits of the bicycle to women, as with all devices, we must understand the benefits within the context of the social and economic conditions that produced such a device.

MOTORCYCLES

Turning to motorcycle history, we can, as with bicycle history—with its bicycle craze, economic collapse, development of racing, and the like—identify moments in which class concerns intersect with those of gender. At the outset, however, one difficulty is that owing to the effects of American popular culture and the history of American motorcycling since the late 1940s, motorcycles and motorcyclists have been beset with an image of motorcyclists as "outlaws." Motorcycle historians point out that motorcycles were not always the exclusive bailiwick of working-class, homosocial males, referencing magazine advertising and letters to the editor, as well as the familiar and impressive achievements of the Van Buren sisters, Theresa Wallach, Dot Robinson, Bessie Stringfield, and others.[29] However, for our purposes, what's most interesting about the comparison of motorcycles to bicycles is how significant American popular culture was, to the exclusion of virtually all other Western countries' media, in creating a public façade of gender relations. While our analysis has focused on the historical transition from the bicycle to the motorcycle, comparing early bicycling to American post–World War II motorcycling may provide a helpful contrast, especially given the powerful international influence of American popular culture on public attitudes toward motorcycling.

Consider Germany, for example, a country absent of any public media image of the motorcyclist (with the exception of the cartoon character Werner).[30] As an advertising campaign for the Messerschmitt company indicated, the motorcycle was viewed by post–World War II Germans as an interim vehicle between the bicycle and the motorcar, one for the younger people, until they gained sufficient funds to *umsteigen* (switch or "graduate") to an automobile. While Britain certainly developed an image for the motorcyclist, most obviously in the films of Sidney Furie and Joseph Losey, these developments (as well as the phenomenon of the Rockers) resulted from absorbing the images of the motorcyclist first proffered in the United States in the early 1950s, most notably in *The Wild One*.[31] And in the fifties and to this day, the motorcycle's connections to gender and class are pronounced and evident.

The images originated in sensationalized journalistic and cinematic accounts of an isolated event occurring on the Fourth of July weekend, 1947, when the small agricultural town of Hollister, California, hosted a motorcycle race. That weekend, a number of uninvited motorcyclists arrived, uninterested in the races, but instead devoted themselves to drinking, roughhousing, and generally upsetting the inhabitants. Accounts differ widely as to what happened, but in the following weeks, *The San Francisco Chronicle* and *Life Magazine* produced articles and photographs that sensationalized the "invasion" of the motorcyclists.[32] The film rights to *Harper's Magazine*'s fictional "Cyclist's Raid," based on the events, were purchased by Hollywood producer Stanley Kramer, who contracted Lásló Benedek to direct Marlon Brando in *The Wild One* (1954). The image of the Outlaw Motorcyclist was born, mirroring the background and appearance of a small number of returning World War II vets and their motorcycle culture, while simultaneously providing an image to emulate for up-and-coming bikers. As the member of one club recalled, "We wanted to be like the gangs depicted in movies—tough sons of bitches who didn't like authority and weren't afraid of anyone, guys who looked out for one another and fought for one another."[33] Like the "scorchers" of nineteenth-century bicycling, these "outlaw" motorcyclists were considered a public nuisance, reinforcing the image of the motorcycle in the public's eye as a masculine-gendered, proletarian vehicle. Unlike the upper-class twits on their scorchers, however, the motorcyclists were decidedly the inverse. And while we have photographic evidence and some contemporary testimony to the contrary, motorcycles and their pilots played a decidedly negative role in advancing gender equality.[34]

This phenomenon of the motorcycle club is often explained in part by an analysis of the youthful California motorcyclists' background: undereducated military veterans whose clubs reflected their military past, and associations based on a rigid hierarchy, military order, and lots of rules, all contributing to a civilian refashioning of their wartime experience.[35] These clubs, sexist if not outright misogynist, reduced women to servants and/or objectified sexual playthings.

Consider, however, the Montreal high-wheeler club, prior to 1890, as described by Glen Norcliffe:

> The club ethos during the highwheeler phase amounted to a version of Victorian chivalry. Many club members were eligible bachelors who, by parading very visibly on what was a somewhat awesome machine, were consciously acting out the role of "two-wheeled knights." Allusions to military chivalry were enhanced by the club uniforms and the parade routines (simple riding patterns looked very impressive to onlookers). Since the thrill and danger of riding a high bicycle was widely appreciated, these riders were viewed by their admirers as gallants—rather as some sports heroes are today—but, being drawn mainly from the upper class, they were also assumed to be gentlemen. The records of the Montréal bicycle club show very clearly that marriage was understood to take a rider out of active club life; indeed, members often presented marrying colleagues with what was, in effect, a farewell gift. Thereafter, it was expected that a married man would not attend early morning or evening practices, or races, or regular Saturday rides, but he would attend social events and the occasional ride.[36]

As this passage suggests, there is no necessary causal factor linking a military background, or a lack of formal education, or a particular economic stratum, to two-wheeled clubs that excluded women from a perfectly acceptable pastime. What we do see here is a structural analogy to the "outlaw" motorcycle club, in which military structure, homosociality, and gender discrimination are significant. The proto-chivalrous attitudes of the nineteenth-century bicycle clubs were as likely to discriminate against women as were the Neanderthal attitudes of the early postwar motorcycle clubs.[37] Yet, these bicycle club structures and strictures were determined appropriate by upper-class men, Canadians, even.[38] In what respect, then, does class play a role in gender discrimination?

By the 1950s in America, there was no confusion. As Randy McBee notes:

> In a 1954 article in the *Saturday Evening Post* titled "Most Unpopular Men on the Road" the working-class influence in motorcycling was also prominent. The article dealt broadly with the typical motorcyclist's experiences from police harassment to the potential injuries and hazards riders faced as well as the organization of motorcycle races across the country. Aside from the so-called "experts" who raced, the men taking part in endurance runs represented what the

> author called an "average bag of motorcyclists"—a crane operator, a half dozen automobile mechanics, a one-eyed man, and a collection of red-faced teenagers out for their first timed run." The working-class rank and file of the world of motorcycling was so pervasive and so complete that a writer for *Cycle* magazine in 1952 noted that simply mentioning, "the word motorcycle in a middle-aged business or professional group" and "eyebrows will be raised. Admit that you ride one and you may find yourself the subject of unpleasantly close scrutiny." Working-class men rode motorcycles; middle-class men frowned upon them.[39]

The class identity of the motorcyclist was fixed in the popular imagination—but not as a consequence of economic forces attached to the vehicle. By contrast, as observed in the case of the bicycle, the collapse of the market, not newly discovered egalitarianism, brought the working class into bicycling. As for simple physical proximity, it was the bicycle show, not clubs or serendipitous street encounters, that brought bicyclists of differing income groups together,[40] while motorcyclists tended to affiliate along class lines.

Clearly, the analogy between bicycling and motorcycling does not hold. While the boom-and-bust pattern of the bicycle industry was followed by an analogous pattern in the motorcycle industry (in America, for example, the industry went from more than two hundred manufacturers in the early twentieth century to two at the time of the Hollister events), economic factors were not prevalent for at least a decade and a half after the war. The solidity of the connection between the working-class man and his motorcycle was a commitment to *a particular identity*, rather than simple economics. What did change at least a sector of the motorcycling demographic was the entry of Japanese manufacturers into the American market, most especially Honda's entry in the early 1960s. Like Italy, which had seen tremendous postwar growth in scooter manufacture, as former airplane factories began turning out Piaggios and Vespas, the island nation of Japan produced small, reliable, "underpowered" motorcycles and, perhaps more important, a stunningly effective advertising campaign, picturing riding as a harmless, fun and utilitarian enterprise undertaken by priests, families and even Santa Claus.[41] Yet, parallel with Honda's Nicest People campaign, American International and other independent film production companies were cranking out films with titles like *Angels from Hell* (1968) and *The Cycle Savages* (1970) that reinforced the proletarian, sexist image of the motorcyclist.[42]

We might then ask, were there "invisible" factors, such as those affecting the bicycle industry, which transformed the motorcycle industry? Certainly one point of connection is tariffs, such as the 1891 McKinley Act, which politically aggressive nineteenth-century bicycle manufacturers used to keep superior British products away from America's shores, similar to Harley-Davidson's successful 1983 campaign to make larger-bore Japanese motorcycles (750cc and above) prohibitively expensive.[43] In this case, the international relation was established from the East, not the West.

At the point of Honda's entry into the American market, we can see a structural analogy with bicycle development that had an unintended effect on gender. Harleys were large-bore bikes, legendary for their problems with keeping the oil inside of the motorcycle. Given the biological differences in upper-body strength between men and women, these motorcycles were seen as too big for a woman to wrestle around, and there is some truth to the observation (keeping in mind that many of the legendary women motorcycle competitors, such as Dot Robinson, rode Harleys). In addition, the noise and the grime, while appealing to the nine-year-old inside some men, were unlikely to be attractive to many women. The smaller, cleaner, better-engineered Japanese bikes had a crossover appeal for both men and women. As McBee notes:

> The motorcycle was not necessarily a lifestyle but an accessory that was used if convenient and just as easily discarded, avoided, or even rejected. . . . Motorcycles were another marker of class for an already acutely class-conscious bunch whose understanding of cycling contrasted sharply with that of their working-class counterpart. . . . Motorcycling was thus a means to an end but not the end itself. In the middle-class imagination or fantasy, motorcycling led to a day at the beach, a weekend at a favorite campground, or even an afternoon of fun buzzing around town on a scavenger hunt with your favorite female friend.[44]

In its class migration, not only had the interest in motorcycling spread from the working to the middle class, the understanding of what the vehicle was for had changed. Rather than symbolizing commitment to a jingoistic, quasi-libertarian, homosocial path in life, the middle-class rider saw it as a utilitarian vehicle. And, in another paradoxical relation to the Safety bicycle, which gave women the chance to make themselves available to men, the motorcycle became an object of consumption that made men "cool" in the eyes of certain women. The image of the smaller Japanese motorcycle mirrored that of the Safety: it brought women and men together for leisure and, possibly, romance.

The outlaw prided himself on his marginalization, and the very public rejection given to bikers reinforced his commitment to his image, one, ironically enough, originating in the movies. In *The Wild One*, Johnny Strabler's (Marlon Brando) defiant retort to the question "What're you rebelling against?"—"Whaddya got?"—defined the outlaw's oppositional stance. With the adoption of the motorcycle by the middle-class male, however, the club biker found himself further marginalized.[45] As McBee notes:

> The outlaw was a threat not simply because of his unruly behavior on and off his cycle but because he patently rejected the consumer culture that is also identified with the nation's postwar affluence and the industrial ethic that valued

Figure 5.2. An ad selling the romantic possibilities of two-wheeling: Starley's Rover bicycle (1885).

productive and disciplined labor. The look, the behavior, and the rootlessness of the motorcyclist riding from town to town with what appeared to be few cares or responsibilities first attracted national attention just as the United States was entering a period of unprecedented prosperity and as labor was reaching the peak of its strength and influence.[46]

While lowering bicycle prices brought more individuals to the market, American postwar prosperity estranged the working-class "outlaw" biker even further from other, more affluent Americans, for whom the motorcycle became another object of consumption and convenience.

The parallels are striking: the Ordinary was male-identified owing to the physical difficulties in riding it and the real potential for injury. The Harley-Davidsons and Indians of the world were also physically difficult to ride and, being motorcycles, were considered dangerous. The Safety bike, like, for example, the Honda Cub, was smaller, easier to ride, and given its mechanical limitations, was less likely to expose the rider to the types of injuries Harley riders were prey to.

But note the curious inversion: in the case of male-identified bicycles, we moved from the upper class to the middle and working classes, owing to bicycle industry economics. With the male-identified motorcycles of the Fifties, we moved from the lower class to the middle, and, eventually, upper classes in the adoption of the Japanese bikes, a phenomenon indirectly connected to Japan's wartime loss and economic devastation. By the late twentieth century, even the working-class Harley-Davidson became the bike of choice among the upper class. The billionaire Malcolm Forbes founded a motorcycle club late in life, The Capitalist Tools, and gained further notice by giving Elizabeth Taylor a purple Harley-Davidson. He was inducted into the Motorcycle Hall of Fame in 1999.[47] His wealth and affection for the machine suggests this upward economic movement in interest in motorcycling. His homosexuality, long concealed, contrasts ironically with the homophobia associated with outlaw motorcycle clubs.

Hence, when we seek to understand gender identification surrounding a technological device, as we argued in chapter 1, we cannot assume the device itself is gendered. Instead, the device manifests itself in a particular economy and culture, and we have to look outside the device for the sources of whatever gendered orientation it might have. As noted, popular culture played a powerful force in gendering the 1950s motorcycle, but it would seem that economic forces a century ago exerted a more powerful effect in rendering the Safety bicycle, during a certain discrete period, a supposed key to the emancipation of women. While the smaller Japanese bikes opened up opportunities for women to ride and socialize with like-minded males, the sense of the motorcycle as a utilitarian vehicle has not, thus far, supplanted the powerful image of the outlaw motorcyclist. As those raised on that image "age out" of motorcycling as an activity, in popular culture we see multicultural youths of both genders representing the contemporary "standard" identity of a motorcyclist. The careful enculturation of children into motorcycling by manufacturers' support of motocross and Supercross, as well as the admittedly risible films devoted to teens on bikes, may well erase the image of the male motorcyclist, replacing it with one that is genderless and classless or, if the films *Biker Boyz* (2003) and *Torque* (2004) are to be believed, a rainbow world populated by male and female models on sport bikes.

Correlatively, we have seen since the inauguration of the mountain bike in the Seventies, a series of novel images for the bicyclist (e.g., the rough-and-tumble mountain biker, the sleek and impeccably attired road biker, the retro-nerd fixie riders, etc.) each of whom is as distant from one another culturally as is the grizzled Harley cruiser rider from the whippet on the sport bike. Note that these images of the bicyclist did not emerge from technological innovation but from a complex series of economic and cultural causes.

Witness the movement toward replacing petroleum-based vehicles with more environmentally friendly forms of power, a development that may affect class and gender understandings of the motorcycle. As well, electric-powered bicycles may create new images of the two-wheeled set, no doubt eliciting scorn from their more conventional brothers and sisters. We should, however, resist the temptation to assign a causal vector to emerging technologies, in which, for example, the electric bike "creates" a new image and class of users, understanding instead that the developing technology is (a) a result of a complex of causes, and (b) new consumer images have their roots in causes in addition to those that are technology-based. We might appreciate such development as analogous to the urban geek-hipster image associated with early adopters (and creators) of digital technology, in which a number of related causes (the development of the microprocessor, government funding for ARPANET, businesses seeking new methods to reduce inventory and supplier costs, the expansion of university-government partnerships, etc.), in popular retelling, reduced to two smart kids in their parents' garage. We are in the midst of observing that digital technology, something that emerged from a decidedly male-dominated field, now supplies images of both males and females. What remains is the need to recognize the independence of both bicycles and motorcycles from their supposedly inherent gender and class connections, and the need to seek other, more complex causal factors in their cultural representation.

NOTES

1. As we have discussed, this has been called the "unilineal development model technological" or "determinism," defined by Ron Eglash as "an account of technologies as having 'social impact' but little in the way of social origins, and with developmental trajectories that are either entirely obscured or seen as governed by a sort of natural law which makes their forms (and presence) seem inevitable" ("Technology as Material Culture," in *Handbook of Material Culture*, ed. Christopher Tilley, Webb

Keane, Susanne Küchler, Michael Rowlands, and Patricia Spyer [London: Sage, 2006], 331). See introduction.

2. As Daniel Headrick has argued, most accounts of technological development "are hardware histories, compilations of pictures and facts about objects divorced from the context of their time" (*The Tools of Empire: Technology and European Imperialism in the Nineteenth Century* [New York: Oxford University Press, 1981], 4).

3. Headrick, *Tools of Empire*, 4.

4. "Was fällt, das soll man auch noch stossen!" (Friedrich Nietzsche, *Also Sprach Zarathustra*, 56:20, http://www.gutenberg.org/cache/epub/7205/pg7205.html).

5. Thomas Piketty's now-famous formula, r>g, seeks to establish the superiority of capital growth over wage increase as an economic law. See *Capital in the Twenty-First Century* (Cambridge, MA: Belknap Press, 2014).

6. "Champion of Her Sex," *New York Sunday World*, 2 February 1896, 10. The Hahn Vineyard has released a *Cycles Gladiator* pinot noir with a label featuring an art-deco image from a vintage advertising poster, claiming "*Cycles Gladiator* wines pay tribute to that spirit of unfettered freedom and expression that graced the era known as the *Belle Époque*." See http://www.cyclesgladiator.com. Making the claim that cycling brought female emancipation as a ploy to sell wine illustrates our point.

7. Robert A. Smith, *A Social History of the Bicycle: Its Early Life and Times in America* (New York: American Heritage Press, 1972), 2.

8. Frances E. Willard, *A Wheel within a Wheel: How I Learned to Ride the Bicycle with Some Reflections by the Way* (Chicago: Woman's Temperance Publishing Association, 1895), 38.

9. "Cycling: Here, There and Everywhere," *Sporting Life*, 1893.

10. Eileen B. Leonard, *Women, Technology, and the Myth of Progress* (Upper Saddle River, NJ: Prentice Hall, 2002), 19, 22.

11. Social Security, "National Average Wage Index," http://www.ssa.gov/oact/cola/AWI.html.

12. We are using the Ordinary as an example to illustrate the high cost of a bicycle, aware that the Safety bicycle would be the appropriate comparison, as it was the model that popularized riding among women. Historical calculations of worth, however, are difficult. According to David Herlihy, James Kemp Starley's Rover Safety bicycle debuted in Britain in 1885 at a cost of £22 (*Bicycle: The History* [New Haven, CT: Yale University Press, 2004], 235). Online calculators of the 2013 equivalent of £22 in USD produce a substantial range, from $1930 to $4770: http://www.measuringworth.com/calculators/exchange/result_exchange.php. While the range itself is unsatisfactory for a more precise comparison, it does suggest that the bicycle was decidedly a luxury item, unavailable to the average working man or woman.

13. Phillip Gordon Mackintosh and Glen Norcliffe, "Men, Women and the Bicycle: Gender and Social Geography of Cycling in the Late Nineteenth-Century," in *Cycling and Society*, ed. Dave Horton, Paul Rosen, and Peter Cox (London: Ashgate, 2012), 162. For a detailed analysis of prices, see Thomas Cameron Burr, "Markets As Producers and Consumers: The French and U.S. National Bicycle Markets, 1875–1910" (PhD diss., University of California, Davis, 2005), 89–92.

14. In Europe, this class phenomenon was not confined to Britain. Consider Michaux's developing bicycle business and French class relations, as noted by James McGurn: "Michaux publicized the new model World Exhibition of 1867 in Paris and he booked an encouraging number of orders. He also received an order from the head of state, Napoleon III, who was an invalid. Once the Royal velocipede was delivered, Michaux (always aware of the value of loyal patronage) supplied the Prince Imperial, Louis-Napoleon, with a velocipede de luxe of rosewood aluminum-bronze. The prince, in turn, presented twelve child-size velocipedes to aristocratic playmates, and such was his enthusiasm that an opposition faction called him 'Vélocipède IV.' His rides along the streets of Paris and the Tuileries Gardens were a priceless public advertisement for Michaux and encouraged velocipeding among the socially high-placed. The wealthy and titled frequented the riding schools or practiced in the seclusion of private courtyards. House-party guests at country châteaux arranged vélocipède races among themselves, and when the rich of Paris holidayed at the coast they took to velocipeding along the sea-front promenades" (*On Your Bicycle: An Illustrated History of Cycling* [Facts on File, 1987], 35).

15. Bruce D. Epperson, *Peddling Bicycles to America: The Rise of an Industry* (Jefferson, NC: McFarland, 2010), Kindle loc. 1665.

16. Burr challenges sources who argue the percentage of women riders approached one-third of the market: "elite legitimation of cycling helped expand women's share of the market yet again. Smith claims that women made up 25 to 30 percent of the U.S. market (*Social History*, 35), yet most other statistics indicate that the real number was probably lower. . . . We cannot infer an exact percentage of the market that women actually constituted from these indirect and qualified pieces of evidence, but a reasonable estimate seems closer to 20 to 25 percent, not a third of the market" ("Markets As Producers and Consumers," 260–61).

17. Smith, *Social History*, 31.

18. McGurn, *On Your Bicycle*, 126. At this temporal distance it would be difficult to assign a motive to the formation of this club. It could be that this was a "high class" activity, and the club was a means to indicate who was and was not a member of that class. Or, given the date of formation, it might be analogous to Malcolm Forbes's "Capitalist Tools" (see following discussion), a way of distinguishing the elite bicyclists from the biking rabble.

19. For a history, see Epperson, *Peddling Bicycles to America*, Kindle loc. 822–1250.

20. McGurn, *On Your Bicycle*, 132.

21. McGurn, *On Your Bicycle*, 94.

22. For an additional account, see James Longhurst, *Bike Battles: A History of Sharing the American Road* (Seattle: University of Washington Press, 2015), 51–62.

23. *Mr. Punch Awheel: The Humors of The Humours of Motoring and Cycling*, ed. J. A. Hammerton, Project Gutenberg, http://www.gutenberg.org/files/29022/29022-h/29022-h.htm.

24. See Tony Hadland and Hans-Erhard Lessing, *Bicycle Design: An Illustrated History* (Cambridge, MA: MIT Press, 2014), 175.

25. See the chapter on roads in part 2.

26. Glen Norcliffe, *The Ride to Modernity: The Bicycle in Canada, 1869–1900* (Toronto: University of Toronto Press, 2001), 180.

27. John Tully, *The Devil's Milk: A Social History of Rubber* (New York: Monthly Review Press, 2011), 57.

28. See Greg Grandin, *Fordlandia: The Rise and Fall of Henry Ford's Forgotten Jungle City* (New York: Henry Holt, 2010).

29. See, for instance, Steven E. Alford and Suzanne Ferriss, *Motorcycle* (London: Reaktion Press, 2008), 67–116. Among accounts focusing exclusively on female motorcyclists see Ann Ferrar's *Hear Me Roar: Women, Motorcycles and the Rapture of the Road* (North Conway, NH: Whitehorse Press, 1996) and Cristine Sommer Simmons, *The American Motorcycle Girls: A Photographic History of Early Women Motorcyclists* (Parker House Publishing, 2009).

30. See "Werner: Amtliche Webseite," http://www.werner.de.

31. The film was banned in Britain from its release until 1968. For motorcycle films, see Mike Seate, *Two Wheels on Two Reels: A History of Biker Movies* (North Conway, NH: Whitehorse Press, 2000), and Alford and Ferriss, *Motorcycle*, 119–31.

32. Among the many accounts of the Hollister events are Alford and Ferriss, *Motorcycle*, 89–93, and Randy McBee, *Born to Be Wild: The Rise of the American Motorcyclist* (Chapel Hill: University of North Carolina Press, 2015), 19–40.

33. Chuck Zito with Joe Layden, *Street Justice* (New York: St. Martin's, 2002), 51.

34. See William L. Dulaney for a definitive, and historically accurate, history of the development of "outlaw" motorcycle clubs, as well as a compelling critique of popular accounts of the Hollister incident: "A Brief History of 'Outlaw' Motorcycle Clubs," *The International Journal of Motorcycle Studies* 1 (November 2005), http://ijms.nova.edu/November2005/IJMS_Artcl.Dulaney.html.

35. See Alford and Ferriss, *Motorcycle*, 84–85.

36. Norcliffe, *The Ride to Modernity,* 197.

37. John Hall, a member of the Pagans, has described his club's embrace as a knightly ethos: "The Pagans were a one-percenter outlaw motorcycle brotherhood, medieval and mystical, far more like the religious warrior brotherhood of Teutonic knights than some sort of modern criminal enterprise like the government and media were always trying to tell people it was" ("Memorial Day Weekend 1967," in *The Devil Can Ride: The World's Best Motorcycle Writing*, ed. John Klancher [Minneapolis, MN: Motorbooks, 2010], 74–75).

38. Like the Canadians, early American clubs were more comfortable with a patina of militarism: "American clubs first copied British club customs but many switched to regular military titles, such as first and second lieutenant, and even committee posts were militarized. Also, American club bugle calls were taken directly from the *Cavalry Tactics Manual* of the U.S. Army" (McGurn, *On Your Bicycle*, 53). They also emulated the British cyclists' dress, which consisted of double-breasted, close-fitting patrol jackets, with a straight waistcoat and breeches or knickerbockers (Phillis Cunnington and Alan Mansfield, *English Costume for Sports and Outdoor Recreation from the Sixteenth to the Nineteenth Centuries* [London: A. C. Black, 1969], 232).

39. McBee, *Born to be Wild*, 53.

40. Smith, *Social History*, 31.

41. "In 1963 Grey Advertising created a campaign designed to present riding a motorcycle as a benign and practical activity. Ads with the slogan, 'You Meet the Nicest People on a Honda', deliberately divorced the rider from the outlaw image prevalent in America. Featuring sunny photos of housewives riding on errands, parents and children commuting to school, joyriding young couples, grandmothers and even Santa Claus, the ads offered an alternative image of motorcycling as safe, simple, fun and—crucially for a Japanese company—all-American. In fact, the corporation became the first foreign company to sponsor the Academy Awards. . . . The campaign was an astonishing success: in 1962 Honda sold 40,000 bikes a year; by 1970 they were selling 500,000" (Alford and Ferriss, *Motorcycle*, 132). The Beach Boys 1964 song "Little Honda," also gave the brand an unexpected boost. A television commercial featuring a young John Travolta is posted on YouTube: http://www.youtube.com/watch?v=d1CuZRPM0Aw&noredirect=1.

42. See Alford and Ferriss, *Motorcycle*, 127–29, as well as Bill Osgerby, *Biker—Truth and Myth: How the Original Cowboy of the Road Became the Easy Rider of the Silverscreen* (Guilford, CT: The Lyons Press, 2005), and John Wooley and Michael H. Price, *The Big Book of Biker Flicks: 40 of the Best Motorcycle Movies of All Time* (Tulsa, OK: Hawk Publishing Group, 2005). The book's subtitle is misleading for Wooley and Price focus almost exclusively on the "biker-sploitation" films.

43. For the McKinley Act, see Epperson, *Peddling Bicycles to America,* Kindle loc. 2537. For the Harley tariff, see McBee, *Born to be Wild*, 181–84.

44. McBee, *Born to be Wild*, 113–14. This recalls claims of early female motorcyclists in the 1920s. Twin sisters Betty and Nancy Debenham, both ardent motorcyclists, enthused, "Motor-cycling is an ideal hobby for the tired business girl. She can seek health and pleasure during her precious week-ends by exploring the countryside and the seaside." They envisioned female riders gathering "violets and primroses from the woods" ("Motor Cycling for Health," *Daily News*, 16 March 1926).

45. See Alford and Ferriss, *Motorcycle*, 93–98, 114–16.

46. McBee, *Born to be Wild*, 120.

47. His January 1987 article in *Popular Mechanics* gives some sense of his attitude toward motorcycling: Malcolm Forbes, "The Art of Motorcycle Touring; Driving a motorcycle across the country or around the globe begins with the right equipment—and lots of friends," *Popular Mechanics*, June 1987, 90–94, 132.

Chapter Six

The Embodied Cyclist and Freedom

In *The Wild Angels* (1966), Heavenly Blues (Peter Fonda) tells a judge, "We wanna be free! We wanna be free to do what we wanna do. We wanna be free to ride. We wanna be free to ride our machines without being hassled by The Man!" He voices a familiar, if unintentionally comic, refrain: central to riding a bike, whether motorized or not, is the experience of "freedom." Riders repeatedly report that they feel free when riding, that riding frees them from their daily concerns. But what does "freedom" mean?

"Freedom" is, for riders, ultimately a somewhat murky, subjective concept. As we will discuss, possible explanations for this feeling of freedom have emerged from the realms of neurology, genetics, psychology, and metaphysics. But, in addition to this subjective experience of freedom, there is also an objective dimension that becomes manifest in politics, as well as the social dimensions of bicycling and motorcycling. Does the subjective experience of riding and freedom translate into a coherent objective sense of political and social freedom as well? To put it another way, is there an objectively correlative ideological concept that meshes with our subjective sense of freedom while riding? More simply, we might ask, does the experience of freedom while on a two-wheeled vehicle bring us together politically after we dismount? Cycling history suggests not.

POLITICAL FREEDOM

The goal of any modern political order legitimized by popular participation is individual freedom, consisting in a set of rights guaranteed by the government: freedom of religion, assembly, press, speech, trial by a jury of our peers, and so on. One of the implicit guarantees of modern freedom is, within certain limits, freedom to move about, and certainly freedom to move within one's nation's borders.[1] How does this democratic, social contract ideal mesh with two-wheeled-vehicle riders' sense of the political dimensions of their activity?

For instance, early female riders associated the mobility granted by the bicycle as a source of emancipation: freedom of independent movement, freedom from constricting garments, and even freedom from confining domestic roles. Marguerite Merington, writing for *Scribner's* in 1895, had advised, "Now and again a complaint arises of the narrowness of woman's sphere. For such disorder of the soul the sufferer can do no better than to flatten her sphere to a circle, mount it, and take to the road."[2] The act of riding widens her horizons, granting her "absolute freedom," as Marie Ward explained:

> In travelling, the country all about soon becomes, as it were, your own domain. Instead of a few squares, you know several towns; instead of an acquaintance with the country for a few miles about, you can claim familiarity with two or three counties; an all-day expedition is reduced to a matter of a couple of hours; and unless a breakdown occurs, you are at all times independent. This absolute freedom of the cyclist can be known only to the initiated, and as proficiency is acquired, it becomes a most attractive feature of the sport.[3]

While, as we have noted, such emancipation depended on class in the nineteenth century, that liberation of the sort Merington and Ward described was limited to those with the means to purchase a bike, contemporary programs across the globe have extended such freedoms to women of various classes, nationalities, ethnicities and religions.[4]

Historically, the connection between women and freedom of movement began with the 1885 introduction of the Safety bicycle. Prior to this, during the era of the Ordinary or high-wheeler—an era dominated by male riders—bicyclists were considered nuisances, but not exactly "outsiders," given that bicycle prices insured that their riders were affluent and did not adopt the oppositional stance of traditional outsiders. What set them apart was their disruptiveness and novelty. With the contemporary dominance of automobiles everywhere except in developing nations, the bicyclist's status has changed, especially given the rider's physical vulnerability on the roads.

Illustrations in then-contemporary magazines, newspapers, and even songs took full advantage of memorializing and satirizing both "scorching" young men and female bicyclists. In our own American contemporary popular culture, images of the bicyclist and the motorcyclist clearly differ. An "outsider" bicyclist might be a wild-and-crazy dispatch rider (see, for example, "Wilee" in 2012's *Premium Rush*), an urban-romantic figure who, like the motorcycle dispatch rider, is disappearing from the roadways

Figure 6.1. Popular songs documented the phenomenon of "scorching" in the 1890s. Courtesy of the Lilly Library, Indiana University, Bloomington, Indiana.

as digital communications become dominant. Since the 1970s, the go-for-broke mountain biker is the pastoral mirror of the dispatch rider, although the mountain biker exhibits a non-commercial skill. Given the origins of mountain bikes and mountain biking in California, the mountain biker is, culturally, a land-based analogue to the surfer, a lone, gentle figure with a singular skill who pits him/herself against a natural barrier, whether it be big waves or big hills. Another figure from the more conventional sport of bicycle racing would be the OCD privateer cross-country racer,[5] one who, in many cases, literally destroys his/her health in pursuit of a physically punishing goal, an ultramarathoner on wheels.

In contemporary culture, the functional equivalent of the original "outlaw" bicyclist, the "scorcher," would be not a bicyclist but the squid, the youthful sport bike rider who (so goes the image) endangers both himself and others with his (and it's invariably a "he," just as in the age of the high-wheeler) antics on public roads, from high speeds to death-courting wheelies.

In the political arena, however, contemporary bicyclists seldom arouse public ire in their quest for, for example, safer and more extensive bikeways.[6] Like their nineteenth-century counterparts, they simply seek space and safety on the roadways. Where once their rivals were horses and oxcarts, today their adversaries are automobiles, buses, and trucks. Their political campaigns center, literally, on space: space on the roadways.

However, a significant segment of bicyclists avoid roadways altogether and, in so doing, create public conflicts with political dimensions: mountain bike riders. While the nonriding public registers displeasure with trail-riding bicyclists, the bicyclists themselves see as their opponent not their fellow citizens, but the government, in particular land management bureaus. Land management officers, more precisely, those of the US Forest Service, are charged with stewardship over public land, providing opportunities for citizens to use it while protecting the land for the long term against damage that might prevent future users from enjoying it.

Mountain bike riders ride on trails. Like horse and hiking paths, they need to be created and maintained. However, instead of employing pathways created by foresters, some bicyclists have taken matters into their on hands on public lands, creating pathways, jumps, and other elements of the mountain bike experience without planning or permission. Accordingly, given that the trails are unauthorized, forest service officers have destroyed their wooden jumps and effectively prevented the mountain bikers from enjoying the forest.[7]

In this respect the mountain bikers are literal outlaws, breaking the law through unauthorized modification of public land. From their point of view, they are citizens employing public land for their enjoyment, and find themselves hassled by the Man.

Ironies abound in this political conflict. For one, bicyclists are back to scaring the horses, 150 years later: horse trails on public land have intersected with the self-made bicycle trails. While urban bicyclists campaign for more bicycle awareness on public roads, mountain bikers create their own "roads" for their own use, ignoring the interests of others. The final irony may perhaps be that, while the original bicyclists were public campaigners for better roads, the mountain bikers have reverted to using trails for their exclusive use to pursue their passion. Unlike their contemporary "outlaw" counterparts, motorcyclists, these self-propelled outlaws have moved off the road onto the trail.

Politicized motorcyclists are a different matter. Their gatherings at state capitols to assert their rights and support motorcycle-centric legislation are god's gift to local news organizations, who depict them as noisy, smelly, and hairy, and help entrench in the public mind the notion of the motorcyclist as an angry, aggressive, one-note political operative. What is the ideological basis for their anti-helmet crusade, or their insistence on jailing motorists who hit motorcyclists? Why do they all share such a narrow, common agenda? Why do they dress that way? The evidence would suggest that this popular image is reductive and in no way represents a monolithic motorcycle community.

Consider the ideological spectrum of some well-known motorcyclists. The late Malcolm Forbes, whose riding group was known as the Capitalist Tools, and Jim Rogers, author of *Investment Biker*, are traditional and committed capitalists, political libertarians, who see entrepreneurial economic enterprises, free from government regulation, as the essence of freedom.[8] Sonny Barger and his Oakland chapter of the Hells Angels of the 1970s saw the United States' military incursion into Vietnam as the expression of America's right to employ its military forces to fight what he saw as the threat of global, expansionist communism, an expression of rightist political ideology.[9] The women of Dykes on Bikes®, along with Ann Ferrar, Barbara Jones, Karen Larsen, and others see motorcycling as an arena for the assertion of women's political, social, and sexual rights. Patrick Symmes's *Chasing Che* and Barbara Brodman's *Looking for Mr. Guevara* evoke the connection between leftist ideology and motorcycling. Many motorcycle travelers, such as Ted Simon (*Jupiter's Travels*), Christopher Baker (*Mi Moto Fidel*), or Christoper Hunt (*Sparring With Charlie: Motorbiking Down the Ho Chi Minh Trail*) are essentially apolitical, and see the motorcycle as a means to establish human, rather than ideological, connections among people. Klaus Schubert and Claudia Metz's *Abgefahren* shows how for those committed to the romantic hippie ideal of disappearing into nature, motorcycling can free one from political society altogether. And we mustn't forget Werner Bausenhart, whose books demonstrate how motorcycling freed him from having to spend any time with his wife.[10]

Clearly, there's a subjective, psychological dimension to motorcycle freedom but, ideologically, motorcyclists are seemingly all over the map. Or are they? Some of the more visible political manifestations of motorcycling may isolate some ideas they hold in common.

First, there is the area of motorcycle rights, motorcyclists' ongoing quest to not be hassled by the Man. MROs (Motorcycle Rights Organizations), in

America and elsewhere, concern themselves with a variety of political issues, from motorcycle licensing to motorcycle modifications to motorcycle helmets. In the latter instance, does the government have the right to impose a dress code on a specific subset of the motoring public? While they might not explicitly say so, the key to understanding the political dimension of the helmet controversy can be found in John Stuart Mill's Harm Principle, stated in his work, *On Liberty*: "The only purpose for which power can be rightfully exercised over any member of a civilized community, against his will, is to prevent harm to others."[11] Motorcyclists argue that the government has no right to impose requirements on individuals that interfere with their liberty of action unless that action would result in harm to others. In this case, we can clearly identify the ideology in question: MRO advocates are libertarians.

Note, however, that MROs are *reactive* organizations that arose to combat apparent government interference in the daily life of motorcyclists. The libertarian quality of MROs functions as an oppositional stance to what members see as "totalitarian enactments."[12] If the government and police agencies didn't spend their time singling out motorcyclists for what they consider to be unfair treatment, MROs wouldn't need to be so active, or, perhaps, to exist at all.[13]

However, MROs do not exhaust the political dimensions of motorcycling. Consider the example of the motorcycle club. Motorcycle clubs are ubiquitous, from Australia to Romania to Canada.[14] Clubs can be organized on the basis of a specific brand. Clubs can organize themselves around an era—such as classic bike organizations—or an activity, such as road racing or off-road activities. Other than the occasional association of a brand with nationalism, such as Harley-Davidson with America or Honda with Japan, none of these clubs is inherently political. However, the most famous type of club found internationally is exemplified by the Hells Angels, which could be said to have a political orientation. Unlike the MRO, internally the post–World War II motorcycle club is anything but libertarian, once an individual chooses to become a prospect. The clubs (usually identified as "outlaw" clubs) emphasize "loyalty, masculinity, discipline, independence and courage," but they do so within a rigid, hierarchical structure governed by a constitution-like set of rules.[15] As such, the "outlaw" clubs are governed not by libertarian principles, but those of the traditional social contract: no one is compelled to make the contract with the other brothers, but once done, one is obligated to abide by the rules of the contract. Contracting exhibits the traditional liberal democratic principle of individual choice. However, in agreeing to the contract, one is by no means entering into a democratic union, but instead one governed by more military notions of subordination and conformity. The implicit and announced purpose of this structure is group survival in a perceived hostile environment inhabited by police and turf-endangering other clubs.

Note again that the military model is reactive to a sense of threat from two ongoing opponents, the police and other clubs. Without police "hassling" motorcycle clubs, the two groups would not be opposed, especially considering the remarkable structural similarity in their military-style organizations.[16]

Opposition between clubs is another matter, seemingly founded on the idea of turf. In this respect, conflict is not inherently political, but tribal.[17] Club conflicts, while interesting sociologically, don't seem to have a political dimension.

Hence, we could optimistically say that, absent of state opposition to motorcyclists and their voluntary individual and club-related practices, most of the political dimensions of motorcycling would disappear.

Another significant difference between bicyclists and motorcyclists should be noted: the tendency of the contemporary male motorcyclist, regardless of nationality, to draw on the American past as a model for identity. The beards and flowing hair of the frontiersman, fringe (whether it be on the rider's jacket or flowing in the wind from the handlebars), various visual markers on the motorcycle itself (decals or airbrushed images of Amerindians, southwest landscapes, flintlock rifles, and other western icons), bumper stickers ("Let's mount up!"), all point to a rider imaginatively participating in a past era laden with nostalgic value. Bicyclists don't seem to have a nostalgia-laden sense of themselves (which might manifest itself in dressing in nineteenth-century sporting dress: tweed knickerbocker suits, golf stockings, and cloth caps). In terms of larger group identification, many road bicyclists choose to dress like bicycle racers, complete with the advertisement-laden, skintight shirts characteristic of competitive bicyclists. In emulating their idols, they more accurately mirror soccer fans than motorcyclists.

In seeking a clear political dimension to either bicycling or motorcycling, one finds confusion. The best that can be said is that for both groups politics is largely reactive. If we do seek to explain the differences (why aren't bicyclists more demonstrative? Why aren't motorcyclists less hostile and aggressive?), we might consider that generally, for most bicyclists, riding is a practical transportation choice or recreational *pastime*, while for a segment of the motorcycle-riding public, motorcycling is an *identity*. Hence, for motorcyclists, threats to their ability to ride as they wish ("totalitarian enactments") are threats to their person, not to their transportation choices.[18]

Hence, neither bicyclists nor motorcyclists seem to be aligned on the basis of "freedom" as an ideological concept. However, from road bikes to sport bikes, from mountain bikes to cruisers, all the riding public can agree on the *emotional* sense of freedom granted by riding.

EMOTIONAL FREEDOM

By definition, an emotional response is most often outside the realm of verbal description, although the consequences of an emotion seem sufficiently uniform (anger can lead to violence, erotic passion can lead to sexual activity). Can we describe the *feeling* of riding "freedom"? In addition to the socio-political ideas of freedom, discussed above, there are three possible approaches to explaining the feeling of two-wheeled freedom. The first is the neurological approach: can the wiring of our brain explain why we feel free while riding? Are their certain chemicals, genes, or tissue sites that are stimulated by cycling, resulting in the feeling of freedom? Second, a psychological approach: is there something in our psychology that, for example, impels people toward cycling and the thrills it provides, while causing others to run the other direction? Finally, a philosophical approach: is there something metaphysical, connected with the idea that not only do we have a body, but we are conscious of *having* a body (unlike non-human animals) that might help us explain this phenomenon? In what follows we do not argue in favor of one approach or the other, but offer a prolegomena, setting out possible approaches to the answer to the question of emotional freedom, and suggesting some of the potential consequences and limitations of each approach.[19]

BIOLOGY: NEUROLOGY AND GENETICS

In April 2013 President Obama announced "The White House Brain Initiative," seeking to unite research from the National Institutes of Health (NIH), the Food and Drug Administration (FDA), the Defense Advanced Research Projects Agency (DARPA), the Intelligence Advanced Research Projects Activity (IARPA), the National Science Foundation (NSF) with partners in the private sector, including, but not limited to, companies, universities, and philanthropists.[20] News media periodically report on discoveries about the brain and brain sites.[21] Much of contemporary research has followed from the introduction of fMRI (functional magnetic resonance imaging) scans of the brain, beginning in the 1990s. For example, most researchers agree that the amygdala is the site of the brain's response to fear.[22] However, significant doubt persists as to what fMRIs reveal about the brain's structures.[23] Perhaps those with a tiny amygdala are thrill seekers. Another explanation, dating from the 1960s, was the postulation of the limbic system, the so-called seat of our emotions.[24] While research continues on the amygdala, the argument favoring the limbic system has gone out of fashion, principally because no one could agree what belonged, and did not belong to this system, with the hippocampus being most problematic.[25]

To further complicate the picture, we can say, with philosopher Martin Heidegger, that we are the beings for whom our being is an issue.[26] Neurologically speaking, that means that, as part of the capacity to sense and respond to external stimuli, we have an internal, mental model of ourselves as part of our higher consciousness. Conscious knowledge is, as Antonio Damasio claims, "the relationships between organism and object,"[27] but part of that relationship is a representation of the conscious being to him/herself. Hence, while emotion can be located in neural sites, in particular the brain-stem region, hypothalamus, and basal forebrain,[28] it would be a mistake to say, for example, that the speed of the motorcycle stimulates those sites, resulting in an emotion we call freedom. The systemic nature of the brain, combined with the self-modeling inherent in having a human brain, makes such claims far too simple an account of emotional sourcing. To put it another way, "we only know that we feel an emotion when we sense that emotion is sensed as happening in our organism."[29] While the sight of an object may elicit a response in a conscious being (e.g., the cheetah that sees a wounded antelope), for us to have an emotional response involves first, the stimulus, and then the recognition that *I* am feeling that emotion, a *self*-conscious response. A ride on a bicycle may engender an emotion during the ride, but to step off the bike and say, "Wow, I felt free coasting down that mountain road," suggests situating the emotion within the context of a reflective self: "I had a lousy morning until I mounted that bike."

With this complication of self-consciousness in the background, let's look just at the brain, uncharacteristically shorn of its relation to an object. What we can say with certainty about the brain today is that it is a system of systems.[30] The traditional Cartesian division of the human being into a mind and a body, or our communicative self as a division between emotion and reason is not supported by the neurological evidence. Thus, learned responses to the environment that involve both acting and reacting, such as cycling, cannot be reduced to conscious, rational choice in responding to road and traffic conditions. Despite attempts to isolate areas dealing with generalized human faculties, such as reason or emotion, what is becoming increasingly clear is that despite certain areas being devoted to specific tasks, such as optical or olfactory functions, even these sites do not exist and work in isolation.[31] They are indeed nothing at all without their connections to other systems within the brain. From an evolutionary perspective, we can distinguish the medulla, say, from the cerebellum, but on the synaptic level, there is less to distinguish; instead, we have areas of synaptic concentration working interactively with other areas to produce human behavior. Attempting to isolate a brain site devoted, for instance, to pleasure, and then to claim that cycling pleasure, what we call freedom, emanates from there, results from a naïve notion of the brain as an organ, rather than a system of systems.

From aficionados of peyote to Ambien poppers, from amateur hippie drug takers to those imbibing physician-prescribed Mother's Little Helpers, everyone recognizes that certain chemicals produce feelings of mood elevation. Researchers have, in particular, noted the effects of the monoamines or neurotransmitters (including serotonin, norepinephrine, and dopamine) involved in mood elevation and senses of well being.[32] LSD, for example, induces serotonin emission into the blood stream, causing plasticine forests and marshmallow skies to manifest themselves. Perhaps riding down an Interstate at 95 mph causes the release of certain brain chemicals, and our uneducated response to the chemical reactions is to call them "freedom." Unfortunately, scientists have discovered that this molecular approach to mental states is too crude, and that our level of knowledge about the functioning of these molecules is simply not far enough along. Certain brain chemicals produce a set of synaptic conditions we may identify as euphoria in one instance but can, in another situation, have a completely opposite effect. As Joseph LeDoux notes,

> Although it seemed in the early 1960s that there might be a particular chemical code for different mental states—molecules of pleasure, fear, and aggression were proposed—this notion is now viewed by many as naïve. Mental states are not represented by molecules alone, or even by a mix of molecules. As we've seen, they are instead accounted for by intricate patterns of information processing within and between synaptically connected neural circuits. Chemicals participate in synaptic transmission, and in the regulation or modulation of transmission, but *it is the pattern of transmission in circuits, more than the particular chemicals involved, that determines mental state.*[33]

Thus, trying to reduce an emotion to a flood of chemicals released owing to a particular activity is highly problematic.[34]

A related biological explanation can be found in genetics, which seems to be another potentially exciting research area that could help explain cycling freedom as having an organic origin. Following the mapping of the human genome, perhaps we could isolate genetic areas that would explain our predisposition to risk-taking behavior, such as motorcycling, and, given the genetic differences among humans, we could claim that the propensity toward seeking out motorcycling freedom could be found on a particular unit of a particular chromosome. "Freedom" would then be a particular sequence of amino acids, all shared unknowingly by the motorcycling community.

Despite the science fiction scenarios, from *Brave New World* to *Gattaca*, stressing the malleability of genes and thus behavior, the genetic approach fails to understand a key element in genetic expression, namely that a genetic predisposition is *epigenetic*. That is, gene expression as we develop into adults is not like the sprouting of a seed, but instead involves the relationship of the gene to its environment. How genes get expressed has as much to do with where and under what conditions they get expressed as with which biological person is doing the expressing. The preponderance of African-American stars in American sports such as basketball and football has given rise to the argument that these men and women possess a "sports gene" not shared by Caucasians or those of other races. However, David Epstein's 2014 book, *The Sports Gene*, decisively debunks this theory, supporting instead the argument that the environment of one's upbringing seems to have a substantial influence on athletic performance, despite or because of a genetic predisposition.[35]

The biological sciences of neurology and genetics, then, offer three possible approaches to discovering the sources of freedom: identifying a brain site, identifying a brain chemical, or identifying a specific gene whose expression would induce, on some level, a feeling of freedom. Each, however, fails to recognize the systemic aspect of neurological behavior and/or environmental/genetic interaction, whether within that system of systems we call the brain, or between the biological and environmental systems involved in human growth and development. Further, in activities involving our higher consciousness, such as reflecting on a ride just completed, we have to take into account two things. First, stimulating the brain in a certain way, such as high racetrack speeds, means nothing except in relation to a particular brain; what is freedom to some is terror to others.[36] Second, the stimulus-response model of cycling does not account for the process of consciousness wherein it makes a model of itself internally, what we call "our self." That representation of the self to itself is what the self reflects on, not something called "the brain."

PSYCHOLOGY

Psychology might be another fruitful area, although one not substantially different from neurology. As LeDoux notes, "Brain circuits and psychological experiences are not different things, but rather, different ways of describing the same thing."[37] Herein lies the problem for psychology: historically, it seems to have simply made up names for the origin of observed behaviors or internally sensed states. Self-destructive behavior is owing to our thanatos, or death-drive. Our cultural productions result from redirecting the libidinial energy from our repressed id. Thanatos, libido, id: these seem to be metaphors in search of a nonexistent referent. Behavioral psychology, recognizing the lack of scientific rigor in cognitive psychological jargon, threw the baby out with the bathwater in asserting that only behaviors were worthy of scientific study, not internal states. While what is now termed cognitive behavioral therapy seems to be effective as therapy, as an explanatory model it suffers from the limitations of its predecessors.[38]

One of the seemingly counterintuitive elements of cycling is that the activity exposes the rider to danger and even death. "I wouldn't ride a bicycle in a major city; that would be courting death." "Who in their right mind would ride a bicycle down Alpe d'Huez? Those turns, those speeds: those Tour de France guys are crazy." "I think motorcycles are beautiful, but I'd never ride one. Too dangerous. You're exposed to automobile traffic, and at those high speeds one false move could kill you. I've looked at the statistics, and motorcycling is incredibly dangerous." Yet, millions of people worldwide, especially those who do not need to ride two-wheeled vehicles for work or transportation, seem to ignore the sober observations of nonriders and continue to expose themselves to danger. Why?

Michael J. Apter's 1992 book, *The Dangerous Edge: The Psychology of Excitement*, seeks to provide an answer. Apter points out that anxiety and excitement have the same physiological roots; they are both phenomena we could classify under the more general rubric of *arousal*. He says, "An emotion involves both arousal, which is physiological, and some kind of subjective interpretation, which is psychological."[39] The question of whether an experience evokes fear or excitement is secondary to whether it is arousing.

According to Apter, we exist mentally in three zones: safety, danger, and trauma, the latter meaning actual physical injury. From a psychological standpoint, arousal is achieved the closer one moves away from safety, toward danger, but stops just short of trauma. He notes that "the danger is needed to produce the arousal, whereas the perceived lack of real danger is what produces the feeling of protection that allows the arousal to be felt as excitement."[40]

We are able to experience danger as excitement because we construct a psychological protective frame, insulating us from the anxiety that emerges from a sense of impending trauma. These frames may differ in their origin and disposition (Apter provides three different models), but the result is the same: a framework within which to have an experience that is exciting rather than anxiety producing. He notes, "Danger is used to give rise to arousal which is experienced as excitement rather than anxiety."[41]

We might become aroused by watching other people do exciting things, such as witnessing a sporting event or watching an erotic film. Or, we might become aroused by engaging ourselves in an activity involving danger, such as cycling. For Apter, cycling falls into the activity category of "overcoming a basic physical limitation," in this case, our inability to move very fast through space. Other examples include "rollerskating, skateboarding, go-karting, … hotrodding … skiing, and powerboating."[42]

Thus, Apter provides a context within which to understand excitement-seeking behavior. We desire emotional arousal that is interpreted as exciting through experiencing danger within the protection of a psychological frame, skirting the dangerous edge between safety and trauma. But why? Apter offers several explanations, among them the ever-popular evolutionary biological one, that we need people willing to explore limits for the good of the group. Perhaps there might be cultural reasons, since transgressing boundaries is part of cultural progress. There might be individual reasons, that mastering a dangerous skill helps the individual in enhancing his or her character.[43]

Apter does not provide a definitive answer as to why one chooses to mount a two-wheeled vehicle, but one clue can be found in the intensely *private* appeal of riding. Sure, we may like the play-acting elements of a ride (dressing as a bicycle racer or as an "outlaw") but one of the central rewards of riding seems to be psychological.

Apter provides a framework of talking about the dangerous edge, the psychology of cycling's appeal. However, one must take a further step, and that is communicating cycling's allure through *language*. While neurological and genetic explanations seek physiological evidence to explain the emotion of "freedom," for a psychological explanation to be convincing, it must be communicable. Akin to logotherapeutic models of psychiatric analysis, to understand "freedom" we should be able to communicate it through means other than a broad smile after dismounting.

One component of riding "freedom" is the intensity of the pleasure that results from a good ride. And here is the nub of the problem: communicating pleasure is like communicating pain. There's an inherent difficulty with a type of experience that is, after all, not intellectual but somatic.

As the German phenomenologist Edmund Husserl has argued, consciousness is always consciousness of something.[44] And feelings, whether pleasurable or painful, are always feelings *for* something or someone: I love my wife; I hate going to parties where I don't know anyone; I fear the police. But the pleasure one takes in cycling has nothing to do with an object, such as a love for the machine itself (an obvious feeling experienced by most all owners), but love of the *riding*. Finding a language for what it means to ride is, while not impossible, certainly challenging.

Cultural critic Elaine Scarry has addressed the issue of finding a language, not for pleasure, but for pain. In her 1995 book, *The Body in Pain: The Making and Unmaking of the World*, she explores the difficulties of writers of both fiction and nonfiction in communicating the experience of pain. She notes that,

> for the person in pain, so incontestably and unnegotiably present is it that "having pain" may come to be thought of as the most vibrant example of what it is

> to "have certainty," while for the other person it is so elusive that "hearing about pain" may exist as the primary model of what it is "to have doubt." Thus pain comes unsharably into our midst as at once that which cannot be denied and that which cannot be confirmed.[45]

The same, one could argue, could be said about pleasure as Scarry has noted about pain: as an interior state, it "has no referential content."[46] Many people, when confronted with the chance to ride a two-wheeled vehicle, refuse because it is dangerous, and it is difficult, if not impossible, to communicate to a frightened friend the appeal of riding.

Scarry herself notes that the difference between pleasure (of play, for example) and pain is that one is enslaved to pain, while one can separate oneself, move in and out, from an act of play. Moving down the highway at 80 mph could be construed as a type of play, but not a type that one can separate oneself from quickly and at will.[47]

Another scholar of the incommunicable is Michael Polanyi. In *The Tacit Dimension* and elsewhere, he has examined the issue of connoisseurship, the difficulty of communicating in any teachable fashion the acquired skill of, for example, wine tasting.[48] However, cycling is not an example of tacit knowledge. While, for example, motorcyclists differ in their competence, the statistical difference in accidents between those who have taken an MSF (Motorcycle Safety Foundation) course and those who have not demonstrates that skillful riding can be taught.[49] Ironically, while we may use the phrase "it's like riding a bicycle" to refer to an effortless action, cycling requires learning and mastery of skills (balance, steering, etc.) that only become "effortless" after practice and the creation of "muscle memory."

The answer to why cycling "freedom" is so difficult to communicate is that the specific form of pleasure we experience in motorcycling is what Apter, Mihaly Csikszentmihalyi, Susan A. Jackson, and others have described as "flow."[50] In Apter's terms, cycling is about experiencing change (such as curves, road conditions, speed, other vehicles, etc.) and successfully adapting to it. When the rate of change of external conditions puts us at the edge of our abilities, employing them becomes extremely pleasurable. Apter says, "At this rate the challenge never becomes too great for the individual's resources of knowledge and skill, but remains great enough to elicit continuing interest and response." Such an individual is experiencing flow, "a state of mind in which one is so totally and deeply absorbed in what one is doing that one feels one is 'flowing along in it,' typically losing all sense of time and selfhood. . . . We could say that the flow experience is likely to take place when the problems are *not* so great as to break through the protective frame, but *are* great enough to elicit high arousal."[51] The experience of flow imparts new complexity to our mental states:

> Following a flow experience, the organization of the self is more complex than it had been before. . . . Complexity is the result of two broad psychological processes: differentiation and integration. Differentiation implies a movement toward uniqueness, toward separating oneself from others. Integration refers to its opposite: a union with other people, with ideas and entities beyond the self. A complex self is one that succeeds in combining these opposite tendencies.[52]

Here Csikszentmihalyi may well be describing what we observed above to be a neurological process, explaining its "feltness" not at the level of synaptic firing, but through language.

Imagine yourself as an NBA basketball player bringing the ball up the court. Five tall men are trying to prevent you from reaching the basket. Adapting instantly to changing court conditions, you slam dunk the ball. The crowd goes wild. Then imagine the postgame interview. Postgame interviews with athletes are right up there with watching paint dry, and the reason is not that athletes are dumb or inarticulate, but that few words describe the flow they attain in practicing their sport.[53] In making the play, shooter is no longer "himself": the self has become absorbed into the action. While fans see the shooter dunking the ball, for the shooter there is the unity of self-ball-hoop. The self has disappeared in the act of dunking.

Key to this explanation is the disappearance of the self in the activity. There is no cycle when you are riding, and more important, there is no *you*; you and the cycle are one. Traditionally, this experience has been described as ecstasy, or ecstatic: literally standing outside oneself. Standing outside oneself, freeing oneself from oneself—perhaps this approaches the meaning of freedom. One is not free of everyday cares and anxieties, although that is true. One is free of the sense of oneself as a self, disappearing into the moment of skillfully plunging down a hillside or accelerating out of a curve.[54]

One should point out, of course, that an experience of flow is not continuous in the performance of whatever act elicits the phenomenon. Cyclists must be constantly scanning their surroundings, seeking to avoid, among many possible threats, dogs and turning vehicles. However, in the absence of ongoing external threats, the experience of a "good ride" (i.e., the experience of flow) can be had for periods of time, depending on environmental and emotional conditions.

The freedom-as-flow explanation has the virtue of shared recognition. While neurological accounts sound better suited to a medical school classroom, psychological accounts sound like something we have experienced. Yet, for all their familiarity, they also seem to be talking around the subject rather than addressing it directly. We can name something "flow" and describe its parameters, but we are no closer to an understanding of the relation of the sensorimotor events induced by it and the connection to our conceptual apparatus, whereby we say that we feel "free."

METAPHYSICS

Both the difficulty and strength of scientific descriptions of human beings, such as neurology, is the assumption that the body is an object. However, as human beings, we experience ourselves and others as subjects. Only through a reductive act, considering, for example, the brain as a spongy, grey mass (as opposed to *my head*), do we understand the brain as a neurological system of systems. Outside of a narrow scientific context, however, we encounter ourselves and others as *people*, not as bodies. In our daily experience we are always-already people, and only through a conscious reductive act can we consider ourselves objects for the purpose of scientific study or parts of ourselves as limbs or organs for the purpose of observing their behavior.

The branch of metaphysics known as phenomenology aspires to begin its inquiry with, and maintain the human encounter with, the world as the fundamental way to talk about ourselves and our connection to the world. As Drew Leder notes, "The notion of a lived body provides a potential mode of escape from cognitive habits of dualism deeply entrenched in our culture. . . . If the body as lived structure is a locus of experience, then one need not ascribe this capability to a decorporealized mind. The self is viewed as an integrated being. . . . The lived body is thus first and foremost not a located thing but a path of access, a being-in-the-world."[55]

The irony of this conception is that, in using the body, it disappears. While we can focus on our eye if there is stray matter in it, to see we necessarily have to forget the eye; it recedes from view, as it were, in order to function. Leder describes a general principle: "insofar as I perceive through an organ, it necessarily recedes from the perceptual field it discloses."[56]

Hence, we can use phenomenology's insights to point out at least two key weaknesses of neurological and psychological accounts of the sense of freedom. First, the objectified body is not the body we experience; we experience the world as *my body*, and, for example, *my* body's disappearance into an act of flow is the significant part of that equation. Second, as noted above, from a phenomenological perspective, there is no such thing as consciousness; there is only consciousness of an object. As Maurice Merleau-Ponty says, "consciousness always finds itself already at work in the world."[57] To speak of a consciousness independent of the object of its focus (whether external or internal) is to engage in a reductive reification that subverts the process of understanding it.[58]

Phenomenologists from Husserl to Heidegger to Merleau-Ponty have pointed out that our essential experience is not, for example, the exercise of our reason (the explanation of what it means to be human from Plato to Descartes to Kant), but our "thrownness" into the world: one finds oneself always already in the world, not as a passive, "scientific" observer. To consider oneself somehow detached from it, and to name that thing as the "essential me" is to fail to understand that we are, in the words of the phenomenologists, beings-in-the-world. There is no being, and indeed no consciousness, without a connection to some aspect of that which is outside of us. As Merleau-Ponty notes, "Consciousness is being-toward-the-thing through the intermediary of the body." Further, he notes that "the body is essentially an expressive space . . . the body is our general medium for having a world."[59]

If we follow the lead of the phenomenologists, we can see that the defect in both the neurological and psychological accounts is the assumption that a set of specific types of tissues (neural ones) is the me-ness of me. The program of the phenomenologists—in particular Merleau-Ponty—is to rediscover the inseparable bodiliness of our embodiment in the world, and our connection to the world as part of our embodiment. Certainly, the neurological component of our body is important, since it models to ourselves our body as a body-in-the-world, but severing it from both the rest of our body and the body's orientation toward the world is a reification or objectification of what it means to be human.

Merleau-Ponty claims that the experience of the world arises fundamentally from our motility, not our reflective capacity. Even a seemingly passive activity such as perception, he argues, is a type of prospective motility.[60] Movement is what we are as bodies—even when we're not moving, we experience our relation to the world as one of motion, or prospective motion.

One further component: while everything lives and occurs *in* time, only we have an experience *of* time. This experience of time, for example, gives rise to the anxiety we have about death, and, in turn, the emergence of a moral sphere in humans. We are, according to this view, bodies-in-motion who always already find ourselves as beings-in-a-world. In explaining the temporal component of this experience, Merleau-Ponty quotes Kant: "Time is 'the affecting of self by self.'"[61] Time is not some property of the world out there, but emerges through our capacity to present our self to our self. The mystery of the origin of self-consciousness is, for Heidegger and Merleau-Ponty, the mystery of the origin of time. This would suggest a connection with the earlier discussion of neurology and psychology, and science's Newtonian assumptions of time's flow, of our living in the container of space while observing, and being the selves affected by time's cause and effect. As Merleau-Ponty says of time:

> Change presupposes a certain position which I take up and from which I see things in procession before me: there are no events without someone to whom they happen and whose finite perspective is the basis of their individuality. Time presupposes a view of time. It is, therefore, not like a river, not a flowing substance. The fact that the metaphor based on this comparison has persisted from the time of Heraclitus to our own day is explained by our surreptitiously putting into the river a witness to its course.[62]

We must avoid the mistake of considering that we are witnessing time's flow: "We must therefore avoid saying that our body is *in* space, or *in* time. It *inhabits* space and time."[63]

Merleau-Ponty wants to argue that freedom, metaphysical freedom, is the name for this opening up of consciousness, *as consciousness*, to its connection to the world. Freedom is the pure possibility of a relation to the world, and in that relation we become who we are as beings-in-the-world. This freedom occurs because of bodily motility. Pure, unreflective movement is, phenomenologically, one way to describe that moment before all other moments, or freedom, when we as beings become who we are, the origin of our temporal relation to the world. High-speed cycling, in which we lose all sense of differentiation between ourselves and our machines is indeed freedom. The loss of self-experience in cycling, described by the psychologists as "flow," is metaphysically a re-enactment of our primordial nature, our unreflective absorption with the world. We enact our metaphysical freedom when we ride down the road on two wheels.

The near-simultaneous advent of the bicycle and the motorcycle inaugurated the possibility of a bodily experience that, with the exception of riding in a chariot, was unknown until the nineteenth century. The possibility and capacity for bodily speed, whether though the pumping of legs or pumping of pistons, induced a type of emotional experience that cyclists sought to express and then explain. Unlike forms of communal high-speed transport, such as railroads and airplanes, cycling happens directly to riders owing to their own behavior: pedaling or twisting the throttle. And how to describe it? Well, it makes a person feel free.

We have examined here the dimensions of "freedom." There is no question that cycling raises questions of political freedom, of freedom within the confines of a specific cultural community, but, as we have seen, there are few ways to characterize how this kind of motile freedom is expressed, as the question arises largely as a reaction to a perceived repression of movement by the culture on the individual. At the same time, the devices themselves can be used to express a political point of view (for example, bicycling as a means of defense against environmental degradation). So, both the political conflicts and the various texts inspired by them help us understand the continually contested relation of the individual to the community, but these events help clarify individual and community rights more than they characterize the particular, static ideological dimensions of a bicycle or motorcycle.

Neurology and psychology are two characteristic ways to explore the meaning of "freedom" on a bodily level. The assumptions behind a neurological approach are themselves, however, suspect. Specific brain sites have been determined to either be nonexistent or to rely on other elements of the neurological system to complete their functioning, and the assumption of a brain "site" is an unfortunate metaphor allied with an incorrect understanding of the brain as an organ. The release of brain chemicals can cause neurological effects, but their mode of transmission trumps their function: they do not work like a targeted drug, and they cannot be relied on to manifest a certain kind of reaction in everyone. Finally, identifying a specific gene fails to account for the role of epigenetics in gene expression. In general, we should not, of course, dismiss neurological approaches, but understand that the study of neurological systems is still in its infancy.

As noted, psychology is simply another way to talk about neurological events. The advantage of the psychological notion of "flow" is that it sounds convincing; the disappearance of the self in a state of arousal (in this case, at high speed) is plausible, but it fails to account for what bodily processes originate the response. In addition, such explanations may well work for some individuals, but the event that may evoke positive arousal ("freedom") in one individual may well evoke terror in another.

The phenomenological approach to freedom has the advantage of offering a compelling critique of scientific approaches: a science of the human body is not "wrong," but reductive, for it treats the body as an object, when our fundamental encounter with ourselves and others is as subjects, not objects. If we are talking about something as incommunicably private as an experience of "freedom," we should begin with the assumption of ourselves as fundamentally subjects, indeed, as subjects in motion. Subjects in motion whose connection to the world is fundamental to their identity (their "throwness" and "being-in-the-world") cannot be better understood by separating them from the world, the connection to which is a fundamental element of their identity. With the metaphysical approach we are, however, left with a problem analogous to that of psychology: it's all well and good to talk about the "primordial openness to being" as the source of freedom, but it's not clear what we've said after we said it. Philosophy is fundamentally an activity, and we can continue to explore the question of the relation of being to freedom, but it is not as if philosophy gives us an answer in the same way that, say, physics or mathematics does. This is not a criticism of philosophy but a recognition of its function and the properties of its findings.

So, like the cyclist moving down the road, we have made some progress in our understanding of freedom, mainly by detailing the limitations of contemporary discourse about it. This does not mean that an understanding is impossible, nor that we lack the tools to pursue it, but we have a few miles yet to go on our journey.

NOTES

1. Political freedom as freedom to move becomes most evident in its absence: one of the hallmarks of repressive regimes is limiting the mobility of those citizens who oppose it, from Myanmar's Aung San Suu Kyi to the youthful female members of Russia's pop band, Pussy Riot. In America, consider how issues of right-of-way still emerge in conflicts in the political sphere, from access to beaches adjacent to beach house property owners to struggles about eminent domain when planning new roads.

2. Marguerite Merington, "Woman and the Bicycle," *Scribner's* 17 (June 1895): 702–4. Reprinted in *The American 1890s: A Cultural Reader*, ed. Susan Harris Smith and Melanie Dawson (Durham, NC: Duke University Press, 2000), 288–91.

3. Marie E. Ward, *The Common Sense of Bicycling: Bicycling for Ladies* (New York: Brentano's, 1896), 4.

4. In Amsterdam, for instance, bike share and rider education programs focus on Muslim women, providing them with means of independent travel outside the home, freeing them from dependency on male relatives.

5. The denizens of the Race Across America (RAAM) give much food for psychological thought. See Amy Snyder, *Hell on Two Wheels: An Astonishing Story of Suffering, Triumph, and the Most Extreme Endurance Race in the World* (Chicago: Triumph Books, 2011).

6. In the legal arena, note some of the cases outlined by Fred Oswald at "Bicycle 'Right to the Road' Cases": http://bikelaws.org/Rt2Road.htm, as well as in James Longhurst, *Bike Battles: A History of Sharing the American Road* (Seattle: University of Washington Press, 2015).

7. While this is not an isolated phenomenon, our narrative is relying on the account presented in the 2011 documentary, *Pedal-Driven: A Bikeumentary*, which chronicles the conflict between the U.S. Forest Service and bicyclists in the area surrounding Leavenworth, Washington. Contemporary newspapers have reported on conflicts, particularly between bicyclists and horses, in various states, including California and Washington, as well as in Britain.

8. Jim Rogers, *Investment Biker: Around the World with Jim Rogers* (Holbrook, MA: Adams Media Corporation, 1994). For an account of Malcolm Forbes's motorcycling, see *American Motorcyclist*, October, 1988, 18–19. See also Karen Bettez

Halnon and Saundra Cohen, "Muscles, Motorcycles and Tattoos: Gentrification in a New Frontier," *Journal of Consumer Culture* (March 2006), 33–56.

9. For a discussion, see Randy McBee, *Born to Be Wild: The Rise of the American Motorcyclist* (Chapel Hill: University of North Carolina Press, 2015), 203–10.

10. See K. Alex Ilyasova, "Dykes on Bikes and the Regulation of Vulgarity," *International Journal of Motorcycle Studies* 2 (November 2006), http://ijms.nova.edu/November2006/IJMS_Artcl.Ilyasova.html; Ann Ferrar, *Hear Me Roar: Women, Motorcycles and the Rapture of the Road* (New York: Whitehorse Press, 1996); Barbara Jones, *Bike Lust: Harleys, Women, and American Society* (Madison: University of Wisconsin Press, 2001); Karen Larsen, *Breaking the Limit: One Woman's Motorcycle Journey Through North America* (New York: Hyperion, 2004); Patrick Symmes, *Chasing Che: A Motorcycle Journey in Search of the Guevara Legend* (New York: Vintage, 2000); Barbara Brodman, *Looking for Mr. Guevara: A Journey through South America* (New York: Writers Club Press, 2001); Christopher P. Baker, *Mi Moto Fidel* (Washington, DC: The National Geographic Society, 2001); Christopher Hunt, *Sparring with Charlie: Motorbiking Down the Ho Chi Minh Trail* (New York: Anchor Books, 1996); Ted Simon, *Jupiter's Travels* (Covelo, CA: Jupitalia, 1979,1996); Claudia Metz and Klaus Schubert, *Abgefahren: In 16 Jahren Um Die Welt* (Koeln: Kiepenheuer & Witsch, 2004); Werner Bausenhart, *Africa: Against the Clock on a Motorcycle* (Toronto: Legas, 2002).

11. John Stuart Mill, *On Liberty* (1869), http://www.gutenberg.org/catalog/world/readfile?fk_files=3278265.

12. ABATE is one of the most well-known and ubiquitous national organizations. The acronym has been understood to have various meanings, among them "A Brotherhood Against Totalitarian Enactments." Despite the aggressive language, state ABATE organizations present themselves as active members of local communities working for motorcycle safety and citizens' legislative involvement. A helpful listing of links of state ABATE organizations and other MROs can be found at the New York ABATE site: http://www.abateny.org/links.html.

13. Compare, for example, automobile associations with MROs. They form a coalition of like-minded individuals around a mode of transportation, but don't have to spend their time fighting incursions into their individual rights by governmental forces.

14. Accounts of the international phenomenon of the motorcycle abound. Note in particular those of Daniel Wolf, *The Rebels: A Brotherhood of Outlaw Bikers* (Toronto: University of Toronto Press, 1991) and Arthur Veno, *The Brotherhoods: Inside the Outlaw Motorcycle Clubs* (NSW, Australia: Allen & Unwin, 2003). See also Steven E. Alford and Suzanne Ferriss, *Motorcycle* (London: Reaktion, 2008), chapter 2.

15. Veno, *Brotherhoods*, 52. See the previous chapter on "Paradoxes of Class and Gender" for a discussion of the relation of these clubs to early bicycle clubs.

16. As Veno has noted, the police are seen not as oppressors, but as mirror-image rivals, who also have a paramilitary organization, a sense of internalized brotherhood, a feeling of apartness that manifests itself as being constantly threatened by outside forces (forces that, ironically, both groups refer to as "citizens"). Hence, the difference between the police and a motorcycle club is not between civilization and

barbarism, but two sets of social values in conflict with one another (*Brotherhoods*, 15). Also interesting in this respect are Randy McBee's comments in the July 2005 issue of *The International Journal of Motorcycle Studies* about Hunter Thompson's *Hell's Angels*:

> Thompson suggests that the Angels did not become the focus of a national campaign for "law and order" because they were not as threatening as they often appeared. Thompson refers to what he called a "psychic compatibility" between the cops and the Angels, who, Thompson argues, "get along pretty well" and "operate" on what he called "the same motional frequency." Thompson claimed that the Angels and the cops "deny this." "The very suggestion of a psychic compatibility will be denounced . . . as a form of Communist slander." But he argued that this compatibility was obvious to anyone who has ever seen a routine confrontation or sat in on a friendly police check at one of the Angel bars. Apart, they curse each other savagely, and the brittle truce is often jangled by high-speed chases and brief, violent clashes that rarely make the papers. Yet behind the sound and fury, they are both playing the same game, and usually by the same rules.

("A 'Potential Common Front': Hunter Thompson, the Hell's Angels, and Race in 1960s America," *International Journal of Motorcycle Studies* 1 [July 2005], http://ijms.nova.edu/July2005/IJMS_RT.McBee.html.)

17. The image of the "tribe," a band of brothers, is politically ambiguous, in the history of modern political philosophy. The Rousseauian primitive of *The Second Discourse* and the Hobbesian primitive of *Leviathan* offer contradictory images of the pre-political dimensions of tribal organization.

18. This is not to say that no bicyclists understand their identity in terms of their relation to their bicycle. Along with passionate and devoted mountain bikers, fixed-gear riders see themselves as a band apart, creating their own culture centered around a particular kind of bicycle, as do mountain bikers. For an illustration of these sub-cultures, see the documentary films *Fixation* (2012) and *Strength in Numbers* (2012).

19. In what follows we use the terms "emotion" and "feeling" interchangeably. Antonio Damasio, a principal source in the neurological section, distinguishes between the two: "the term *feeling* should be reserved for the private, mental experience of an emotion, while the term *emotion* should be used to designate the collection of responses, many of which are publicly observable" (*The Feeling of What Happens* [New York: Harcourt, Inc., 1999], 42).

20. See "The White House BRAIN Initiative," September 30, 2014, https://www.whitehouse.gov/share/brain-initiative.

21. For a roundup of such reports, see "BrainFacts.org," http://www.brainfacts.org/news.

22. This, of course, is an interesting observation until we realize that the range of possible emotions precludes us finding a "site" in the brain for each one. Damasio divides them into primary or universal emotions (fear, anger, sadness, disgust, surprise, and happiness), background feelings (fatigue, energy, excitement, wellness, sickness, tension, relaxation, surging, dragging, stability, instability, balance, imbalance, harmony, discord), and moods, which are "made up of modulated and sustained background feelings as well as modulated and sustained feelings of primary emotions—sadness, in the

case of depression" (*The Feeling of What Happens*, 286). The idea that, for example, each primary emotion occupies its own site is on par with phrenology.

23. See the popular account of scans' problematic results in Sally Satel and Scott O. Lilienfeld, *Brainwashed: The Seductive Appeal of Mindless Neuroscience* (New York: Basic Books, 2013), and Robert G. Shulman, *Brain Imaging: What It Can (and Cannot) Tell Us about Consciousness* (New York: Oxford University Press, 2013). Note as well the laboratory work of Nikos K. Logothetis: http://www.kyb.mpg.de/nc/employee/details/nikos.html#=0.

24. Originating with neuroscientist Paul Broca in the nineteenth century, this claim was championed by Paul McLean in the early 1950s. See John D. Newman and James C. Harris, "The Scientific Contributions of Paul D. McLean (1913–2007)," *The Journal of Nervous and Mental Disease* 197 (January 2009), 3–5.

25. See Joseph LeDoux, *The Synaptic Self: How Our Brains Become Who We Are* (New York: Penguin, 2002), 208–10.

26. For a discussion, see Michael J. Quirk, "Martin Heidegger: Beings, Being and Truth," *Sophia Project: Philosophy Archives*, 2000, http://www.sophia-project.org/uploads/1/3/9/5/13955288/quirk_heidegger2.pdf.

27. Damasio, *The Feeling of What Happens*, 20.

28. Damasio, *The Feeling of What Happens*, 60–62.

29. Damasio, *The Feeling of What Happens*, 279.

30. Damasio, *The Feeling of What Happens*, 331.

31. See Damasio, *The Feeling of What Happens*, 15–19.

32. LeDoux, *The Synaptic Self*, 265.

33. LeDoux, *The Synaptic Self*, 261. Italics added for emphasis.

34. Some of the consequences of acting on this assumption in treating mental disorders can be found in Robert Whitaker, *Anatomy of an Epidemic: Magic Bullets, Psychiatric Drugs, and the Astonishing Rise of Mental Illness in America* (New York: Broadway Books, 2010).

35. For further discussion, see LeDoux, *The Synaptic Self*, 297. For the "sports gene," see David Epstein, *The Sports Gene: Inside the Science of Extraordinary Athletic Performance* (New York: Current, 2014).

36. Speed itself is "a phenomenon with a welter of manifestations in sociology, physics, and psychology, as well as popular culture" (Steven E. Alford and Gerd Hurm, "Motorcycle: Beschleunigung und Rebellion? Introduction," *International Journal of Motorcycle Studies* 6 [Spring 2010], http://ijms.nova.edu/Spring2010/IJMS_Artcl.AlfordHurm.html). The most sophisticated treatment of speed in modernity is the work of Hartmut Rosa, extensively examined in his book, *Beschleunigung: Die Veränderung der Zeitstrukturen in der Moderne* (Frankfurt am Main: Suhrkamp Verlag, 2005). For shorter works in English, see "Social Acceleration: Ethical and Political Consequences of a Desynchronized High-Speed Society," *Constellations* 10.1 (2003): 3–33; "The Speed of Global Flows and the Pace of Democratic Politics," *New Political Science* 27.4 (2005): 445–59; and, most recently, "Full Speed Burnout? From the Pleasures of the Motorcycle to the Bleakness of the Treadmill: The Dual Face of Social Acceleration," *International Journal of Motorcycle Studies* 6 (Spring 2010), http://ijms.nova.edu/Spring2010/IJMS_Artcl.Rosa.html.

37. LeDoux, *The Synaptic Self*, 262.

38. LeDoux, *The Synaptic Self*, 291. However, a recent study has called into doubt the perceived effectiveness of talk therapy. See Ellen Driessen et al., "Does Publication Bias Inflate the Apparent Efficacy of Psychological Treatment for Major Depressive Disorder? A Systematic Review and Meta-Analysis of US National Institutes of Health-Funded Trials," *PLoS ONE* 10 (September 30, 2015), http://journals.plos.org/plosone/article?id=10.1371/journal.pone.0137864.

39. Michael J. Apter, *The Dangerous Edge: The Psychology of Excitement* (New York: Free Press, 1992), 14.

40. Apter, *The Dangerous Edge*, 27.

41. Apter, *The Dangerous Edge*, 45.

42. Apter, *The Dangerous Edge*, 97.

43. In sociological studies, the issue of risk-taking is characterized as "edgework." See Stephen Lyng, *Edgework: The Sociology of Risk-Taking* (New York: Routledge, 2004). For an application to motorcycling see Patricia Gagné and D. Mark Austin, "Playing with the Guys: Women's Negotiation of Gendered Leisure and Space," *International Journal of Motorcycle Studies* 6 (Fall 2010), http://ijms.nova.edu/Fall2010/IJMS_Artcl.GagneAustin.html.

44. For a discussion, see Andrew D. Spear, "Edmund Husserl: Intentionality and Intentional Content," *Internet Encyclopedia of Philosophy*, http://www.iep.utm.edu/huss-int/.

45. Elaine Scarry, *The Body in Pain: The Making and Unmaking of the World* (New York: Oxford University Press, 1985), 4.

46. Scarry, *The Body in Pain,* 5.

47. Scarry's complex and comprehensive argument diverges early from ours: she claims that the pain experienced in torture and war "deconstructs" the self of the sufferer, and that the construction, or reconstruction of the self can be achieved through artistic creativity.

48. Michael Polanyi, *The Tacit Dimension* (Gloucester, MA: Peter Smith, 1983).

49. See, for example, an analysis of Alabama motorcycle accidents: Steven L. Jones, Jr. and Saravanan Gurupackian, "The Who, What, When and Where of Motorcycle Crashes in Alabama," *International Journal of Motorcycle Studies* 8 (Spring 2012), http://ijms.nova.edu/Spring%202012/IJMS_Artcl.Jones.html. General information on research into motorcycle accidents, including the Hurt Report, can be found at: http://www.nhtsa.gov/people/injury/pedbimot/motorcycle/00-nht-212-motorcycle/research9-11.html.

50. Mihaly Csikszentmihalyi, *Finding Flow: The Psychology of Engagement with Everyday Life* (New York: Basic Books, 1997); Susan A. Jackson, *Flow in Sports* (Champaign, IL: Human Kinetics, 1999).

51. Apter, *The Dangerous Edge*, 187.

52. Csikszentmihalyi, *Finding Flow*, 41.

53. Guy Martin, a spectacularly successful motorcycle racer at the Isle of Man TT, is also hilariously inarticulate. See his interviews in the film *TT3D: Closer to the Edge* (2011).

54. More contemporary (and generally younger than their grizzled, cruiser-riding counterparts) sport bike riders encourage this harmony of person and machine visually by wearing full leathers and a helmet matching the color scheme of the bike, which, to the spectator, visually melds rider and bike into a single unit, a visible analog to the unitary experience of human-machine *flow* while riding a bike.

55. Drew Leder, *The Absent Body* (Chicago: University of Chicago Press, 1990), 5, 21.

56. Leder, *The Absent Body*, 14. This is an application of Heidegger's famous distinction between readiness-to-hand (*Zuhandenheit*) and presence-at-hand (*Vorhandenheit*) found in his masterwork, *Being and Time* (1929). In the example above, the eye, when in use, is unreflectively present (i.e., it "disappears" in the act of seeing; it is ready-to-hand). The eye, when an object of reflection ("there's something in my eye"), manifests itself *as an eye*; it is present-at-hand). Maurice Merleau-Ponty expresses this idea: "This paradox is that of all being in the world: when I move towards a world I bury my perceptual and practical intentions in objects which ultimately appear prior to and external to those intentions, and which nevertheless exist for me only in so far as they arouse in me thoughts or volitions" (*The Phenomenology of Perception*, 2nd ed. [New York: Routledge, 2002], 95). Note that this is a philosophical version—albeit a very different one—of the explanation offered by Csikszentmihalyi's notion of "flow."

57. Merleau-Ponty, *The Phenomenology of Perception*, 502.

58. Damasio discusses this issue from a neurological standpoint in his chapter on what he calls "core consciousness": "Consciousness depends on the internal construction and exhibition of new knowledge concerning an interaction between that organism and an object" (*The Feeling of What Happens*, 169).

59. Merleau-Ponty, *The Phenomenology of Perception*, 160, 169.

60. "My eye for me is a certain power of making contact with things, and not a screen on which they are projected" (Merleau-Ponty, *The Phenomenology of Perception*, 325).

61. Merleau-Ponty, *The Phenomenology of Perception*, 494. The original reads, "Die Zeit ist ihrem Wesen nach reine Affektion ihrer selbst" (Martin Heidegger, *Kant und das Problem der Metaphysik*, [Klostermann, 1998], 180–81).

62. Merleau-Ponty, *The Phenomenology of Perception*, 477–78.

63. Merleau-Ponty, *The Phenomenology of Perception*, 161.

Conclusion

> The spokes are in a certain sense the opposite of the hub. While the hub is in the center, the spokes are in the periphery; while the hub is empty, the spokes are full; while the hub is still, the spokes are in motion; and while the hub is single, the spokes are many. The spokes represent the realm of the visible and the realm of activity. They are the image for everything that has a definite and "positive" place—although these positions are constantly changing. When the wheel is turning, the spokes occupy every position, top and bottom, left and right. They run through the whole "positive" space of the wheel. Through their constant turning, they mark the space and borders of activity. This space of activity or motion is itself a space of opposition: top and bottom, and left and right. The space created by the turning of the spokes is constructed by the exchanging of opposite positions. Within this process of rotation the spoke on top changes position with the spoke on the bottom and so forth. The whole periphery performs a constant, harmonious alternation, a perfectly regular course of changeovers.
>
> —Hans-Georg Moeller, *Daoism Explained: From the Dream of the Butterfly to the Fishnet Allegory*

The concept of the wheel has been used to refer to far more than transportation: the Wheel of Fortune, the Wheel of Life, the Wheel of Time. The wheel—in Buddhist thought, astronomy or politics—is a metaphor capturing dualism and paradox: revolving wheels cause forward motion, but the wheels themselves don't go anywhere. The revolving wheels remain in place, bound to a motionless center, the hub or axle, mirroring the motion of celestial bodies moving in orbit around a fixed center. In a political sense, "revolution" originally meant restoration, a return or circling back to begin anew, but now is synonymous with revolt or rebellion, a break in the cycle.[1] The spokes of the wheel fix it to the hub, but generate its revolutions, sustaining its structure and movement. Multiple and arranged in opposition, the spokes form a wheel, whole and unified. Wheels represent multiplicity and unity, movement and stasis.

Doubled, they are not only components of bicycles and motorcycles but conceptual keys to understanding the complexities and contradictions inherent in the devices' construction and use. Two-wheeled vehicles have transformed the lives of people all over the earth. More than that: they have changed the earth itself, creating the social and political conditions for improved roads. As with all events and devices looked on as contributions to "progress," these advances in human freedom do not come without their own built-in ironies. Our current inability to breathe, owing to pollution and, soon enough, the presence of beachfront property in many now-inland cities have resulted from a series of decisions and assumptions originating in, among other spheres, the Good Roads movement. If not God, then human history often manifests itself as a grim but smiling ironist.

But, if there is one lesson as we look back on the development of bicycles and motorcycles, it was announced in part 1: it could have been otherwise. As we noted at the time, narratives of evolutionary development or historical inevitability create a story by beginning at a desired endpoint and working backward, demonstrating the glories of the contemporary device/event at the expense of complexity and nuance. This caveat was further extended in part 2: the gifts of the earth that are transformed into objects of use are themselves entangled in cultural epistemology and history. Roads are for everyone, but no one seems to want to share them. One era's toys and environmental annoyances (rubber and petroleum) become the next period's "resources," to be cornered, fought over, and profited from. Materials, from rubber to steel to cotton, find themselves as part of a much larger story of exploitation and misery, whether the object of imperial violence or the quieter tales of domestic mistreatment of factory workers' health. Part 3 suggests that amid all these grand narratives, the issues raised emerge for most of us as a person's individual experience: we don't know much about steel, but we certainly are annoyed by the squid on his Hayabusa doing a wheelie in front of us on the Interstate. We are thrilled by our new carbon-fiber road bike, without thinking too much about its Chinese origins, and we enjoy even more the jealous looks from other, poorer bicyclists. Ultimately, while we two-wheelers may find pleasure in helping forestall the death of the planet, our central pleasures are not moral but biological: there's something about speed that draws us to devices that allow us to whiz down the road.

It could have been otherwise then and, with a sense of environmental stewardship and a conviction that we are, ultimately, members of the same family, it can be otherwise now. We can move forward, secure both in the realization that transportation can change lives for the better, and that any of our achievements should be savored with a sharp sense of irony and enhanced understanding of the infinite complexities propelling—and sometimes impeding—our progress down the road.

NOTES

1. We are indebted to Katherine Sutherland for these insights.

Selected Bibliography

Adas, Michael. *Machines as the Measure of Men: Science, Technology, and Ideologies of Western Dominance*. Ithaca, NY: Cornell University Press, 1989.

Alexander, Jeffrey W. *Japan's Motorcycle Wars: An Industry History*. Vancouver: University of British Columbia Press, 2008.

Alford, Steven E., and Suzanne Ferriss. *Motorcycle*. London: Reaktion Press, 2008.

Apter, Michael J. *The Dangerous Edge: The Psychology of Excitement*. New York: Free Press, 1992.

Aronson, Sidney. "The Sociology of the Bicycle." *Social Forces* 30 (March 1952): 305–12.

Baptist, Edward E. *The Half Has Never Been Told: Slavery and the Making of American Capitalism*. New York: Basic Books, 2014.

Bayly, C. A. "The Origins of Swadeshi (Home Industry): Cloth and Indian Society, 1700–1930." In *The Social Life of Things: Commodities in Cultural Perspective*, edited by Arjun Appadurai, 285–321. Cambridge: Cambridge University Press, 1986.

Beckert, Sven. *Empire of Cotton: A Global History*. New York: Alfred A. Knopf, 2014.

Bijker Wiebe. *Of Bicycles, Bakelites, and Bulbs: Toward a Theory of Sociotechnical Change*. Cambridge, MA: MIT Press, 1997.

Bijker, Wiebe E., Thomas P. Hughes, and Trevor Pinch. *The Social Construction of Technological Systems*. Cambridge, MA: MIT Press, 1987.

Boore, J. P., and V. S. Polansky. *The Seamless Story: A History of the Seamless Steel Tube Industry in the United States*. Los Angeles: Commonwealth Press, 1951.

Burr, Thomas Cameron. "Markets As Producers and Consumers: The French and U.S. National Bicycle Markets, 1875–1910." PhD diss., University of California, Davis, 2005.

Byrde, Penelope. "Dress: The Industrial Revolution and After." In *The Cambridge History of Western Textiles*, part II, edited by David Jenkins, 882–909. Cambridge: Cambridge University Press, 2003.

Cox, Peter, with Frederick Van De Walle. "Bicycles Don't Evolve: Velomobiles and the Modelling of Transport Technologies." In *Cycling and Society*, edited by Dave Horton, Paul Rosen, and Peter Cox, 113–31. Aldershot, UK: Ashgate, 2007.

Cresswell, Timothy. *On the Move: Mobility in the Modern Western World.* New York: Routledge, 2006.

Csikszentmihalyi, Mihaly. *Finding Flow: The Psychology of Engagement with Everyday Life*. New York: Basic Books, 1997.

Cunningham, Patricia A. *Reforming Women's Fashion, 1850–1920: Politics, Health, and Art*. Kent, OH: Kent State University Press, 2003.

Cunnington, Phillis, and Alan Mansfield. *English Costume for Sports and Outdoor Recreation: From the 16th to 19th Centuries*. London: Adam and Charles Black, 1963.

Damasio, Antonio. *The Feeling of What Happens*. New York: Harcourt, Inc., 1999.

Davies, Peter. *American Road: The Story of an Epic Transcontinental Journey at the Dawn of the Motor Age*. New York: Henry Holt, 2002.

Dodge, Pryor. *The Bicycle*. Paris: Flammarion, 1996.

Eglash, Ron. "Technology as Material Culture." In *Handbook of Material Culture*, edited by Christopher Tilley, Webb Keane, Susanne Küchler, Michael Rowlands, and Patricia Spyer, 329–40. London: Sage, 2006.

Epperson, Bruce D. *Peddling Bicycles to America: The Rise of an Industry*. Jefferson, NC: McFarland & Company, Inc., 2010.

Farnie, Douglas. "Cotton, 1780–1914." In *The Cambridge History of Western Textiles*, part II, edited by David Jenkins, 721–60. Cambridge: Cambridge University Press, 2003.

Fitzpatrick, Jim. *The Bicycle in Wartime: An Illustrated History*. Kilcoy, Australia: Star Hill Studio, 2011.

Fransen, Tim, ed. *An Anthology of Early British Motorcycle Travel Literature*. Essex: Essex-Dakar Books, 2009.

Garvey, Ellen Gruber. "Reframing the Bicycle: Advertising-Supported Magazines and Scorching Women." *American Quarterly* 47 (March 1995): 66–101.

Goddard, J. T. *The Velocipede: Its History, Variety and Practices*. Cambridge: Riverside Press, 1869.

Goddard, Stephen B. *Colonel Albert Pope and His American Dream Machines: The Life and Times of Bicycle Tycoon Turned Automotive Pioneer*. New York: McFarland, 2008.

Grandin, Greg. *The Empire of Necessity: Slavery, Freedom, and Deception in the New World*. New York: Metropolitan Books, 2014.

———. *Fordlandia: The Rise and Fall of Henry Ford's Forgotten Jungle City*. New York: Henry Holt, 2010.

Grew, W. F. *The Cycle Industry: Its Origins, History and Latest Developments*. London: Sir I. Pitman & Sons, Ltd., 1921.

Hadland, Tony, and Hans-Erhard Lessing. *Bicycle Design: An Illustrated History*. Cambridge, MA: MIT Press, 2014.

Headrick, Daniel R. *The Tools of Empire: Technology and European Imperialism in the Nineteenth Century*. New York: Oxford University Press, 1981.

Hebdige, Dick. *Hiding in the Light: On Images and Things*. London: Routledge, 1988.

———. "Object as Image: The Italian Scooter Cycle." *Block* 5 (1981): 44–64.

———. *Subculture: The Meaning of Style*. London: Methuen, 1979.

Herlihy, David V. *Bicycle: The History*. New Haven, CT: Yale University Press, 2004.

Holley, Jr., I. B. *The Highway Revolution, 1895–1925: How the United States Got Out of the Mud.* Durham, NC: Carolina Academic Press, 2008.

Holt, Richard. "Women, Men and Sport in France, c. 1870–1914: An Introductory Survey." *Journal of Sport History* 18 (Spring 1991): 121–34.

Hounshell, David A. "The Bicycle and Technology in Late Nineteenth Century America." Tekniska Museet Symposia 2, 1980.

———. *From the American System to Mass Production, 1800–1932*. Baltimore, MD: Johns Hopkins University Press, 1984.

Jackson, Joe. *The Thief at the End of the World: Rubber, Power, and the Seeds of Empire*. New York: Viking, 2008.

Jackson, Susan A. *Flow in Sports*. Champaign, IL: Human Kinetics, 1999.

Jenkins, David. "The Western Wool Textile Industry in the Nineteenth Century." In *The Cambridge History of Western Textiles*, Part II, edited by David Jenkins, 761–89. Cambridge: Cambridge University Press, 2003.

Johnson, Walter. *River of Dark Dreams: Slavery and Empire in the Cotton Kingdom.* Cambridge, MA: Belknap Press, 2013.

Kingsland, Florence. *Etiquette for All Occasions*. New York: Doubleday, 1901.

Larsen, Jonas, John Urry, and Kay Axhausen. *Mobilities, Networks, Geographies*. Aldershot, UK: Ashgate, 2006.

Lay, M. G. *Ways of the World: A History of the World's Roads and of the Vehicles that Used Them*. New Brunswick, NJ: Rutgers University Press, 1992.

Leder, Drew. *The Absent Body*. Chicago: University of Chicago Press, 1990.

LeDoux, Joseph. *The Synaptic Self: How Our Brains Become Who We Are*. New York: Penguin, 2002.

Lemonnier, Pierre, ed. *Technological Choices: Transformation in Materials since the Neolithic*. London: Routledge, 1993.

Leonard, Eileen B. *Women, Technology, and the Myth of Progress*. Upper Saddle River, NJ: Prentice Hall, 2003.

Lewis, Tom. *Divided Highways*. New York: Penguin, 1997.

Loadman, John. *The Tears of the Tree: The Story of Rubber*. New York: Oxford University Press, 2014.

Longhurst, James. *Bike Battles: A History of Sharing the American Road.* Seattle: University of Washington Press, 2015.

Lyng, Stephen. *Edgework: The Sociology of Risk-Taking*. New York: Routledge, 2004.

Mackintosh, Phillip Gordon, and Glen Norcliffe. "Men, Women and the Bicycle: Gender and Social Geography of Cycling in the Late Nineteenth-Century." In *Cycling and Society*, edited by Dave Horton, Paul Rosen, and Peter Cox, 153–77. Aldershot, UK: Ashgate, 2007.

Mann, Charles C. *1493: Uncovering the New World Columbus Created*. New York: Alfred A. Knopf, 2011.

Marx, Leo. "The Idea of 'Technology' and Postmodern Pessimism." In *Does Technology Drive History? The Dilemma of Technological Determinism*, edited by Merritt Roe Smith and Leo Marx, 237–57. Boston: MIT Press, 1994.

McBee, Randy. *Born to Be Wild: The Rise of the American Motorcyclist*. Chapel Hill: The University of North Carolina Press, 2015.

McGurn, James. *On Your Bicycle: An Illustrated History of Cycling*. New York: Facts on File, 1987.

McKendrick, Neil, John Brewer, and J. H. Plumb, eds. *The Birth of a Consumer Society: The Commercialization of Eighteenth-Century England*. London: Hutchinson, 1982.

Merington, Marguerite. "Woman and the Bicycle." *Scribner's* 17 (June 1895): 702–4. Reprinted in *The American 1890s: A Cultural Reader,* edited by Susan Harris Smith and Melanie Dawson, 288–91. Durham, NC: Duke University Press, 2000.

Merleau-Ponty, Maurice. *The Phenomenology of Perception*. 2nd ed. New York: Routledge, 2002.

Miller, Daniel. *Material Culture and Mass Consumption*. Oxford: Blackwell, 1987.

———, ed. *Material Cultures: Why Some Things Matter*. Chicago: University of Chicago Press, 1998.

———, ed. *Materiality*. Durham, NC: Duke University Press, 2005.

Misa, Thomas J. *A Nation of Steel: The Making of Modern America*. Baltimore, MD: Johns Hopkins University Press, 1995.

———. "Retrieving Sociotechnical Change from Technological Determinism." In *Does Technology Drive History? The Dilemma of Technological Determinism*, edited by Merritt Roe Smith and Leo Marx, 115–41. Boston: MIT Press, 1994.

Mokyr, Joel. *The Lever of Riches: Technological Creativity and Economic Progress*. New York: Oxford University Press, 1992.

Molotch, Harvey. *Where Stuff Comes From: How Toasters, Toilets, Cars, Computers, and Many Other Things Come to Be as They Are*. New York: Routledge, 2003.

Mukerji, Chandra. *Graven Images: Patterns of Modern Materialism*. New York: Columbia University Press, 1983.

Norcliffe, Glen. *The Ride to Modernity: The Bicycle in Canada, 1869–1900*. Toronto: University of Toronto Press, 2001.

Oudshoorn, Nelly, and Trevor J. Pinch. "Introduction." In *How Users Matter: The Co-construction of Users and Technologies,* edited by Nelly Oudshoorn and Trevor J. Pinch, 1–25. Cambridge, MA: MIT Press, 2003.

Pacey, Arnold. *The Maze of Ingenuity: Ideas and Idealism in the Development of Technology*. 2nd ed. Cambridge, MA: MIT Press, 1974, 1992.

———. *Technology in World Civilization: A Thousand-Year History*. Boston: MIT Press, 1991.

Pearson, Henry C. *Pneumatic Tires: Automobile, Truck, Airplane, Motorcycle, Bicycle: An Encyclopedia of Tire Manufacture, History, Processes, Machinery, Modern Repair and Rebuilding, Patents, Etc., Etc., Profusely Illustrated*. New York: The India Rubber Publishing Co., 1922.

Penn, Robert. *It's All about the Bike: The Pursuit of Happiness on Two Wheels*. New York: Bloomsbury USA, 2011.

Perry, David B. *Bike Cult: The Ultimate Guide to Human-Powered Vehicles*. New York: Four Walls Eight Windows, 1995.

Petroski, Henry. *The Evolution of Useful Things*. New York: Alfred A. Knopf, 1993.

Petty, Ross D. "Peddling the Bicycle in the 1890s: Mass Marketing Shifts into High Gear." *Journal of Macromarketing* 15 (Spring 1995): 32–46.

Polanyi, Michael. *The Tacit Dimension*. Gloucester, MA: Peter Smith, 1983.

Pratt, Charles E. *The American Bicycler: A Manual for the Observer, the Learner, and the Expert*. Boston: Osgood and Company, 1879.

Rabinbach, Anson. *The Human Motor: Energy, Fatigue, and the Origins of Modernity*. Berkeley: University of California Press, 1990.

Reid, Carlton. *Roads Were Not Built for Cars: How Cyclists Were the First to Push for Good Roads & Became the Pioneers of Motoring*. Washington, DC: Island Press, 2015.

Reutter, Mark. *Sparrows Point: Making Steel—the Rise and Ruin of American Industrial Might*. New York: Summit Books, 1988.

Reynaud, Claude. *Vélos de legend* [Bicycles of Legend]. Geneva: Georges Naef, 2013.

Rosa, Hartmut. *Beschleunigung: Die Veränderung der Zeitstrukturen in der Moderne*. Frankfurt am Main: Suhrkamp Verlag, 2005.

Rose, Mark H. *Interstate: Express Highway Politics, 1939–1989*. Knoxville: The University of Tennessee Press, 1979, 1990.

Rosen, William. *The Most Powerful Idea in the World: A Story of Steam, Industry, and Invention*. New York: Random House, 2010.

Scarry, Elaine. *The Body in Pain: The Making and Unmaking of the World.* New York: Oxford University Press, 1985.

Schneider, Jane. "Cloth and Clothing." In *Handbook of Material Culture*, edited by Christopher Tilley, Webb Keane, Susanne Küchler, Michael Rowlands, and Patricia Spyer, 203–20. London: Sage, 2006.

Schorman, Rob. *Selling Style: Clothing and Social Change at the Turn of the Century.* Philadelphia: University of Pennsylvania Press, 2003.

Scott, Robert Pittis. *Cycling Art, Energy and Locomotion*. Philadelphia: J. B. Lippincott, 1889.

Shannon, Brent. *The Cut of His Coat: Men, Dress, and Consumer Culture in Britain, 1860–1914*. Athens: Ohio University Press, 2006.

Sharp, Archibald. *Bicycles and Tricycles*. London: Longmans, Green and Co., 1896.

Slack, Charles. *Noble Obsession: Charles Goodyear, Thomas Hancock, and the Race to Unlock the Greatest Industrial Secret of the Nineteenth Century*. New York: Hyperion, 2002.

Smith, C. Wayne, and J. Tom Cothren, eds. *Cotton: Origin, History, Technology, and Production*. New York: John Wiley & Sons, Inc., 1999.

Smith, Merritt Roe, and Leo Marx, eds. *Does Technology Drive History? The Dilemma of Technological Determinism*. Boston: MIT Press, 1994.

Smith, Robert A. *A Social History of the Bicycle: Its Early Life and Times in America*. New York: American Heritage, 1972.

Snyder, Amy. *Hell on Two Wheels: An Astonishing Story of Suffering, Triumph, and the Most Extreme Endurance Race in the World*. Chicago: Triumph Books, 2011.

Spiegel, Bernt. *The Upper Half of the Motorcycle: On the Unity of Rider and Machine*. North Conway, NH: Whitehorse Press, 2010.

Swift, Earl. *The Big Roads: The Untold Story of the Engineers, Visionaries, and Trailblazers Who Created the American Superhighways*. New York: Houghton Mifflin Harcourt, 2011.

Tully, John. *The Devil's Milk: A Social History of Rubber*. New York: Monthly Review Press, 2011.

Turpin, Robert J. "'Our Best Bet Is The Boy': A Cultural History Of Bicycle Marketing And Consumption in the United States, 1880–1960." PhD diss., University of Kentucky, 2013.

Ward, Marie E. *The Common Sense of Bicycling: Bicycling for Ladies*. New York: Brentano's, 1896.

Weber, Eugen. *France, Fin De Siècle*. Cambridge, MA: Belknap Press, 1986.

White, Lynn Townsend. *Medieval Technology and Social Change*. Oxford: Clarendon Press, 1962.

White, Richard. *Railroaded: The Transcontinentals and the Making of Modern America*. New York: W. W. Norton, 2012.

Willard, Frances Elizabeth. *A Wheel within a Wheel: How I Learned to Ride the Bicycle*. Chicago: Woman's Temperance Publishing Association, 1895.

Wolf, Winfried. *Car Mania: A Critical History of Transport*. Translated by Gus Fagan. London: Pluto Press, 1996.

Wosk, Julie. *Women and the Machine: Representations from the Spinning Wheel to the Electronic Age*. Baltimore, MD: Johns Hopkins University Press, 2001.

Index

Page references for figures are italicized.

About the Authors

Steven E. Alford and **Suzanne Ferriss** have been at the forefront of motorcycle studies for more than a decade. In addition to publishing *Motorcycle* in 2008, they edited *The International Journal of Motorcycle Studies* for ten years. They have been involved in the study of the intersection of motorcycles and culture, lecturing on diverse topics such as biker fashion, women riders, New Zealand motorcyclists Burt Munro and John Britten, and the psychological effects of riding. They contributed articles to *Harley-Davidson and Philosophy* (2006) and penned the introduction to *An Anthology of Early British Motorcycle Travel Writing* (2009).

They both teach at Nova Southeastern University in Fort Lauderdale, Florida. Steven's areas of research and teaching include early German and English Romanticism, film criticism and theory, and American literature, in particular the contemporary American novel and the work of Paul Auster. His work on motorcycle culture has appeared in *The Literature of Travel and Exploration: An Encyclopedia* and *Studies in Travel Writing*. Suzanne coedited two volumes on the cultural study of fashion: *On Fashion* (1994) and *Footnotes: On Shoes* (2001). She is also coauthor of *A Handbook of Literary Feminisms* (2002), and has written articles about Jane Austen, Mary Shelley, and the Brontë sisters, and about popular films based on literary texts by Austen, Virginia Woolf, and Helen Fielding. She coedited two companion volumes on "chick culture" with Mallory Young: *Chick Lit: The New Woman's Fiction* (2006) and *Chick Flicks: Contemporary Women at the Movies* (2008).